MARILYN:
NOT JUST ANOTHER GIRL

Mill City Press, Inc.
2301 Lucien Way #415
Maitland, FL 32751
407.339.4217
www.millcitypress.net

Printed in the United States of America

ISBN-13: 978-1-54567-364-5

FOREWORD

*A*t age 19, Michele was spending the summer back at her childhood home after her first year of college as a theatre major. One night she discovered her most recent past life, as memories began to present themselves. She suddenly realized her soul lived the life of one of the most troubled and photogenic women of all time, Marilyn Monroe. *This is a journey about the present healing the past, and the past healing the present.* And by the end of this book, the reader will know exactly what happened to Marilyn Monroe on August 4-5, 1962. Michele believes she is the only one still alive who can tell you this firsthand.

Furthermore, this writing is aimed towards those readers who already know reincarnation is real, or those who don't dismiss the possibility. For those who don't believe yet, perhaps you'll change your mind. You never know when you may reconnect with your former self from another lifetime. And if you do, the author hopes this book is helpful in some way.

Michele's memories of Marilyn are only the tip of the iceberg. As her college years progressed, she began to recall many other past lives, a few famous, most not. And with the writing of this book, yet another stepped forward. Each past lifetime is important. Each one deserves to be acknowledged. Michele is the sum-total of all those past selves, plus herself.

By Sheldy Teresa Brooks

DEAR READER,

I never thought I would write a book. But I'm doing so out of a promise that spans two lifetimes. My soul was Marilyn Monroe's.

Note: This book contains some sexual content and is not appropriate for all ages. Chapters 5, 9, 12 Sex in the next life......after Marilyn Monroe.

I still remember that night...August 4-5, 1962. I'm not sure what side of midnight it was because I wasn't watching the clock...I was dying. I saw my body moved around like a rag doll, manipulated by men who only wanted to dispose of me. Alone, surprised, outnumbered, overpowered, betrayed, frantic, disoriented, confused, bewildered, discarded... and yet very, very determined to tell somebody. I vowed to come back and tell what happened. I want to tell the world!

Imagine on December 31st, you make a New Year's Resolution and then you lose focus. A year later, you are wondering, "Why didn't I follow through?" I can't do that with this. Her self-promise is mine. Here is "our story".

In an effort to protect the privacy of those people in my life who may not want to be linked to "the truths" that I tell, I have omitted using people's last names and in some cases use code names altogether. I have done my best to tell my stories honestly, complete with *the nitty-gritty* that comes along with being forthright. I apologize for any offence that may come with it....but I have seen the way every single detail of Marilyn's life has been excavated and gone under the microscope since the day she died and I feel this is my one and only chance to really speak my mind and explain my current lifetime the way I see it...and explain her impact on me.

Perhaps this book is my glorified diary...or rather, "our diary".. Marilyn's and Michele's. I have included a handful of stories that may seem a bit distasteful, but I believe sometimes the worst things each of us goes through are the things we should be willing to share, because someone else may be going through the same thing and need to know that they are not alone.

I will only be successful in this literary endeavor if I manage to rescue Marilyn without sacrificing Michele. But quite frankly, I think this book is "the moment" I was born for.

- Michele

"I was a girl before...I am a girl now. I don't speak 'icon' or 'legend' ...I just speak from the heart."

"People telling me I am crazy, doesn't make my book fiction. Finding Marilyn in-the-nude, doesn't make murder sexy."

"I refuse to compromise The Truth: I would rather tell you 3 things I am sure of, than 20 things to impress you."

"PLEASE PARDON ANY AND ALL TYPOS! I did go to college, but I might have spent more time studying boys than I should have. I have noticed, most guys don't really care where I stick the apostrophe, as long as it is somewhere. And they are generally happy as long as there is an occasional period and a lot of exclamation points. Other than that, I just do my best. If I spelled something wrong....please forgive me. I did consult the dictionary. But, this is the first time I've ever written a book."

DEDICATION.

This book is dedicated to TRUTH...and also actress, author, friend... SUSAN STRASBERG.

Susan Strasberg was a lovely, sophisticated, talented, kind-hearted woman. Susan was perhaps Marilyn's "second sister". Susan shared her family with Marilyn, even when Marilyn's dramatic nature didn't make it all that easy to do so. This book is dedicated to telling the truth about many things...one of which is....Susan was precious, and was never in anybody's shadow. Susan radiated goodness. Even as a child during my Michele-lifetime I felt drawn to her.

When I was about 15, I remember flipping through the TV channels late one night at my Nunny's house. There was a movie in progress... "Mr. and Mrs. Bo Jo Jones" with Desi Arnaz Jr. and Christopher Norris. And there SHE was...an elegant, dark-haired woman with the features of an angel. She played a character named "Lee". I stared at her. Then I saw that name in the movie credits... "Susan Strasberg". I kept wondering, "Why does that name sound so familiar?" I just figured Strasberg must be some important sounding name like Vanderbilt. Several years later, I understood why. Eventually with the help of YouTube, I went on to watch many interviews Susan gave with her usual poise and thoughtful words. She was often asked about Marilyn. I wish I had known her as a middle-aged woman. My friend Tina and I both have her books.

TABLE OF CONTENTS

I/Michele hope this will be at least somewhat interesting.

I will do my best not to confuse you, but I do tend to talk in first person and third person here and there because of my different levels of attachment to these lives. I was trying to explain to my hypnotist how I experience my past life memories. I said, "I never really 'just watch' what happens. I either am 'being that other person'....or.... 'attached like a Siamese Twin'". Most of my past life memories just came to me without pursuing them. I never actually hired a hypnotist until June 2018, when I was 53.

You will notice there are no photos of Marilyn in this book. I would have loved to have had a few choice ones. But due to copyright laws, I have refrained because it is not easy to track down who owns the rights to the ones I like the most. I would have loved to have had at least one shot of Marilyn in front of the Actors Studio sign...because that is what was important to her...her craft...and being the best she could be.

Let me also say that I wish Marilyn's sister and niece would have profited from her image, instead of a lot of strangers.

Diehard Marilyn fans know what the stuffed animal above is from. It is from the photo of Marilyn's house, taken in 1962 as policemen surveyed the area after her death. This toy belonged to Marilyn's cute white pup, Maf. I do not know who took the photo of Marilyn's house, but "thank you". Several different versions of the yard exist and some seem to be copyrighted and some I can't tell. I have not been able to figure out who "owns" the photo from the angle which I have extracted this stuffed animal from. Therefore, this stuffed animal is the symbol I am using to remind us all that this book is about Marilyn......MARILYN MONROE.

Michele M Baumberfield

Chapter One:

MARILYN-MICHELE: "MARILYN CLAIMERS" ABOUND!

Marilyn Claimers

So, let's address this subject. There is a growing list of people claiming they lived a past life as Marilyn Monroe. Some have even written books or had a doctor study them:

-Sherrie from Canada
-Angela from Idaho
-Kate from New Jersey
-Zsuzsanna from Hungary

-Chris from the UK
-Edith from Israel
*-**whoever** comes next...*

*N*ot sure how so many can believe this...or even just one of them can believe it. I'm truly perplexed. I'd like to know what they are actually experiencing. I have read parts of some of their books. Mainly I read the parts about Marilyn's cause of death. I just figured, "Heck, maybe they are psychic and know what happened even if they weren't there."—Nope! These people either don't know how I died or they are afraid to tell.

I heard that one Claimer felt "haunted" by memories of Marilyn. I have never felt that way. I feel a deep "recognition". Recognition of former self. And the feelings are so deep, it still feels like relevant self... current in the moment...and the emotions come flooding back as if they just were or are.

Despite my full belief that my own soul was Marilyn's, I cannot call any of these other claimers liars because I don't know what they have gone through and maybe they are experiencing energies from the past.

I do however have a theory:

Later in the book I will mention that my consciousness bumped into a mirror as I/Marilyn was first out-of-body while dying. It startled me! But I/Michele don't know why it did...it happened so fast. Now I am left wondering whether my energy was diffracted and it attached to other people who maybe I have something in common with without realizing. Just a theory.

At first I thought I could be ok with the lady who was the most interviewed of all the previous "Marilyn Claimers". She really did the publicity circuit a decade or so ago and had a doctor study her and write a book about her and accompany her on some interviews. I figured, "Well, she is pretty, and speaks well, and STAYED IN SHOW BIZ, so who cares if people think she was Marilyn. At least she likes animals and seems like a nice person."

But then when I found out she believes Marilyn merely killed herself, that left me feeling unsettled...COULD I REALLY LIVE WITH

THAT being the message the world is asked to believe? If it were true, I could. But...there is more to the story than that. Let me just say, "That Claimer's take on things is a tough pill to swallow."

WHAT DO I WANT?

I suppose I am expecting people to believe Marilyn and I share the same soul even though I don't appear to resemble her at first impression. I am expecting people to believe that I was Marilyn even though I dropped out of show biz after college. I expect people to believe that I was Marilyn even though I'm not photogenic and don't have many pictures to show. I expect people to believe that I was Marilyn even though I don't remember a gigantic plethora of Marilyn tidbits and perhaps the things that are the most written about. I even expect the diehard Marilyn fans who are fiercely loyal to her memory to be open-minded. I guess I expect a whole darn lot! —-Well, let me say this... maybe I don't really "expect" these things....but I am "hopeful" people will read the rest of the book and then decide.

I am not looking for 15 minutes of fame, or opportunities in the theatre or my own reality TV show. My objective is to tell you about me, so you know that I am not a secretive person and that you can trust me when I tell you how I died during my last past life. I don't know how else to tell people this.

Now, I can just imagine the people who are thinking that it is so sad to be beautiful and famous in one lifetime and then not in the next. But as you will see throughout the rest of my book, sometimes there are trade-offs... other good things besides "Hollywood approved assets". Hollywood is just one part of the world...not the whole world. We all know that....right?

Living another lifetime is a new opportunity to see life from a different perspective and try new things. Coming back to this world doesn't mean constantly reincarnating as an identical twin to your past self. At least not for me. My life now isn't glamorous for sure...yet in some ways it is better.

I have heard it said that reincarnation can be studied scientifically in an earnest attempt to prove a person was who they claim they were during another lifetime. However, my opinion is this: Don't forget about the GOD ELEMENT. Remember it is what's inside that really counts. Sort of like the way a lot of people believe tomatoes and cucumbers are vegetables...but those seeds on the inside make them fruits.

Same with people. It isn't your hair color or size of your hands or shape of your feet that proves anything. It's the soul...that thing we can't see or predict or study. We don't know how our souls may show up in the next life. The outside is temporary. Perhaps for me this lifetime is one to remember many of my past lives and their traumas and to heal. Marilyn's experiences are part of my life ... but there is so much more.

"Mr. Surgeon, I'd like to have everybody else's opinion removed."

Since Marilyn's death, people seem to have gone bonkers digging up every scrap of paper on which she wrote...and trying to interpret it. While people typically deem Marilyn with kindness now, this is very odd to me. I know that when I was living that lifetime I craved attention and approval....but certainly not to this degree. Imagine if every private note you scrawled ...in sometimes your worst handwriting.... was put on display and interpreted by others!

I have seen online that some are concerned about a particular writing which Marilyn wrote during the mid-50's. (I had no recollection of this catharsis, so I read it.) Some people believe her words are about a bad dream. Some think mind control. I believe it is about questionable mental health practices during that era, coupled with my own insecurity and inability to take that leap and change "the image". Marilyn wanted to please others. Marilyn wanted an answer to a complicated career situation. Marilyn was an adult when she sought her acting coach. She knew that acting involved dredging up deep emotion...expression...control. Theatre is a living thing...you continue to work through each role you play...even during the run of a show. It's not a quick fix. I/Marilyn desperately was fearful of disappointing everyone around me...I wrote about Me afraid of Me.

Chapter Two:

MICHELE: WHO AM I THIS LIFETIME?

In the beginning...

irst let me tell you about my family and how I fit in. I think this is very important because of the obvious. <u>Marilyn always wanted a stable family.</u> She wanted to know who her Father was. Marilyn's Mother had mental illness. Marilyn's beloved half-sister Berniece was raised in Kentucky and kept away from her until the later part of her childhood. So.......I am darn lucky to have the family I have during this current lifetime!

My parents Mary and Jim got married less than a year after they met each other. They were planning a wedding for 1963, but suddenly felt the hurry to move up their wedding date. December 29, 1962, they took their vows. I have often thought that maybe they "needed to get married" so I could come along. Afterall, Marilyn had just died August 5th that same year. But more than likely, they were just two pretty people very much in love. I love their wedding photos. My Nunny sewed the bridesmaid dresses, and often said that she had to rush to get them all done!

As a younger man during the early 70's, my Dad was very handsome with sandy brown hair and blue eyes...along with his cleft chin. He flew to California a couple times on business and took his guitar with him.— He just dabbled at playing for fun. Dad said people would mistake him for Glen Campbell walking through the airports, until they got up real close and realized that he wasn't. We thought that that was funny!

I really have to credit my Dad for a couple big things. He gave up smoking cigarettes because when I was a child I saw something about "kicking the habit" and I nagged him a few times. That is all it took. He literally mulled the idea over in his head and gave up smoking because he said he wanted to be healthy for his family. He said he never regretted it, because he saw others later in life who ended up with health issues. And also cigarettes kept going up up up in price. I think I was about 6 or so when he quit.

Dad also gave up hunting because I had seen some news segment about someone who was accidentally shot by their own relative when a few family members went into the woods during hunting season. Friendly fire they called it....sounded awful to me. I told my Dad I was very concerned for him. I was probably 7 or 8. My Dad said he thought that over and realized his two daughters and wife needed him. And besides, he said that with the high power rifles these days, hunting didn't seem so challenging any more...the deer were simply overpowered. My Dad became "the camp cook" while his brothers continued to shoot. Thanks Dad. I really admire him for making such a decision and sticking to it...especially with peer pressure right in his own family. My Dad is the coolest!

My Mom was very pretty, with dark brown hair, brown eyes and quite a noticeable hour-glass figure. I saw a few 1960's beach comedies and thought my Mother could have been Annette Funicello's stand-in. There is one photo of my Mother in her 20's that I particularly like. She was in Philadelphia in the wintertime, all bundled up and sitting on a park bench. She wore bright red lipstick. That was probably late 1950's.

When I was a small child, my Mom would have tea parties at our house. Actually several women in the neighborhood took turns hosting. It always seemed so elegant and I loved to watch her set the table...it just seemed more interesting than normal table-setting to me. I figured that was something I would do when I was older. The whole idea of tea with cookies or cake and the fancy tea pot and nicely folded napkins intrigued me. The idea of my Mommy sitting around the table gabbing with ladies who were my friends' Mothers seemed delightful. And back then, all the mothers literally scrubbed and waxed their kitchen and dining room floors down on their hands and knees. So the floor always had that newly polished look...that you could just slightly smell when it was still drying. I can still smell the wax polish. Mom said she and Laddie listened to the radio while she scrubbed. Laddie was a handsome mild-mannered collie and good company.

My Dad has always been a genius and he worked in science, math and engineering related fields. By the time I was ready to go to college, he was working at a major university. My Mom had a job at The University Creamery doing some kind of testing in the lab. She quit to be a stay-at-home Mom when she was pregnant with me. She went back to work when I was in the 8th grade. Eventually, she was also working again for The University during my college years. They are very good parents and got my sister and me both a bachelor's degree without taking on school loans.

My parents have lived in the same house since I was one year old. I can still go back and sleep in my old childhood bedroom when I visit! Another thing is, my parents have made it clear I can always come back home. If only Marilyn had had a safety net to fall back on. Nothing replaces a good, caring, loving, stable family...nothing. It's easy to take a close-knit family for granted because most people assume we "should" just have one. But people who don't have one KNOW what I mean. In the pages to come, readers may look at my life and think I have back slid...nothing seems too amazing. I'm quite ordinary and so is my life. I work hard to live modestly. However, I think perhaps Marilyn would have traded places with me.

I was born in Pennsylvania... July 10, 1964.
This was almost 2 years after Marilyn died.
My name is Michele Marie...my childhood nickname "Missy"

7

Prior to going off to college, the only time I remember being called by my formal name was if my Dad called me "Michele Marie". I never thought I looked like a "Michele". I thought "a Michele" should be tall with long dark hair. But once in college, a handsome green-eyed Italian boy insisted on it, and I suddenly decided it was time...I became **Michele**. That same boy took me out on Friday, August 13, 1982...so that is why I never think of Friday the 13th as a bad day. Mike R. talked me into using my own name.

I am the first daughter of two. My sister Chris is "the cute one" in the family, and the one who had naturally pretty blond hair up until it turned dark during her teens. She is athletic and I am the daydreamer.

As a kid, I liked dolls, listening to show tunes, pretend acting in my room, and watching psychological thrillers into the wee hours of the morning on weekends. My sister was confident and bold...I tended to be shy. Despite the fact I often felt unattractive and insecure, I always felt destined to be famous. Was this because of Marilyn?

I was very close to my Mother's Mother who I called Nunny. And thankfully Nunny and Papa only lived an hour from us, so I grew up spending many weekends and holidays visiting them in their 1930's two-story, dark-red brick home. Old red brick homes are my "dream home".

Papa was half deaf due to severe childhood earaches that weren't attended to on-time. Papa always had a great vegetable garden and specialized in tomatoes. He was a quiet man who never carried on long conversations. He loved football and baseball and my Mother acquired an autographed picture of Joe Paterno, which he proudly displayed above his TV-set. I can only imagine that Papa probably loved Joe Dimaggio back in his heyday.

Papa got me a collie dog named Laddie because I loved Lassie. My Nunny always said he was very good with animals. I hope to have a collie again in the future...maybe when I don't work long hours and can let a doggy outside in the middle of the day. Dreamin'.....

Nunny didn't wear much make-up or jewelry, but she always had a touch of glamour. Her finger nails and toe nails would be painted a matching cherry red, and she smelled like Wind Song perfume. She was a very talented seamstress, and often made clothes for everyone. Nunny had a good sense of humor, loved to gab, and had a kind and accepting way about her. She used to throw little New Years parties and play piano. She was an amazing cook and baked pies. Nunny loved to make in fun of 70's songs because she said they just kept repeating the same word... "baby baby baby baby baby".

Nunny and I used to paint with watercolors together. We would drink hot tea with cream and sugar and put on our best fake British accents and mimic people we saw on the TV show "Upstairs, Downstairs". We loved to laugh at ourselves and how mediocre we sounded. I idolized Nunny. I loved hearing about the good old days. Nunny was born in 1917, and she used to say, "I was born the same year that President Kennedy was." I was lucky enough to have Nunny in my life until I was 40. Spending time with Nunny was the very best part of this current lifetime. She just seemed magical.

My family is very very Catholic on both sides. My Great Grandparents said the Rosary every day. They were Nunny's parents. In my 20's, I did tell Nunny I believe in reincarnation. **One day she said to me, "Missy, I don't really think reincarnation is real. But just in case it is, promise me if it is, you will be my mother in another lifetime."** I told her I would name her Francesca and we would live in France and go to an amusement park together and have lots of fun. She said it was a deal. I was glad she wasn't totally closed off to the possibility! I look forward to seeing her again.

I never knew my Dad's Dad, because he died the year before I was born. But my Dad said he was a really hard worker and he got a scar on his face when he once fought a man who he saw abusing a dog.—I'm sure I would have liked him!

My Grandmother on my Dad's side was a lovely lady who raised 13 kids of her own, and helped raise one step-son. She painted ceramics, made homemade candy at Christmastime, and was constantly entertaining visiting relatives. I once had a sleepover at her home when I was 19 and we had a great conversation. Grandma was in my life until I was 23. I feel badly for people who don't get to know their grandparents. Grandparents are a great blessing.

Nunny and Grandma each repaired the red paws on my favorite stuffed dolls. Grandma repaired Emily's and Nunny repaired Mary's.

**At this point, I need to mention two of my very best friends...
Mary and Emily.** They are my two favorite dolls I got when I was
under 5 years old. My Dad got them for me. They are my "childhood
children". Mary and Emily are two yellow rubber faced stuffed bunnies...vintage 1960's. Their long bunny ears are behind their heads like
pony tails now...they got floppy over time. I used to hold them when I
slept at night and play with them when I was listening to show tunes
on my record player.

Mary was named after my Mom and Emily after my Nunny. **I used
to look at them and think, "Who do they remind me of?" and
"Mary is the sassier one."** I have loved them into a very delicate state,
so therefore they still reside in my parents' home for safe-keeping, and
sleep in a doll cradle in the same room I had as a child. Nunny used to
say she thought I called her "Nunny" because it rhymes with "bunny".

Years later I realized they had "Marilyn Monroe like faces" with
cute button noses. I have been told I'm nuts for seeing that in them...
but I do! And also, one day I realized that their initials spell ME. Mary
and Emily. My Nunny painted a picture of them and it hangs in my
bedroom even now.

Some girls have Barbies...some boys have ball cards...I have
Bunny Dolls.

I truly believe that during my childhood they subconsciously
reminded me of Marilyn. I felt extremely bonded with them. I think
it was almost like when a person is out of body and sees their own face
from the outside.

I remember my Nunny had a neighbor several doors down and her
grown-up daughter's name was Marilyn. Marilyn wasn't home much so
I never really got to know her. I remember telling Nunny that there was
something I really liked about her name. Nunny said, "Really, why? It's
an OK name." I said I didn't know why, I just did. I said I thought the
name was kind of beautiful. The name just stuck in my mind.

Throughout my life I have been a TV addict. I would say the only
time I wasn't was during my college years when I lived in the dorms.
My Dad used to call the television "the one-eyed monster" and he said
it would suck my brains out if I watched too much. I am still guilty

of working quite a dose of TV into my schedules even now. I like the sound...which some people call "noise".

I do remember the 1970's when Joe DiMaggio and Jane Russell were doing ads on TV...coffee makers and bras. I remember really being perplexed about why Jane was selling bras. But I didn't actively recall that she had been a big star in the 50's who I knew. I remember asking my Mom why Jane was selling bras. She explained that, "Big busted gals need extra support." I didn't know what to make of it. One time when we were at Nunny and Papa's house, my sister Chris and I made a prank phone call and thought we were so clever rattling off stuff about 18 hour bras and hanging up. But eventually Nunny got her phone bill and wondered what the call to the odd area code was about. We confessed. That ended our pranks. As far as Joe's coffee maker ads, I remember being more interested in the coffee maker than him. But my parents drank instant until I was an adult. I recently looked up one of his old ads on youtube. I think he was more attractive as an older man than as a younger man. He seemed nice.

On an amusing note, I have often heard people debate, "Ginger or MaryAnn?" They are referring to who you prefer on the 1960's TV show "Gilligan's Island". Well, I like them both...but...I always related more to Ginger, even when I was little and far from stunning. There was just something about her that was both exasperating and fabulous. My favorite show of the whole entire series was when MaryAnn hits her head and has amnesia and thinks that SHE is Ginger. So MaryAnn goes around acting like Ginger most of the show. Who knows....maybe I saw Norma Jeane turn into Marilyn in that episode. Maybe the past was speaking to me.

Halloween party....what's wrong with me?

When I was a kid, my Halloween costumes were typically pretty cheap and premade. During the 70's you could buy a box with a mask and a jumper type costume in it. The masks always had a funny feel and smell to them and the band that held them on your head kind of hurt and it was hard to breathe behind the plastic.

I recall one year when I was about 8, my Nunny and Mom helped me get a better costume, because the girl down the street was having a costume party. I got to wear a pretty light blue party dress which looked like the 1950's, and a blond wig. I recall everything being ok until they announced there would be prizes for the funniest costume, scariest costume and prettiest costume. People voted by applause for who they wanted to win.

When someone dared to put me in the "pretty category," I immediately felt the worst sense of embarrassment and shame and I looked down and shrank as much as I could. I didn't want the prize and I didn't win the prize. I never understood why I felt the way I did in that moment. It was very, very odd. I think the lady who nominated me was a bit surprised too. She was being nice, I was being elusive. I simply couldn't handle that moment...something about it disturbed me to the core.

I wanted so badly to be pretty but admitting I wanted to be pretty made me feel very ashamed and this is something that continued throughout a lot of my childhood up until the time I went off to college. I never understood the irony. I told myself it was because I was raised Catholic and should be modest. I told myself that wanting to be pretty was asking for too much attention. I told myself it was just plain egotistical. Yet I wanted it so!

I'm not ready for sexy!

When I was in high school I auditioned for a murder mystery the Thespians were going to perform. I got an understudy role. I was so afraid of being called upon at the last minute that I memorized all the lines, even though the Director never actually worked with the understudies.

One day our group of actors was told we could go along on a Saturday trip to a news studio an hour away. —I don't recall anyone ever saying what the purpose was. Only the Director and a few of us kids showed up...and not the girl I was understudying for. Turns out we were taping some short promo for our play.

So they had me and a guy named Ron do a scene with about 2-3 lines. My character spoke in a British accent, his character choked me. The way we played the scene really wasn't like in the actual play, but we were on a little set and just improvising something since the camera was already in position. I think I was sitting on a newsroom "interview seat".

I loved doing British accents because Nunny and I used to fake them with our tea. And I used to "seriously practice" them because Julie Andrews, Princess Diana and Hayley Mills had them.

Anyway, after the taping, the studio staff were whispering to the high school Director. Then I was pulled aside and asked if I would be interested in doing any kind of work. Of course I was! **But then one studio guy looked at me with a glimmer in his eye and said, "You know, I hate to say it but sex appeal sells."** (It must have been the accent that did it!) I blushed and I'm sure looked totally not up to the tasks they had in mind. I never got called. I was also underage, so maybe they decided to scout out an 18 year old to be sexy for the camera...or whatever.

It is probably just as well. Marilyn probably didn't want me to land that kind of work! I had plenty of time to decide what kind of "sexy" I wanted to be. No need to rush it! I did not appear in the play, but the girl who played the role was her usual good self. I was relieved because I never got to rehearse.

Cleopatra eyes...

When I was in junior high, I remember my Mom saying that young girls who wear a lot of make-up "look like painted ladies". I knew the connotation was BAD. I wanted to wear make-up when I was just a small child and my Mom bought me some pink frosted lipstick one birthday, but that was "just for play around the house". I was allowed to wear light lipstick or lip gloss when I went out. But other than that, I didn't wear make-up or do anything special with my face until I was in 10th grade. Maybe she would have let me wear it sooner, I don't know. But I was afraid of "looking cheap" and "painted" and "harsh". So I remained pale.

Then during 10th grade I bonded with an 11th grader who said her Mother had been a model for a while. We were instant friends. She wore very thick eye-liner and I began wearing it too. I don't really recall my Mother reacting to the make-up at that time. But many years later she tried to get me to "tone it down". I have not! It's my trademark—ha!

Finally, people noticed me and told me I had pretty eyes. I still felt uncomfortable when people complimented me, and I rarely believed them. But at the same time I also still craved to be noticed. One neighbor told my Mom I had very expressive eyes that sparkled a lot when I talked. This helped counteract how unattractive I always felt. Eyeliner does wonders!

As a matter of fact, going forward, my eyes were the one thing I liked about my appearance. **And I often told myself, "Well, if nothing else, at least you have nice eyes."** Many years later, I would have to deal with not having this crutch. The flaws of skin cancer surgery changed all that.

What decade do I belong to?

During 11th and 12th grades, one of my favorite things to do was to use my study halls to get a pass to the school library. I would read the big Life magazines that had lots of groovy 1960's photos in them. I loved the 60's and often felt badly that I/Michele was just a child during that period and not able to experience it as an adult. I didn't know why I was so obsessed with that era, but I felt a powerful connection to it... the styles I saw in those pages felt mysteriously life-sustaining to a girl who felt like a misfit. I really loved *that* particular style of sex-appeal too. Big hair, blue eye-shadow, go-go boots, short dresses, the whole fabulous over-the-top works!

During my high school years, I would often pray that I would go to sleep and not wake up the next morning and have to go to school... but I always heard the call to get up to catch the bus. **Now and then I used to think, "I feel like I should be a different person."** But the idea seemed so weird and sci-fi. So, I'd push the thought out of my mind. How far-fetched!!!

Who is this woman....?

The first time I recall ever hearing about Marilyn at all was during the 1970's when I watched the TV movie "The Sex Symbol" with Connie Stevens in the starring role. The lead character was not called Marilyn. She was called Kelly. My Dad walked into the room at the very end when the Kelly character is dead. **He said, "Oh, that must be a take-off of Marilyn Monroe's life story." I asked "Who?"** He explained Marilyn was a sexy actress who overdosed before I was born. His saying that really stuck with me, but I didn't know why.

Prior to college, I remember seeing about two scenes of "The Misfits," two scenes from "The Seven Year Itch," half of "Bus Stop", and the diamonds number in "Gentlemen Prefer Blonds". But overall, when I would see Marilyn's movies advertised on TV, I would think, "Yuk, that's the dumb blond image." For some reason I felt like I didn't want to watch. The idea seemed annoying actually.

Years later as a 53 year old woman, I watched some of Marilyn's movies at last. I only watched them because I was severely depressed at the time and could easily see them on cable TV. I figured I had nothing to lose. I felt almost stupid choosing them because I expected to be disappointed at every turn. However, I was pleasantly surprised and liked a few afterall. Most of the time I thought Marilyn had talent. Some of the time I just saw that odd blank far-off look in her eyes... which I understood.

I personally like "River of No Return" as it is actually a serious drama. And I recall during the later part of Marilyn's life, I thought the same thing. "Niagra" is also very good. I like the musical numbers in "Gentlemen Prefer Blonds," but not the dialogue. I love Jane Russell. Two of Marilyn's movies are too bad to even mention.—I want to forget that they even exist! I'm just so, so relieved that at least there are a few pretty-good movies among the collection. A few I have yet to watch and maybe never will.

Summer 1982....

When I graduated high school, my Dad told me I HAD TO go to college. So I did. I went to the best University around! I immediately started attending classes close to home. I proudly majored in theatre. I moved into the dorms and I was propelled into one situation after another where I needed to mingle, mingle, mingle and get over my shyness. I had to grow up socially at an accelerated rate. I went from "very shy" to "must try". I had to put myself out-there a lot more than before.

This was actually new to me. Accept for participating in community theatre during summers and hanging out with the high school Thespians a little bit, I was really a homebody before I turned 18. The first semester I moved into the dorms I had a very spunky, popular roommate who took it upon herself to include me in some things and push me a bit. She was a lot more out-going and she didn't want me to miss out on all the FUN.

I did go to about three or four parties and had a few sips of beer when I was only 18. —But I never liked it. And one time I remember spending a good bit of the night talking with some attractive older guy, who wore red glasses, and looked like he was a little teary-eyed when I said good-night. But what really sticks out in my mind was one night my friends and I had to run really fast in the dark, through some grass and I was wearing big wedge heals. I'm still not sure how I managed not to trip or what we were running from. Someone shouted "Run!" and we ran. I think it was because we were underage. After that, I just stopped going to parties.

My roommate's name was Jackie. She started out as an art major who later turned health and nutrition expert. I was extremely lucky that the computer program used to randomly match us that semester did so. Oddly enough, she was a very cute, very blond, blue-eyed gal with a curvaceous figure. Who knows what that happenstance subconsciously unlocked for me.

I suddenly had to figure out who I was, and what I wanted to be ... but I had no idea I was about to remember a whole other lifetime after my first year of acting classes.

Marilyn Monroe was just an old movie star, I thought. She was someone beautiful and tragic who played dumb roles. She was the blond lady who married the guy who advertised coffee makers... and she dated the President. She was the sexy woman who did things my Mother would never approve of.

I always wanted to be pretty and famous in show business, but I NEVER saw Marilyn as a role model or "a favorite"...never. I collected some posters and records, but I never had anything with her on it even when I was a teen and had a lot of my own money because I babysat all the time.

Marilyn was just "out there"...she belonged to "The World" but I didn't think of her as part of "my world" at all. I never thought much about President Kennedy either...I thought more about Abraham Lincoln. President Lincoln always seemed like a real hero.

Chapter Three:

MICHELE: MIRROR-MIRROR: ALL THOSE DAMN IMPERFECTIONS!

My mirror hates me!

At an early age I never felt "right" and I constantly pursued reasons to hate my image, even if no one else was critiquing me. I must say, I was pretty brutal. You would have thought the girl in the mirror was a leper. I knew I was pretty average and that truly devastated me.

My Eyes
Around age 10, I began to constantly wish for blue eyes. I couldn't figure out why I didn't have them. I really felt like I *should have*. My Dad has blue eyes....my Mom and sister Chris have brown.....

and mine are greenish-brown hazel. Nunny told me to just be happy I could see.—I wasn't. My fixation on blue eyes went on for years... years...I felt deficient. And I really felt things ran much deeper than just being superficial.

I finally figured I must be obsessed with blue, because I was a big Julie Andrews fan and she has blue eyes. So do Shirley MacLaine and Patty Duke. And Melissa Sue Anderson who played Mary on "Little House On The Prairie" was on my TV screen every Monday night throughout my junior high and high school era....and her eyes were simply gorgeous. With many of my favorite performers having blue eyes, I concluded that that must be why I was so obsessed with them... and concerned about my lack thereof. I literally used to feel heart-broken as if something was horribly wrong with me. Then my Mom informed me that my eyes were blue for a short time when I was a baby... but they changed. How could that be?

But once I began to recall my past lives, it put a whole new spin on things. Now I believe that during my Michele-childhood, I sub-consciously remembered having blue eyes during my last two lifetimes. And of course during Marilyn's I was photographed constantly and much was made of my appearance on a regular basis. Is it any wonder why I felt as I did?

I love Sir Elton John's song called "Blue Eyes". I remember hearing it during my 4th year of college. It is so hauntingly sad, yet very sexy. I got blue eye contacts at about age 27, but they hurt my eyes and I gave them up a few months later. Then in my 40's I got them again and they were much more comfortable. But by then I was with my current boy-friend Jay and he said, "You don't look like you now." He seemed to actually like THE REAL ME. I gave them up.

My Hands

By the time I was a teen, I hated my hands. Big hands...not at all delicate. No matter what rings I put on them, they aren't pretty. Years later, I would recall being Marilyn and thinking that my wrists sometimes seemed weak when doing certain things. So, maybe God and The Universe gave me big hands this time around so that I would feel stronger....who knows. <u>Be careful for what you wish for</u>! Marilyn's hands look so lovely in her photos. My sister got the cute little hands like my Nunny had.

Throughout my own 20's and 30's, I spent so much money buying jewelry, especially rings, in an attempt to look prettier. I painted my nails constantly, mostly reds and bright pink. But inevitably I pawned most of my jewels off when times were tough and I needed the cash. To this day, my longtime boyfriend Jay and I laugh about the "Seinfeld" episode about "man hands". Anyone who hasn't seen it is missing something hysterically funny. Jerry tries to cope when he realizes that the pretty blond woman he is dating has huge beefy hands like a man. The lobster dinner scene is so funny!

Anyway, especially during the time I grew up, kids in school hand wrote everything. There was printing and script (cursive writing)....but no computers in the classrooms! You got somewhat judged on neatness. I was always judging my writing for "prettiness" and at a young age I hated it. I knew some people's penmanship was so pretty without really trying. In later years, I would finally recall that when I was Marilyn I worried that my handwriting was too messy when I signed autographs one after another. I really focused on making fancy loopy M's but got down on myself for not making every autograph super-pretty. As a child, I/Michele didn't understand why I cared so much. I just drove myself crazy picking things apart. My hands are big and they don't write pretty like I want them to!

My Nose:
I never fixed it but used to think I wanted to. The first time I remember becoming obsessed with my nose was after I saw "The Sound of Music". I was 9. Julie Andrews was my hero and I thought that movie was the best in the world. I wanted a nose like she had. Her profile looked much smoother than mine. And of course there is that profile scene in the gazebo where she and handsome Christopher Plummer declare their love for each other (as Maria and the Captain). My nose is lumpy in the middle. I had no means to change my nose then, so I cut my hair like hers and I'd go around singing songs from the musical.

Years later my ex-husband told me I should be ok with my nose because he said it looks like it belongs on a Greek sculpture. That somehow made it seem better!

When it was time to take my senior portrait in high school, oddly enough the photographer fixated on my profile and said my right was the best one. For a girl obsessed with her deviated septum, this was amazing to hear!

I remember this situation from my senior year of high school. One of my senior portraits was put in the newspaper. I was taking an art class and there were two male instructors co-teaching. They both were walking around the room looking over people's shoulders to see where they were in their projects. The one man said, "Missy, I saw your picture in the paper and I think it is very nice." I'm sure I blushed. The next instructor couldn't keep his mouth shut. He had to say, "I like *so-and-so's* the best."

Hmmm....they both are entitled to their own opinion and there is freedom of speech. But I don't really know why the second guy had to pipe up. He couldn't have just let me have a moment? Yes, I already knew the other girl was much prettier...thanks for pointing out the obvious!

My Weight:

Lots of designer jeans ads on TV. The first time I remember hating my weight and body was at about age 12. I was still very thin but not developing at a fast pace so I still didn't have curves. I was somewhat underweight really. However, when I was on a vacation, someone took a picture of me in my pink bikini and that photo horrified me. I saw a little belly fat, and that sent me into years of body shame and believing that that was the first thing anyone always noticed about me. I seriously thought people must notice my fat stomach before my smile, my eyes or even my lumpy nose. But this is proportionally how I'm built. I could be thin and still have a gut. I learned to constantly hold it in.

At age 12, I immediately went to work to rid myself of this "deformity" which I felt sure would keep me from having the future movie career which I dreamed of daily. First I started off with some funny exercise contraption that you attach to your door knob and get down on the ground to use. You pull it with your arms and kick up your legs and ....nah! It never did anything for my tummy. Maybe it worked for other people. I think it gave me a back ache....or maybe the countless sit-ups hurt my back. —I joined my mom at the chiropractor a handful of times. I also faithfully began bust exercises thinking if I had a chest that would distract from the lower half of my pear-shaped body.

Then, by the time I was 15, I began torturing myself using food. This was the year I finally got my period, and also blossomed up-top. But I still felt inadequate. Probably the fact that I was constantly watching TV and looking at movie stars didn't help. I told myself I would someday get a tummy tuck. (I haven't.) I went from 118 lbs to 105 lbs in a couple weeks by eating mostly celery and raison bran... sometimes yogurt. But that was hard to maintain and I went back up to my normal weight.

I'm 5'6", so 118 wasn't terrible, accept in my own eyes. I began wishing I was taller like a model. I wished this throughout high school and college years. Eventually I was glad I was average height because some of the men I liked weren't tall. I also wore heels as soon as I began working in an office.

When I was 17, one day my Mom had some fancy frozen chocolate cake with cream and cherries on top. She usually baked cakes but for some reason she had this brand-name delight at the house. I think we had company. Later in the evening, I got the brilliant idea to eat extra and puke it up. I'm not sure what possessed me because at the time I hadn't heard of bulimia, just anorexia. I really have no idea how that idea got into my head.

I found the "right formula" for purging pretty easily...I knew what combination of foods made it easier. I emptied my stomach that way most of my junior year of high school. Sometimes I did it 5 times in one day. It got to the point where there were very few days in the year that I wasn't binge-purging, and it was making me feel quite imprisoned by that whole vicious cycle. My self-hatred continued.

I would also get up extra early on weekends so I could binge when no one was looking. But the truth is, when you over indulge so much, you don't really taste it. It becomes about quantity all of a sudden and just "the action" and not even enjoyment or nutrition anymore. I only felt powerful the first few times I purged, but after that it turned on me and made me feel disgusting. My desire to be in control, felt like it was controlling me!

One time I remember puking into a garbage can at my Nunny's house late late at night after I ate chips. I could barely even do it but I was trying to force the food up.—I think their only bathroom was occupied at the time.

Another time I went on a long weekend trip with my sister, Mom and Nunny. We went to see my Uncle David and I really wasn't sure I could even manage a whole weekend without my usual ritual. But as hard as it was, I did. And that break in my behavior enabled me to break free of it somewhat. I still went back to purging but stopped for a month or two, and then went back to it but not as many days in a row.

One thing I did notice was I was beginning to get red dots all under my eyes. I think this was from the constant pressure on my face because of vomiting. One day I looked in the mirror and decided to just give it up. I was afraid that I might pop something in my head or eye and be left disabled. Once that became my reason for stopping, it wasn't hard to refrain...at least not from using that method of weight control.

Then I began the laxative phase. But I was too embarrassed to actually purchase laxatives themselves, so I used some other things that I heard would have the same affect. The one thing did and the other thing just made me feel like dying. It was all pretty horrible and I did it now and then over the next few years, even beyond high school.

The lowest point was probably when I drank some colorful shampoo. It was a brand I didn't even like using on my hair because it smelled so nasty. But my Nunny had once told me to "Make sure you really rinse the dishes off, because soap can mess up your stomach". So, I figured if I drank a little shampoo that would take the weight off like a laxative. Uh, no. It just gave me a sickening taste in my mouth that I will remember for the rest of my life! And also a headache. I stopped because I was afraid of brain damage. (No, do not blame my past life memories on that, please!)

Then my interest in exercising went to a whole new level...obses-sion! Jumping rope...lifting weights...jogging. My Dad got me started jogging when we were getting ready to go to the shore the summer between my junior and senior year of high school.—That is a really fond memory. We just jogged around our neighborhood and the new one across the way. Neither of us was a "real jogger" but it felt good to do an exercise that actually got my blood and air pumping.

I joined track my senior year, but only in the sense that I went to the practices and did the work-outs with the slower people. I never competed. I wasn't strong enough, didn't like competing for things, and never would have wanted to go to a meet because I always had to pee more than normal and if I had been nervous too, I would have been a wreck. (This is discussed in the next chapter.)

I still hated myself for being imperfect the whole darn time I did all these things. But loud and clear, I heard that incessant chanting in my head. "You...aren't...good...enough!" I suddenly realized that I was so mean...to myself. If I ever witnessed someone else going up to some-body else and saying the same things to them, I would be appalled and angry and want to slap them! (I wouldn't slap them but I'd want to. I don't condone violence.)

There comes a time in your life where you have to say to yourself, "If God made me a cute salamander, then I'm never going to be a cute bunny-rabbit." What I mean is, some things you can change and some things you can't, and you have to accept yourself at some point. And then surround yourself with people who love you for you and walk as fast as you can from those who don't!

I was actually sitting in a college group counseling session for eating disorders the day I heard Karen Carpenter had died. All of us in the room were pretty quiet...speechless. Karen was a great talent and seemed like an extremely sweet lady as well. She is missed.

I had a silver tiger's eye ring that I got at an arts festival. I wore it all junior year and senior year of high school. Then I tucked it away in a drawer as I got other jewelry. When I came across it years later, I looked and looked at it, but all I could think about was how often I washed the puke off of it. I threw it away. Around age 21 I had given up on eating disorders, and I didn't want a reminder of those times... not even in my drawer. Thankfully by my senior year of college I was freed of anorexia and bulimia, although I still continued to exercise. I just did it more moderately with less anger and sadness and self-hatred and fear of what other people thought about me.

I will say, my family never told me I was ugly or homely or fat… never. My Mom told me I was attractive and she loved me just because I was hers. My Dad always said both his "little girls" were smart and attractive and could do whatever they wanted. My Nunny told me many times that a neighbor called me "a rare beauty". No one was down on me, accept ME! My sister even wrote a blurb in my senior yearbook about how she was happy that I had joined track. She was very competitive and did well at sprinting and hurdling herself. So, this was all ME… listening too much to society. The part of society that is narcissistic.

Was Marilyn's image a culprit?

There have been times I have pondered. "Did I, as Marilyn, help to set an unusually high precedent which others feel they must obtain?" I know I had good bone structure, but I also got a bit of a nose job, and had Hollywood style costumes and make-up and great lighting and multiple takes to create the illusion of beauty I represented. And on top of that, I hid behind my beauty when I was lacking in other areas.

So, I am not picking on my former me, but I am very sorry if I, as Marilyn, have ever made any other girl feel "less than" because, believe me, I have been on this other side during this lifetime and I know it is HARSH!

The whole "super model" era was something I felt was telling me how I had to be to be acceptable. Ultimately we have to see our own beauty and not wait for other people's approval to come first…or sometimes ever. I really hope Marilyn didn't make anyone feel badly about themselves. To me that would be very tragic. I know that it is hard to escape caring about image.

Enter the Heroine....

I love Princess Diana because she seemed so sweet and caring... and also had a prominent nose and eating disorders like I did. I first remember hearing about her when I was still in high school. She was three years older than I was, but still so relatable. I got up early to see her get married on TV.

Princess Di used her glamorous life to highlight charities and compassion for others. She was the epitome of true beauty...in photos and in life. Special indeed. Lovely. My favorite photo of Princes Diana is where she and Mother Teresa are meeting. And oddly enough, both of these great ladies died within the same week. Let me say this, there was NOT near enough coverage for Mother Teresa...not nearly. What is wrong with the media?!?

Princess Di made short hair cool...just like Julie Andrews. Of course, Princess Di also had blue eyes...I don't. I still love watching stuff about the Royal Family on TV. They seem like really good people. And no doubt Diana's influence is still present. Marilyn once met Queen Elizabeth. I don't remember that, I've just seen the film footage, which is sweet.

During my 30's I had a Princess Diana calendar and then long after that year was over, I hung up the pictures from each month around my apartment. She always felt like a friend. A very pretty, graceful, kind, caring friend.

It really touched me when Sir Elton John converted "Candle in the Wind" to "Goodbye England's Rose" for Princess Diana. She was/is my favorite non-actor celebrity. She and Marilyn both died at age 36. Elton John was amazing. Imagine writing a big hit and singing it over and over one way...then quickly converting its lyrics and singing it flawlessly in front of millions of people, at a tear-jerking occasion. Talk about pressure. Talk about delivering a masterpiece! Bravo! Amazing, amazing, amazing.

My Spine:

I noticed something was a little off when I was 13. I was pretty slim up until age 15 and people always told me I was lucky for that, even though I was doing lots of exercises for my tummy fat. But one day I was just about to step into the shower and I caught a side-glance of myself in the bathroom mirror. I was horrified! I called my Mom to come quickly and I told her I was deformed. **She said, "Michele Marie, you should be grateful God made you healthy"** and she walked away. I felt ashamed for being so vain and complaining. I didn't want to go to hell for criticizing God!

I noticed that I didn't have a normal sway in my back at the bottom of my spine. Of course, I was always looking at adult models so I hoped I was just going through an "awkward stage". I figured if my butt was bigger and rounder it would make the dip look "more dippy" and normal. I thought over time things would change.

I remember during one of the years of junior high the school nurse did a scoliosis test in gym class. Everyone was scared to death. We watched a video about the condition and it showed untreated worst case scenarios. Then we were told to line up and we each took turns bending over in front of the nurse. No one wanted to be singled out, but a couple people were and they stood to the side so she could talk to them further. I don't know if the nurse or gym teacher called their parents to make sure they got medical attention or what. But I remember one girl had tears in her eyes and I felt horrible for her.

I remember when it was my turn to bend over, my heart was pounding and I held my breath...because I really expected to be told I had it too. I wasn't. And I was grateful. But I just knew something was still not right with me. I just figured I must have it but they didn't notice, but that was fine with me! It still seems incredibly insensitive to me that the test was conducted the way it was with everyone being able to see what was going on and the afflicted few standing in full view of the rest of the kids.

Anyway, I continued to do all my exercises throughout the years because I was always weight conscious and body shape aware. Fast forward to my late 40's. I suddenly went through a couple months where my right leg hurt very badly and would lock up. I had severe pain in my hip and if I bent over to put down food for my cat my knee would be so stiff I could barely get up. If I drove for more than 15 minutes, I could barely get out of the car. I would limp into work in the mornings. This was really concerning me. I knew I had a habit of lifting things that were heavier than I should. I would lift boxes of legal files at work and very large economical size bags of bird food or sometimes furniture I would get at the consignment store. I also had been falling asleep a lot on an uncomfortable couch that hurt my back. I figured that all of these factors created the issue. I decided to look for a chiropractor close to home. I had not been to one for decades...not since I was a teen and went a bunch of times with my Mom.

The doctor was rather intense and about my age and handsome. His place was always packed and he seemed in a great big hurry. He snapped me into place but then said I should get x-rays since I was a new patient. I stood in a paper gown and a bunch of shots were taken. They were developed by my next appointment and I was horrified to see how weird the one shot looked.

At the very base of my spine it looked all crunched up on one side. I am uneven. It really looked like I was crushed. **I commented on that and the doctor said, "It could be scoliosis."** I told him that all the kids in school were tested and the nurse didn't say I had it, but I suspected that I might. It also explained why I moved one leg more than the other while jogging. A kid following me around the neighborhood on a bike once pointed it out.

I knew that since I always had to pee more than normal and often was very uncomfortable in school, I had a habit of sitting funny while riding the school bus or in classes. If I shifted my weight and sat on one of my legs tucked under me it made me feel less like I had to go sometimes. So who knows, I might have warped my spine myself, I thought. I figured I might have developed funny because I was constantly sitting in an abnormal position during my developmental years. Or, on the other hand, maybe one of the reasons I had to pee so often was because my spine was messed up from birth and maybe that affected me. I have no clue. It was just interesting to see that the inside of me looked as messed up as I had always felt I was. From the outside I don't look uneven, but inside I sure do!

For years I had done all kinds of exercises and couldn't figure out why I couldn't get my butt rounder and my back more curved-in looking. My sister looked great in that area. I consoled myself by saying I got the thinner legs. At least I finally had a doctor show me x-rays that explained why years of toil always seemed so pointless, at least in terms of changing certain things. The pain in my right leg then shifted to my left side...which was very odd. But eventually the leg issues all seemed to go away, accept for I was left with an ache in the middle of my lower back which continues.

As Marilyn....

I have a memory from Marilyn's lifetime which I think says a lot. I don't have explicit memories of having sex with my husbands, just little things. But I remember one time one of my husbands was begging me to come into the bedroom to fool around and I was upset about something. Finally he coaxed me to the bed and I was thinking, "OK, let's just get this over with so he stops pestering me." I sometimes had a hard time feeling sexy at the end of the day because I felt like that is all people wanted from me all day long. "Be sexy."

I remember thinking my husband and I would have some loving kissing and then he would crawl on top of me. But he just ordered me to get up on the bed and get on all fours. In that moment, it really pissed me off! I remember thinking, "Oh, so all I am is an ass to you?"

I told myself that it really didn't matter what position we were in because it was sex either way, and afterall I was with my husband. And furthermore why shouldn't he want to look at my backside when I was spending half my career wearing tight clothes to show it off.

There was nothing wrong with him wanting what I was flaunting in front of the rest of the world really. But I was always such a hurt little girl inside a woman's body, that I took offense. I remember saying that he was just like everybody else and only cared about my body and not me. That's the end of that memory and I don't recall if we did or didn't engage in activities. But it is somewhat odd to me that I remember this very clearly.

Then as Michele...

So, then here I am in this current Michele-lifetime and no matter what I do I can't get a round butt. I have done lots of exercises on the floor where you kick up your leg...and sometimes even with leg weights strapped to my ankles. I used to jog a lot. I used to lift weights at the gym and I made sure I did the leg curls up that supposedly help define your butt muscles as well as leg. I have come to the conclusion that I'm being punished! Either that or I'm being saved. Not sure which.

Maybe God and The Universe thought, "OK Marilyn-Michele, see what it is like when you can't play that card and get away with so much for being beautiful. And you can't get mad at people for wanting what you have spent all day flaunting."

Or maybe God and The Universe are also saying to each other, "You know she hasn't changed, she came back to earth within two years of her last death. We better do something to put the brakes on her way of dealing with things because otherwise she will go right back out there and repeat some of her same patterns just because she can. Especially since her former self is all over the media still."

It's hard to say if my own Michele-circumstances are all just a genetic thing or a karma thing. I kind of think both. I believe I was given the genetics that handed me my karma.

I, as Michele, felt so completely flawed when I was growing up. I would constantly try to pretend I was happy but I was very very sad. I remember sometimes I would hit my own self. Yes, I would punch my own upper legs. I'd say I only did it about 10 times.—I thought I was just being weird. I would do it when I felt exceptionally suppressed and depressed and dismal about how my life was going. I would do it when I hated my physical self the most. It was all during my high school years. I told myself I was beating on myself "so I would feel something." Clearly since I would do this while I was bawling, I was feeling something. But it wasn't what I wanted to feel.

I think it meant that I wanted to feel proud of myself, and pretty and sexy. I wanted to be a fighter and a go-getter and all the things that all my various issues made me feel I was too unworthy or incapable to do or be.

Still despite all this, I had the very weird notion that I would someday be beautiful. (Was this because I knew down-deep about Marilyn?)

In high school I never sat at "the popular table". But I had amazing friends from the theatre group and some others as well. I remember a girl named Sandy who was in a gym class with me. She liked the cartoon "Ziggy" and said that we were both "Ziggys" together.—It sounded better than "nerds" and I thought it was a nice way of looking at things.

So many wonderful people helped me get through my growing years this lifetime. So many wonderful people who didn't seem to give a damn if every day was a bad hair day. So many people who didn't care if I wore handmade clothes my Nunny made me instead of fashionable "label" designs. So many people who didn't care if I was underweight or overweight or had a nose like a witch. And I liked them just as-is too.

And there was a period of time when I was obsessed with watching psychological horror/suspense movies on late night television. I was only allowed to stay up til 3:00AM on weekends. But on Monday morning, my study hall friends would ask me what I saw and I would go on-and-on retelling the film plots as best I could. I was told I was good at that...which made me laugh. But perhaps that desire to "story tell" is back afterall...?

By the time I went to college and wore short skirts, I didn't want to risk being bruised. I was also studying theatre and happier despite all my damn imperfections. And hurting myself never made anything better. It never changed any of my issues.

Years later I heard about people who were "cutters" and I heard that sometimes people cut themselves to "feel something". Although I'm afraid of sharp knives in general, I totally get it. It's hard to keep trapped feelings in. Fear, sorrow, hatred don't hide forever. They come out one way or another. Despite being shocked that people cut them-selves, I empathize. And I'm very sorry people are hurt enough to do that to themselves.

Did Marilyn like either of her selves?

One of the things I specifically remember about "being Marilyn" was seeing myself as two different people...brown-haired Norma Jeane and blond Marilyn... "the before" and "the after". I literally thought of them as different people. Logically I knew they were the same, but for the rest of my life I tried to separate them in my own head. I had high hopes that Marilyn could bury Norma Jeane, and by doing so save her. I was wrong. It didn't take long to find out. I loved Norma Jeane (me) but hated her experiences. Sometimes the things I said to the cameras was different than what I thought in my own mind. No one was harder on me than ME.

The truth is, I used to be upset that other people wanted me to "be Marilyn" at the expense of Norma Jeane, even during off-hours. But I myself was just as guilty. No one played mind games with me, more than I did myself. No one exploited me, more than ME...I...the girl... the enigma in the mirror.

When I/Norma Jeane was first "becoming Marilyn," I remember thinking, "Norma Jeane is dead now, and the public will never know about all of the embarrassing things in that part of my life." I really hoped. It didn't work. During the first year with my new blond image and name, I experienced periods of memory loss and crying without a reason I understood. I would lose track of several hours at a time, and be frightened by feelings of overwhelming confusion and sadness. Often this would happen during late afternoon. I would have to think and think, and try to talk myself through the events of the day, retracing my steps to ground myself in current reality.

Obviously I could not escape my history. What you don't deal with, will haunt you somehow, some way. The harder I tried to play the image, the more I fell apart. Norma Jeane would not allow Marilyn to leave her behind. Marilyn was just the picture of what people wanted from me...or so I thought. But unfortunately I can't live that life over a different way.

This makes me think of the movie "Norma Jean and Marilyn" which used the very interesting concept of playing both sides of Marilyn using top notch actresses in both roles...Mira Sorvino and Ashley Judd.

Marilyn...and the dinner....

I, as Marilyn, remember the early years of my career. Several male buddies were going to take me out for Italian food. It was a good crowd. I was already watching my weight and a bit chubby, so I gave myself a few lectures. But I really didn't care. I was starving. I was craving tomato sauce. I wore a white dress and realized I better be careful not to mess it up, as money was tight and I had already done a few unsavory things to increase my wardrobe.

Men would buy me meals and clothes. I wasn't really a prostitute per se, but I would do what I had to do to not be alone at night after dark. Night time terrified me. The benefits of these encounters was often gifts. Most of these encounters were <u>extremely boring</u> and there was an inane sense of "So this is what I've become now? When is the real part of my career going to start?" running through my being.

How absurd that a young girl at the height of beauty was throwing herself into the arms of men who were twice her age and most of them significantly less attractive and drastically less exciting than MUD! It was just "the deed," devoid of any romance. Yes, ABSURD. I told myself that this was the way the business world works. I told myself I could handle it. We were all using each other. I planned to survive.

I was living for some big payoff. I had a vision for myself and it wasn't sucking some random guy's dick for a dress or a pair of shoes. I was going to be a serious dramatic actress and a star! But often it felt like that time was far off and I would die of boredom in some old dark-suit executive guy's lap before <u>my time</u> ever arrived.

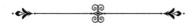

Anyway, I went out for a meal with my jovial gang of friends. Italian food. White dress. Happy to go. However, at some point in the evening I went to the ladies room and found that I couldn't come out. I locked myself behind a stall door, I wept. I couldn't go back to the table. I had no idea what was wrong with me. This was a totally unexpected rush of emotions. I was paralyzed by sadness and loneliness even as I was the nucleus of the group. Eventually someone knocked on the restroom door and I realized I had no choice but to return to the table. Comments were made about how they thought I'd gotten lost. I pretended that was funny. I was among friends. My biggest enemy was all in my head. The truth is, I really truly had gotten lost. I took a detour down the bottomless pit of despair, which was a place I would visit increasingly often as time went on.

I often felt that there were bigger secrets just underneath the surface of my mind. I felt that regardless of how many childhood traumas I could recount, there was still something... not sure what...that I wasn't quite remembering...but it was lurking and reeking havoc. And yet, there were times when I felt as if I almost knew what it could be, that I just couldn't handle the feeling and I would submerge whatever it was back down, underneath to the depths of my being again. I'd put it back where it belonged, so to say. Kind of like saying, "Another day...another day. Now that I know something is there, I can choose to access it on another day when I feel stronger." But I never did...because I never was....stronger.

I, as Michele, remember this situation at the Italian Restaurant with the oddest mixture of happiness and hurt. Was this the point in my/Marilyn's life when I should have run away from Hollywood? Was this a pivotal point in time when I could have changed everything? And if I had, who is to say that doing anything different would have been any better? Would people have loved me even if I hadn't bought into the blond charade? It was the beginning of the climb towards the highest platform...adulation beyond expectation....and also the greatest fall. And it all started when someone colored my hair.....at least I saw it that way.

The real problem is, a new image doesn't cover up your past. So until you work out your past issues, the new image may only temporarily solve anything and in the long run it may complicate things x-100.

During this Michele-lifetime I have often used hair color in a super-ficial attempt to "feel different" about myself. It only works short-term. I'm still me. Do blonds have more fun? Well, there are so many factors. How short is your skirt, how low is your neckline, how big is your smile, how confident are you walking, and do you have anything interesting to say. Nice perfume is a good thing. Kindness matters. It's not just about the hair. But for quite a few years I colored my hair every few weeks as if my life depended on it.

The first time my hair changed colors was by accident during 8th grade. A perm made it somewhat red and it stayed that way for a while. I liked it! Then my Mom helped me turn it back to brown and it became extra dark and more dramatic than my norm. Then at age 22, during my last semester of college, I made it blond. And right before finals I made it red. This is where the decades of constant alteration began...1987.

At age 19 I tried waitressing. I only lasted two months because I got out before I dumped a whole tray of food like I saw one girl do. But anyway, the eatery was changing hands and the new owners-to-be came by. They were an attractive middle-aged couple with big ideas to improve the place. The woman talked to me at length. My hair was blond.

She came back a week later and talked to me again. Then she commented, "So where is blond Michele?" She didn't recognize me! My hair was dark brown when she had come back. I explained to her I was the one she was referring to. She didn't believe me at first.

I will also admit this is about the same time period I used to shave part of the side of my hairline also, in futile attempt to have a higher looking forehead. After about a year I gave up...I had to accept my lower hairline. I also took a break from hair color for a while. I started back up my last semester.

P.S. Tip your waiters and waitresses well!

Another time I was in my 30's and walking in a stairwell at work. A maintenance guy told me I looked like Princess Diana. Of course, she is someone I really thought highly of, so I was extremely flattered. But I did my usual transformation and within a couple days I went from blond to redhead...again. I bumped into the same maintenance guy and he seemed quite confused.

I have sometimes felt almost powerless over those little boxes of chemicals. Coloring my hair was a big hobby. I knew which brands cost less and which brands smelled the best, and which ones had the better rubber gloves included in the box. Finally, in my 40's, I slowed down because I suddenly realized I'd be lucky if my hair didn't all fall out. One of my bosses actually warned me about that. She was very concerned.

What's LOVE got to do with it? ......EVERYTHING!

Some people speculate that Marilyn would have never attempted to kill herself when she was planning to change her will. The truth is, sometimes people do kill themselves, even when they have appointments. I have read that some people are upset because many of Marilyn's belongings ended up in the hands of someone who didn't know her. Well, this is my take on matters. Yes, Marilyn definitely would have liked it if her sister Berniece and niece Mona Rae, as well as John and Susan Strasberg would have benefitted....afterall, she was fond of them. It would have been nice if this had been done early-on after her departure. However, I believe, with all my heart, that the reason Lee Strasberg kept her things stored away was because he couldn't deal with the pain of handling the items and even watching them go away. This would have meant dealing with the loss. Also remember, "the Marilyn times" also were "the Paula times". So maybe Mr. Strasberg was holding onto a whole "something bigger" than Marilyn's memory. Perhaps it seems a bit funny, right? Someone who taught others to "go to that place and feel" might have had a hard time doing that himself sometimes. But afterall, even people at the top of their profession, are in fact....human. The Truth: Marilyn studied with Lee Strasberg to change her image...and indeed it helped.

Chapter Four:

MICHELE: MY INCONVENIENT TRUTH.

I was very tempted to leave this chapter out of my book. But because I read online that younger people can have over-active bladder as well as older people, I decided to talk about this. Personally, I used to feel very alone, dealing with this issue during my impressionable younger years. And most ads on TV are geared toward older people. But younger people also need to know they are not alone. The personality you develop during youth, can impact who you become as an adult.

The condition: I know others have it too.

I grew up during the 1970-80's in a world that worshipped Brooke Shields who was/is beyond beautiful and just one year younger than I am. She's also a very good actress, especially in "Lipstick Jungle" <u>which should have stayed on-air</u>.

But I always felt more like I was Meg Griffin on the "Family Guy" cartoon. (The show wasn't around at that time, but that is how I saw myself.) Then to make matters even worse was the fact that I had always had a small bladder... or overactive bladder...one of those I think. I guess that was the issue. I finally heard of such a thing when I was in my 20's.

I have always had to pee abnormally often. This condition means always looking for a restroom while others are relaxing and enjoying themselves. It means never wanting to plan long drives, hikes in the woods, or sitting in the window seat of an airplane. Even an hour-long church service is sometimes uncomfortable. And as a kid, riding the bus to school, especially on winter days, was just awful because the wait at the bus stop was longer and so was the drive. And rainy days...torture!

I remember going on family vacations to the beach, and 30 minutes after plopping down in the sand, I would be staring up towards the boardwalk and trying to figure out if I could find the restroom on my own. It was often miserable being me. So many situations in life have not been what they should have been because I was distracted. (And oddly enough, despite being a different type of issue, in many ways my bladder issues have created for me what mental health issues subjected Marilyn's consciousness and life to. —-Distraction.)

I first realized I had a problem when I was in first grade....just age 6. At that age you often have to ask the teacher for permission to go use the restroom. I remember watching film strip presentations and knowing I would have to pee as soon as the teacher turned the lights up. I told my Mom that something was wrong with me and she just said to "not think about it." That didn't help. Things were always a little uncomfortable. But I surely never expected things to get as bad as they did by age 12.

In junior high, 7–9th grade, we only had 4 minutes in between classes. I went to a very large school with a couple levels and a long-long staircase that was often packed with other students. Imagine having to walk from the 2nd floor...down the staircase....to a restroom....and then to your next class....in 4 minutes! I did it all the time, and it was nerve-wracking. Now and then I'd have consecutive classes that were thankfully much closer together, but not usually.

I almost never had the chance to socialize in between classes either, unless someone talked to me in a bathroom line. And during my junior high years, kids used to put a lot of graffiti on the bathroom stalls... drawing pictures of pot leaves, bongs and other references to drug paraphernalia. This scared me. I didn't want to encounter "a druggie" while peeing.

One time I had just entered a bathroom stall, and latched the door. A teacher burst into the room, knocked on the door and ordered me to "not flush and open up." She sternly asked me if some older girl had left something in the toilet bowl. I shook my head NO....as the girl, who was much taller than I was, stood behind the angry woman and gave me a fearful yet threatening glance. I didn't need to get beat up for telling the truth. There was indeed some weed in the toilet but it had floated to the side of the bowl ...I had seen it. I remained standing between the bowl and the teacher, who thankfully didn't make me move. So I lied, and they left.

Each school day, there was simply no chatting with friends, flirting with boys, touching-up make-up, or going to my locker for something I forgot. And I drank as little water as possible out of the strange hall fountains, which pre-dated the bottled water everyone has these days. I was always just trying to be responsible, stay out of trouble and get from point-A to point-B on time. I did this during every single classroom change ... every... single ...classroom...change! I think that's probably why I walk so fast even to this day...even in heels. Thankfully I talked to kids during lunch hours and sometimes in locker rooms before/after gym class, which wasn't as quiet and rigid as math and history. Then I'd dash to the next class.

I remember during junior high years, I saw a made-for-TV movie about a bed-wetter. Although I never had that particular issue, I still could relate to the constant inconvenience and embarrassment. This wonderful 1977 movie is called "The Loneliest Runner" and it stars actors Lance Kerwin, Michael Landon and Melissa Sue Anderson. This movie was a Godsend. Even though my condition was still a menace, the film made me feel somewhat less alone in my plight.

In 10th grade my parents sent me to an alternative school which was supposedly for independent, motivated, creative kids. There was some good going on there, and also some things that weren't all that helpful. My parents always said I was very intelligent, so I suppose they thought this place might give me the chance to blossom. Academically the school was a bomb, although I did make a good friend there.

Anyway, because the school was another 20 minute ride up the road, that meant getting on two school buses a day...in the morning... and in the afternoon. I would bus to the regular high school and then catch another bus to the alternative school. And visa versa on the way home. This, of course, was really not great for someone who had to pee more than normal. But somehow I survived. That same year we also had a school bus driver who looked like Jesus and he was really nice to me. His name was Fred.

In 11th grade, I went back to the mainstream high school. That year things got a little less bad as far as my bladder issues went, but make no mistake things were still far from normal. Sometimes I could actually go for two classes in a row without stopping by the restroom. —That translates into about 108 minutes...less than 2 hours. And that was only now and then, not most of the time.

At that point I sometimes wondered how much of my condition was physical and how much psychological. But I knew for sure that at least some part of it really was physical and beyond my control, because of the pain I felt when a urologist tested my bladder holding-capacity the year before.

I sometimes believe part of my issue may be about a fear of "being trapped," although I'm not sure why. I think having to do things in monitored "blocks of time" at school put some strange kind of fear in me. And maybe that felt similar to some past life situation where I was cornered and controlled. I don't know. But I didn't realize in 11th grade that I even had any past lives. Reincarnation was still not a real thing to me then...it was just a weird idea that I didn't believe in because my family didn't.

Trying to get help...

My Mother and Father knew I was constantly struggling with this issue. As a matter of fact, my Mom called my teachers during 7th grade and explained what I was going through and told them I would try to get to class on time but if I was a couple minutes late to please excuse me.

I actually didn't even realize that she was going to do this until it was done. As you can imagine, I was both grateful and also completely embarrassed. But I was more grateful. My Mom was probably embarrassed herself having to make the calls, nevertheless she did because she loves me.

I don't think I ever was late for a class in junior high because I just walked very, very fast. But oddly enough, one time in 10th grade, a teacher did call-me-out for being about a minute late and I will never forget that. It was in an art class.

Teacher:

"OK folks. I'm tired of people being late. Now look at Missy here, even she is late today. Now if a good Girl Scout type of girl like her can be late, then what is going on? You need to start showing up on time, all of you!"

Of course the class was staring at me. I didn't get it, all the times the kids on drugs would show up really late or completely blow off the class, they never got pointed out in front of everyone. But ME...yes. Why? I just couldn't skip going to the restroom. I told myself I must have a face people just like to pick on. Or maybe they do it because I won't fight back.

My parents did take me to two urologists, but it didn't do any good. The first doctor did some tube stretching procedure that made no impact... I was 13. The second doctor was actually a real uncompassionate ass, who ran a test on me and said I was normal, even though I was doubled-over in extreme pain. He said, "All girls go a lot." His "expert help" was a prescription for blue pills that tasted funny and only made me thirsty, as he said they probably would. At the time I was in 10th grade and taking an evening acting class. I discontinued the pills after about a month, because I had a hard time speaking with a dry mouth.

Coping...

I was very fortunate because during my teen years there were several families in my neighborhood who called upon me to babysit often. On top of that, my sister was constantly busy with track-n-field, marching band and hanging out with friends, so we didn't compete for jobs. I had a steady stream of funds to use on fun things and holiday gifts.

Instead of dating, I ended up spending 8th through 12th grade babysitting on a regular basis. I loved all the kids and those experiences hold a special place in my heart. I sincerely babysat the best group of kids around.

However, later on, I decided I was never going to have kids of my own. I had heard a number of pregnant women talk about how much a baby presses on the bladder as it grows inside your tummy. They would claim they <u>always</u> had to pee during the later months before giving birth. The idea of things getting even worse than "my norm" was hard to imagine. I knew I could never go through that!

So, despite the fact I had always loved dolls and pushed a few around in a red plaid baby carriage much longer than normal, I decided I would probably never be a mother. I realized fairly young that that was my reality. As time went on, I just got more and more used to arranging my life around the need to be comfortable, and that really contributed to keeping me both smart and naïve.

I was smart because I hung out with my parents longer than most teens and didn't get into trouble and didn't try drugs and didn't drink alcohol, and didn't get pregnant in high school. (I don't think getting pregnant in high school is the end of the world, <u>as long as you have the child</u> and raise them or give them to a loving home...and find a way to get your degree.)

But I was also naïve because I never experienced all the ups-n-downs of high school love, parties, having a wide group of friends, going to games ...or even being dumped for a prettier girl. I learned things later in life.

Nope, not me!

I didn't even consider going to a prom. And then when a boy did ask me to one, I told him I was babysitting that night. It wasn't actually true, so I feel kind of bad for saying that even to this day. But I didn't know him and I was really shy. —It was just my natural reaction to count myself out.

A decade later I was working in an office with another girl from my high school and we were talking. It turns out the same boy had asked her out too. I don't know who he asked out first, but she didn't go out with him either. I have no idea if he went to prom alone or with someone or not at all. I felt pretty bad. I am sure it took a lot of courage for him to ask out two girls....at least us two...maybe he asked out someone else also. But I didn't really know him because he only talked to me once before asking me out.

Overall, this whole bladder issue just made me more of a homebody and also a bigger daydreamer. I constantly imagined my life being completely different. I constantly thought about all the successes one dreams of if you actually feel able to go to all the places you want and really focus on what you are doing. I constantly dreamed about acting.

I developed my overall view of life from whatever I saw in the movies. I was once told I even talk dramatically and succinctly, and I figured it was because "my friends" all spoke from scripts. People told me all the time that I was mature for my age, but I think what they really meant was that I knew how to be reserved and not impulsive. Mature....me...nothing could have been further from the truth! And as my life has unfolded it has became more and more clear to me that I was acting 35 at age 15 and acting 15 at age 35.

I really think that my condition somehow influenced my personality in ways one just wouldn't imagine. Probably in some ways good, but I know for sure in some ways not. It is hard to tell how I might have been different throughout the years if early on I hadn't had a "handicap" which kept me home so much. I cried enough for a whole lifetime during my junior high and high school years. But...I'm not going to cry over that anymore...we all have some challenges.

Just because we may not always see someone else's challenges, doesn't mean they don't have any and that their life is perfect. We all have things we just don't want to tell the whole world. And people should respect that. Sometimes people who seem aloof are really people who have some problem that keeps them worried and on the side-lines.

When I was growing up, I always thought other people had things a lot better than I did. Sometimes it is easy to look around and see people who seem to have it all...and be tempted to be jealous that they do. But, we should really never be jealous of others who seem more fortunate because we don't know what they may be going through, or may have to go through in the future. **Plus, I have learned, a big part of being happy, is learning to be happy for others. Be happy for others!!!! It's crucial.**

We all deal with difficult things. The longer you live, the more you are likely to shed tears. If for no other reason, than because nobody lives forever so we all suffer loss. Even the richest prettiest people can't avoid losses. Nobody wins every ballgame. There is always a prettier or more handsome person than yourself. Money can buy a lot of things but sometimes even rich people can't buy the cures they need for an illness. Pet lovers lose their companions. It happens to us all.

I definitely think that the one good thing sitting on the side-lines during my teen years taught me was to look around and appreciate the variety of people in the world and know that just because someone isn't just like me, doesn't mean that they aren't working very, very hard to fit in. We all want to be accepted...especially if we have an embarrassing problem. We are all more the same than different. It's more obvious as life goes on.

I finally figured it out!

So...writing an auto-biography has some interesting perks. When you put your life stories down on paper, you suddenly see how more and more things connect with each other...epiphanies that eluded you before. Past life influences come to light.

When I was under 10 years old...not sure what age exactly...I went to a camp, about a half hour from where I lived. I took a bus home by dinnertime each day. It was at a nice campground with a main cabin and then a bunch of other areas where you could pitch a tent or sit under a very rustic picnic area type gazebo. And then there was the dreaded stinky outhouse! Oh, the horror!

Now some outhouses are a little better than others, but this was one with several seats and no privacy between them...and the first one I ever saw. When I was introduced to it, I was shocked. Seriously I remember feeling like I entered another dimension. Spiders, darkness, a putrid smell mixed with moth balls, and pulling down my pants in front of someone who was almost a stranger.

I remember that one of the girl's mothers was a "camp helper" for the day and she walked me up to the smelly building. I remember her commenting, "We are all girls here, don't be modest, just have a seat." I had to pee so badly, I had no choice. I went. And I simply couldn't understand how she could so casually do all this with no privacy walls. I kept telling myself over and over that it didn't matter, but it did!

A year or so later when I was still going to this camp, I was on the other side of the grounds, but the outhouse there was competitively creepy with the first outhouse. Camp was fun and I just tried not to think about the fact that I had to visit the crude facilities several times a day.

One day it was pouring rain...and I had to go pee so badly, that I knew I had to walk down a little hill and enter the restroom-of-gloom before I got on the camp bus. Suddenly, I realized that even if I used an umbrella, I would be all wet anyway because the rain was pouring so darn hard. What was the point?

So....I did the only thing I could think of to do. I walked out in the rain, and just peed my pants on purpose! It beat walking to the outhouse which horrified me. I figured the rain was like taking a shower. I was soaked! It made sense...at first...but then I felt stupid.

I rode the bus home and no one was the wiser because my hair and shirt were wet too. I just told my friends I got rained on.

Now, I know no one really likes an outhouse compared to a room with running water. But I had a serious mental block when it came to using the one at that camp.—Why? <u>Now, I think I finally realize why.</u> I think the little outhouse reminded me of the tool shed which I mention in the chapter about Marilyn and her baby boy. Marilyn was attacked in a tool shed when she was still a teenager named Norma Jeane. And I think that subconsciously that dark outhouse reminded me of the tool shed. I think there was just something about that little building that was disturbing me on some other level. And maybe also the idea of being partially naked around someone else played into a sense of shame, just like being attacked did in my last past life.

I actually remember the outhouse behind my house during another lifetime I lived during the 1800's...when I was named Charlotte. And that was all I knew...people only had outhouses. And it didn't scare me at all. So that is why I think that it is Marilyn's lifetime, right before my Michele-life, that made me feel weary of small, closed in, isolated buildings like that. Maybe that is a stretch...but it makes sense to me.

I've had friends who have had accidents and I never have... yet... knock on wood. But I just shake my head when I think about peeing my pants on purpose to avoid the outhouse. "Normal" kids would have just waited until they got home, but I couldn't. —My inconvenient truth.

When I was in second grade, our class went to a circus an hour away. During intermission I stood in a long line to the restroom, and it wasn't moving fast enough for the girl standing next to me. She peed her pants and I felt so badly for her. I felt compassion for her. I didn't want to make in fun of her. I just thought I was luckier at that moment.

Anti-Bullying:

You hear more and more people these days speaking up against bullying. We should all strive to be the person we would want our own child to encounter out in the world. I am sure there are a lot of bullies who are scared to death their children will encounter someone like they used to be. No matter what you've done in the past, you can be nice today. Be nice today..... every day is "today".

Chapter Five:

MICHELE: YOU DON'T OWN ME! (MY INTRODUCTION TO SEX)

**Sex-education: So, this is how I learned about sex...
in the 1970's...80's.
Before I lost my virginity.**

When I was in 4th grade, I was on a swingset in the playground. Just as I hopped off, a boy in the 3rd grade walked over and pulled down my flowered skirt. He and several other kids roared with laughter. I didn't think it was hilarious in the least, as a matter of fact I was mortified and it bothered me for several days. I was far from naked, but I felt very exposed. I had always liked boys...I had a crush on Burt Ward who played Robin in the "Batman" TV show. But the boy on the playground made me feel degraded. Eventually I put that behind me. I just figured he was showing off to his friends...at my expense. But it was over.

When I was in 6th grade, my sister and I watched a movie on late-night TV at Nunny's house. We were all excited because it starred beautiful Elizabeth Montgomery, the woman who played in the whimsical TV show "Bewitched". But, the movie was not about magic. It was called "A Case of Rape" and made in 1974. Although I had always been attracted to boys, I never had a "sexplanation" before. And Nunny didn't give us one either. She just said, "Sometimes men force a woman to have sex with them and it is against the law." The movie was about a woman's attempt to prosecute her attacker. Chris and I had no idea what sex was. We still watched...with a bit of confusion. The ending was as disturbing as the beginning.

My Nunny must have told my parents about us seeing the movie, because a couple days later my Dad tried to explain sex and rape to us in a very abstract way.—That took about 15 seconds. He told us we had to be careful. I am sure he didn't really relish that conversation. And we pondered "being careful?" The subject faded from my mind.

Stop-it at the bus stop!

Right around 6th grade ...not long after our first "sexplanation" ... something uncomfortable happened. My sister and I were getting off the school bus and she was a few paces behind me. As we made our way up from the middle of the bus towards the door, a boy in the front seat grabbed me in the crotch...and then let go. I was so surprised, that it registered in my mind for about two seconds and then I dismissed it as my imagination. I guess I didn't want to believe it. However, my sister saw it happen and ran home and told my parents.

My Dad was livid and demanded to know the boy's name and where he lived. Typically our bus dropped us off before going up that part of the route past our neighborhood, but occasionally it took us to some of the farm houses and that boy's house which stood alone along a road. So, we knew exactly where to find him. I just stood in my bedroom feeling as if I was the center of a mess, and I felt kind of guilty because I didn't think I needed to make a big thing out of it. I just wanted to forget it, especially since whatever had happened was fleeting and I almost made it go away.

My Dad charged off to speak with the boy's father. When he came back, my Dad said that the other man was very understanding and happy to have been told because he wanted to make sure it never happened again. And it never did....at least not to me.

The thing I remember the most was that it was more embarrassing to have multiple people know about it than it was the split-second it occurred. I also felt bad for the boy because he was a couple years younger, and I hoped his father would firmly talk to him and not yell. But I never knew how the man handled whatever took place. It seems weird that I cared about the boy in a way, but I did.

Since he was so young I guess I felt like the boy made a stupid decision instead of really meaning to upset anyone. And who knows where he learned to do that in the first place. But on the other hand, learning bad behavior young isn't good either and needs to be stopped.

When all was said and done, I can say that I DO understand why victims of bad experiences are slow to report. I don't really feel that that happening did any damage to me overall, and it was, of course, nice to have a sister who cared. And my Dad was very protective. But I understand. There is a wide range of emotions that comes into play with watching other people get upset for you...and having to explain things. And it's odd knowing that someone else can just choose to involve you in something you don't want.

Years later, I was in a situation where people were talking about "if they had ever been molested or not" and this incident never even crossed my mind. The boy was just a kid and it was a one-time thing. I only think about it about once every 10 years, and it just "seems weird". But of course, had my Dad not said something, who knows if the boy would have tried it again.

The centerfold…

About a year later, my Mother decided we girls needed to "have the big talk about sex"…this time for real. She said some other mothers in the neighborhood had already explained things to their girls a couple years earlier, because the kids started asking questions. We were shocked our friends knew about this mystery before we did and hadn't spilled the beans and told us. What was this activity…and why was it such a big secret?

So…one morning, as I was eating breakfast alone, my very religious Mother, who was definitely touting "virginity", came up to the kitchen table, and opened up a Playgirl Magazine. She pulled out the center-fold and I was stunned. There before me was a well-tanned, dark-haired man, standing in a "come-and-get-it" pose, by an athletic bicycle…and holding a bottle up to his mouth. My sister wandered in and saw it too. We couldn't unsee it!

I was trying not to stare, but I was trying to take-it-all-in.–Odd choice of words! This was how I saw my very first naked man…and he was definitely a "man" and not a boy. The picture was both intimidating and spellbinding all at once. My Mother said she just wanted us to know what a guy looked like, and, baffled, I tried to comprehend that there was a forbidden magazine devoted to showing off this male body part that seemed to have a life of its own and apparently changes in size. A+ on visual props!

Kama Sutra?

A few months later, my Mom called me into the bathroom and said to close the door. She very quickly showed me some drawings in a book, which she seemed to guard with her life. I'm not sure if it was the "Kama Sutra" but I saw about five different contortions and then quietly was told, "You can have sex in many positions, but you should wait until you are married." She closed the book and I was a bit puzzled, wondering how exactly it all worked out. It seemed like this sex-thing is supposed to be fun, and yet somehow it provokes anxiety. It also requires a "husband"?

That was something I heard many times throughout puberty. "Marriage" seemed to be the key. But what I never understood is the idea that a woman is somehow more special if she is still a virgin, yet men seem to want women who know what they are doing, and furthermore do it like a pro. Unless that one man is the be-all-and-end-all instructor, how is the woman who devotes herself to only him supposed to get so good?

I have to give my Mom lots of credit for being so upfront.... I'm sure it was uncomfortable for her. My Mom talked about the importance of virginity...in terms of the church ...in terms of not getting pregnant...and in terms of protecting your reputation as a woman. It seemed that "respect" was hanging in the balance...and with one little poke it could vanish!

Sex-ed teacher...

While I was in junior high, the hit movie "Grease" came out. I loved the promiscuous Rizzo character as much as the Sandy character. Then in 8th grade I had to take a sex-ed class in school. Our teacher was an extremely attractive man named Mr. Jones and I think every girl had a crush on him. He had blondish hair and a mustache and seemed squeaky clean...but never-the-less sparked desire. I would guess he was in his late 20's or early 30's ...he was just older and very nice. Mr. Jones talked about some student from another class who approached him because he had VD. "Sexperimentation" has a downside! All of the practical talk definitely put a damper on things. But it was all part of the package of that mysterious act.

Cute boy...

In 10th grade, I went from the mainstream high school, to one that was supposed to be for kids who were "creative and independent". That year a very cute boy began talking to me. He was about my height, had curly hair and he was two years older. He asked me, "Why don't you wear jeans?" My Nunny used to give my sister and me lots of home-made clothing for Christmas presents and all year around. I had resisted wearing jeans even though they were the big style. However, I quickly got some.

That same boy then asked me, "Why are you wearing Leif Garrett on your breasts?" —He made me blush. (I had a pink shirt with my teen idol on it.)

And then one day as I was minding my own business, the boy boldly came up and put his arm around me. As his friend glanced in our direction, the boy said, "She's old enough." I figured I knew what he meant. But I was shy and kept to myself and a few weeks later I heard that he had lost his virginity with some older girl. After that he never went out of his way to talk to me again, but would still say, "Hi" in a way that seemed rather thrilling.

Years later this boy's Mom was a counselor I went to at the time I was getting a divorce. I told her I had had a crush on her son and she proudly showed me his wedding pictures. She was a very nice lady.

Pretty scary...

That same year, during 10th grade, I was "trying to be pretty" and began getting noticed, but I still was my awkward mousy shy self. An older girl who was very brainy in math and science began talking to me a lot. She seemed to have a chip on her shoulder about something, but she also seemed sad. So I would converse when she would come up to me.

Then one day, the Father of another student came to the school. He was waiting in the hall at the end of the day for his son to appear. This is a man who I knew because I saw him at his family business several times. Anyway, the brainy girl literally came up to me...in front of the man...and began choking me. She put her hands around my throat and squeezed. I couldn't believe it and then of course grabbed her hands off. And the man...never moved a muscle. He just smiled. He never said a thing to stop her, or tried to make her quit. He actually had a look on his face as if he was amused by "the show". I thought it was the most peculiar thing.

A few minutes later, the man left and the girl said to me, "You're pretty and you're the type guys will want to have sex with." And she walked away. I was baffled. For one thing I wasn't that pretty, and secondly the man acted like it was normal to watch one kid choke another, and on top of that I was basically sent the message, "If you're pretty, you should die." How odd. I never told anyone about that until many years later. I think I was still in shock for a long time.

Fighting to keep your man...

In 11th grade I was riding home from school and two girls from my neighborhood were clawing at each other as they were in the middle of a full-blown fight on the floor at the back of the bus. Hair was being pulled, names were being called, and I just looked in dismay. A third girl said they were fighting over the same boy.

I ran home and told my Mother about the brawl and she said, "Oh yes, girls can get very nasty over a boy. You have to be careful. Where love and sex are involved, things can get ugly and dangerous." It was so hard to believe. The girls who were fighting were really nice, smart, non-threatening types. Yet they were reduced to acting like THAT!?!

I wondered if the boy even liked either of them. Or if the boy preferred one of them...afterall, it was his decision to make, not the girls'. What was the boy supposed to say, "You have beaten the other girl up, which is very erotic, and now I want to go have sex with you."

Religion and sex...

Despite being choked and despite watching two girls pummel each other over a boy, nothing put me in my place as much as the fear of "being bad" in terms of my soul. The message I got was "sex and religion don't mix".

The whole religious aspect was very real to me. My Mom even used to tell me, "Maybe you could be a nun...your Uncle almost became a priest." While I have respect for women who are, I knew that could never be my choice. Even Maria in "The Sound of Music" ends up marrying the Captain. Giving up boys was not an option...ever! Insane! Besides I was going to be an actress. My Mom said she had fleetingly considered being a nun.

Coital poses...

By my senior year in high school, I had never dated, kissed, or seen more than a photo of a naked man. I think my Mother was a bit concerned because she knew I was interested in going into a profession where people were a little lax on morals and scruples...in comparison to a strict religious point of view. She warned me about all the pressure out-in-the-world, and she wanted me to be prepared. Lots of pressure...I got the message.

One time my Mom showed me a Playboy magazine. It had a pictorial with Sarah Miles and Kris Kristofferson appearing to be having sex for a film. —I thought the actors were very devoted to their craft, but, I didn't know what to make of it. At the same time my Mother gave me a glimpse of this activity, she seemed appalled the actors were so explicit for a movie.

So this is sex....and this is a part of acting now? I had not realized that could be a requirement.—Sex ...or simulated sex?!? I told myself that such a thing was just limited to occasional scripts and not a mainstream thing. At least sex would not be aired on television...and I absolutely love TV. Of course, movies in the cinema seem like "the big time success", but being a TV actor would be great as well...I could "settle" for that if I had to. (Foolishly thought by someone who believed the climb to fame would be a snap!)

I didn't want to do anything to upset my parents. Nevertheless, being an actress was evermore on my mind... and so were boys. And soon it became apparent...all the pictures in the world could not truly prepare me, because dealing with real living breathing virile men was another thing all in itself! And acting class was harder than I thought because this lifetime around, I didn't have "an in". This lifetime, I am not "Marilyn Monroe"... I am "Michele Who?"

Marilyn's beauty...and nudies... paved the way...

When I was Marilyn, I was pretty and people all looked at me and said, "Looky, she really cares about her craft, she's studying acting now. She's hanging out at the Actors Studio." I remember that and I didn't mind a bit! I was taking class to be a better performer, but I was already performing.

So many people thought I was initially "dumb" (stupid) that any sign of intelligence seemed to impress them. All I had to do was hold a book, and suddenly my IQ soared. Nevermind, if I was having trouble concentrating on the topic because of hallucinations...books made me look smarter in photos. I wasn't dumb by any means, I was reasonably smart! But the point is, people were unduly fascinated with me because I had "an in".

I was beautiful...and unusually photogenic because of my soft rounded facial features. So I stood out in the crowd. Yes there were haters...and that hurt my feelings. But there were always people who appreciated what I brought to the table. The point is, I never just sunk to the bottom of the crowd. I was always present. Love me, hate me... you couldn't escape me. The camera made sure if it. And it was in one's best interest to give me special attention with all the flash bulbs around...and journalists documenting my every move. But that was *that* lifetime...1926-1962.

The average person is just "in the great big crowd". And the average pretty girl is just "in the crowd of pretty girls". As much as Marilyn had a love-hate relationship with her image, it was a definite "in"...and she knew it. I knew it! I remember being her and it wasn't the image itself that I hated. It was the idea of being pigeonholed into it. My image was a vehicle.

Marilyn also had the advantage of living during a time when most actors weren't doing nude photos and scenes as "the norm". Nudies were still a bit of a scandal...or a treat. So, at that point in history, posing in the buff meant "doing something extra" that most stars wouldn't do. But these days, it is far more common place, so again, "join the crowd". That attention-getting stunt doesn't have quite the lasting impact anymore. It's nice .... but........NEXT! (Your replacement is coming in the door.)

I am sure that people wanted to be seen with "Marilyn the movie star" as well as she wanted to soak up the "smart appeal" that she got from associating with skilled artists. I believe I was good publicity for people who in turn made me look more respectable in the eyes of judgmental idiots. I look at the photos of Marilyn and Arthur and it seems like the perfect example...people mating because they balance each other out in some way.

Marilyn always knew that despite all her hardships as a child, she had one fantastic glowing "in" as an adult. God and The Universe gave me beauty...and, although it attracted lechers, it also inspired people to take me under their wing and help. Helping "the orphaned sexpot" was good for the soul, and assured a mention in some article somewhere probably. People helped me...for which I'm truly grateful. If someone hurt me, someone else helped me. I was lucky in that. I'm not saying I didn't have to sometimes "give someone something" for their help... but at least I had the option.

So what is the point I am making? In my Michele-life, I had to decide if acting was really my passion...one which I felt defined my existence and I couldn't live without. I had to decide and then work hard to distinguish myself if so. —And no one was going to miss me if I walked away. But with Marilyn, I think performance sought her. I think God and The Universe created that lifetime for the specific purpose of going public.

And what does all this blathering about Marilyn's "in" have to do with anything? Well, Marilyn knew early on that beauty...and more specifically "sex"... was "her thing", and, furthermore, Marilyn used sex as a survival tool. But, as Michele, I wasn't sure in the least what to do about that 3-letter word. Marilyn's Mother had issues and ceased to raise her by the time Marilyn was a teen. Her Father wasn't around. No one back home was going to disown her...or even lecture her...for any kind of conduct she adopted. (Maybe I exaggerated everything?!)

But my dear Mother, during my Michele-life, was one of my best friends and we actually spent a lot of time together before I went off to college. And my Dad was proud of his girls. I wanted to keep it that way. So that just made all the sex-topics a little confusing. It's good... it's bad....you'll do it someday...don't do it anytime soon...and don't show off too much.

Imagine...the first year of college in my Michele-life....I probably had my own thoughts...my Mother's expectations...and then "the ghost of Marilyn" all competing for attention in my head. And if "Marilyn's ghost" was there...what position was she taking? Was she taking the "you did this before, do it again" stance? Or was she taking the "try something new, this might kill you" approach?

How would I know. I didn't even realize that past lives were real the first year away from home. I just looked to my right and looked to my left and I got the distinct impression it was taking me a lot longer to decide what I believed in than it did for most of my peers.

Initially.....

During my college years I/Michele thought I needed <u>everybody</u> to think I was special. I think I was really trying to make up for lost time and all the years I felt invisible in school before.

I immediately began wearing mini-skirts to look 1960's-ish. I loved the clothing styles from movies of that decade. Now and then guys would stop me on the street and ask if I was from England or France. When I would say "no" sometimes they would actually argue with me because they thought that I was lying, despite my having no accent. (I had/have never even been out of the country.)

***My first year of college, the campus had 4 terms in a school year. After that, they switched to a semester system and there were 3 semesters. The semesters are longer than the terms used to be. So throughout this book when I talk about the school years, sometimes I word them differently.

Pure Naivete...

My second term in college was Fall 1982, and I had a crush on a guy who approached me at the salad bar in the dining hall. He thought I was from England, and inquired. His eyes were very blue, his hair was thick wavy blondish-brown and his name was Christopher.

In the following weeks, he came to my dorm lobby once and talked to me awhile and told me about "The Shining" movie. And one time he also showed up at my room unexpectedly. He asked me for some hand lotion for his arm. As he was rubbing it on himself, he said something nice to me about the shape of my hips and I deflected the compliment. Christopher responded, "Typically in most species the males are the better looking ones, but the females are the smart ones and the organizers."—He said this while giving me the extra blop of lotion he had squirted on himself.

I thought he was very sexy. However he was several years older than I was and I was thinking "what a nice boy" while he was probably thinking "let's get it on." We didn't kiss or anything. Just talked a little and he left.

A few days later, I went alone to an evening Halloween party across the street from my dorm area. I dressed in a dark wig and I stuffed a Mickey Mouse t-shirt with two big athletic socks. I was very slim at the time and had small boobs. I said I was dressed to be Annette Funicello.

I saw Christopher there and he was slow dancing with another girl. I wasn't sure what to do so I just stood and looked around. But when he saw me, he immediately left the other girl and came to me. He told me to go outside with him and then he said he wanted to show me something. I followed him across a grassy area...at some point he picked me up...and there was his van.

I naively got inside and he laughed at my stuffing and snapped my bra and the socks fell out of my shirt. We were eagerly making out and then he began putting his hands in other places. But each time I stopped him. Finally after multiple attempts Christopher was ticked off at me and told me he would walk me back to my dorm. I knew he wanted to get rid of me so he could go back to the party and find the other girl who might put-out. I really didn't blame him, she was really pretty. Yet I was heartbroken.

As stupid as it seems, I really had hopes that we could just kiss. I had next to no experience with guys. I had barely kissed the guy who gave me my first kiss, and I had made out only twice with another guy.

The walk was short and I tried to hold his hand but he refused to let me. He told me, "You need to be careful what you do, because you give guys the wrong impression. Someday when you get married, you will make your husband really happy because you are very physical." As soon as my dorm building was in front of us, Christopher walked the other way. That was that!

From there on in, Christopher never talked to me more than a few words. About a week after our encounter he saw me and just stared and then asked, "Are you ok?"...nothing more. I cried quite a bit the rest of that semester and then I also gained weight, which most of my friends claimed made me look healthier. My chest actually did get bigger. **I was on an emotional roller coaster, and I got the message loud and clear, "Put out, or get out."** I felt I was being punished for "being good".

My friend Cathy lived in the dorm room at the end of the hall and she was friends with Christopher. **She said, "You just have to decide what you want in a relationship."** —But that was very hard for me to do. I still had all the things my Mother said to me colliding with all the things I felt were "my choices". I still felt like I was going to hell if I stepped out of line, because I was raised very religious. I still had a lot to reconcile within.

The next term in college began in January 1983. Cathy told me Christopher had left school. I knew he was older than I was, so he may have just completed his degree. I also heard some other things could have been the cause. I didn't know why he was really gone, but I was sad. I ended up talking for a while with a couple friends of his, one of which wanted to be a film maker. But I never found out anything more about Christopher through his buddies. So he just remained a fantasy in my mind the rest of that college year. Eventually, I got sick of crying...

Oddly enough when I was 38 and just about to move to California, a flukey thing happened on the internet. Somehow I got into some IM that someone else was also on. It was like some weird thing in The Universe. We were both unwittingly using the same user ID and password, and somehow our IM's intertwined. When we realized something mysterious was happening, the other woman and I began talking. She called herself "Kelly".

When she told me where she was from, I kiddingly asked her if she knew Christopher. (I gave her his full name.) Kelly said she didn't think she knew him but her husband had a good friend with the same first name. I asked her if the friend had a specific facial feature. She said she never looked at him very closely, but she would ask her husband.

And it turned out... her husband was friends with the guy I had had a crush on 20 years earlier! It was very good to know he was still alive and well! I knew then that he was still in Pennsylvania. I am sure he still had very blue eyes too. I told Kelly I knew him a long time ago... and that was that! I moved to California...where everything fell apart. (Story in another chapter.)

Various other experiences while in college...

Christopher wanted sex, but he wasn't scary. I actually liked him. However, throughout my first year of college, I remember a couple different times guys would get a female friend to walk them up to my dorm room and <u>there</u> they would be. One time a guy even told me he went into my room looked around, went through some photos, and then left when I didn't come back after a few minutes. These were guys who I spoke to over breakfast in the cafeteria. We had pleasant conversations over yogurt and oatmeal...but I never extended an invitation. It made me uneasy. I didn't want miscellaneous guys randomly invading my living space!

One time a guy in a class asked for my number. I gave it to him. It was winter semester and I was wearing heavy clothing, nothing skimpy. He called me and immediately began talking about sex and I was shocked. He said, "Hi. You're pretty. You know most guys like sex up the butt. It is more common than you think." Click!—I wasn't going to discuss that!

The following year, when I was waitressing, a guy in a sailor's uniform followed me back into the kitchen area to ask me out. I was wearing a fake engagement ring which I got for my 16th birthday. So I told him I had a boyfriend. He said, "So?!" I'll admit he was cute, but he kind of scared me. He didn't want to take no for an answer, and I was afraid I would get fired.

And then of all things...there was the time I went out with an extremely handsome guy, who took me dancing at a frat, walked me back to my dorm room, kissed me a little, and then when I wouldn't do more he said he would rape me. I just stared at him and he stared back. I don't know what reaction he expected. Did he think I would take off my pants? Did he think I would scream? What? Then he said, "I can't do that to you, you are too innocent." And he began telling me about how he was sad because he lost a puppy... and also someone's husband tried to beat him up after he screwed her.

Over a very short time, I realized I didn't need to "be popular". I simply didn't even like it. I liked being more low-key. I don't like aggression. I don't think anyone does. I wanted to be safe. I don't need adulation from the masses anymore, just one devoted boyfriend... a few best friends... and my family. Marilyn's life was different than mine.

Naked for the first time... 3rd term to 4th term in college...1983.
I am electing to use code names for these two men because of the content of the stories. I don't want to make waves in anyone's life.

Christopher had just left campus never to be seen again. And I had to focus on my studies. I will admit, I was a terrible student and tearfully begged my Dad to let me quit college. He agreed, but changed his mind the next day.

In the theatre department, if you didn't get a part in a play, you had to join set construction crew. So by the middle of my freshman year I was taught to use electric saws and I was painting a lot. Between taking classes and set crew in the evenings, I was almost always around theatre people. And sometimes set crew ended rather late.

There were times I would go home in the middle of the night with a buddy who had several housemates and I'd sleep on their couch....or with them on the floor. They were straight but didn't try to force me into anything. They were actually very respectful and saved my first year of college from being a big drag. I am still grateful to this day.

There was the green-eyed guy named Grant. He was a year older than I was, had adorable dimples, and dark brown hair that swept across his forehead like Robert Redford's in "The Way We Were". He was also studying acting. He was cute with a charming smile and we palled around on campus, walking from one theatre building to the next in between classes. I never took his company for granted because it was so nice to have a hot guy who actually spent quality time with me.

Grant and I made-out at length several times. We always stayed in the livingroom. He was a good kisser, but he never tried to get anything more from me and I enjoyed our times together. I was told by his friend that he had been previously hurt in a fling where he got more emotionally hung up on the girl than she had on him. So perhaps he was happy to have found a girl who didn't move fast.—I don't know. He was in my life at just the right time. He gave me hope in the whole boy-girl thing!

Then there was the blue-eyed guy named Khail. He was a few years older than I was. He had medium brown hair and kinda resembled Mikhail Baryshnikov. He was built pretty solid and had a funny little laugh. He wore nice cologne and played music by the band "Chicago" on his stereo. –I thought "Color My World" was oh-so sexy!

Years later when a dentist told me to listen to one of his CD's to relax, I chose the "Chicago" one because it reminded me of Grant and Khail and that time in my life.

I had actually met Khail before Grant but then met Grant when Khail took me home after construction crew. The whole situation was all pretty buddy-buddy. Khail served me coffee and hot breakfast cereal and we'd sit around and talk...and then drink more coffee.—This is where my love for coffee began. Then later in the evenings I'd end up making out with Grant. It was actually quite amazing how things would work out. However...I grew increasingly curious about Khail.

On several occasions Khail told me he thought I was "refreshing" because he said, "Too many girls throw themselves at me...and all the other guys." Khail restored my faith in the man-woman thing! I continued to live in my "Sandy from Grease" world, but we all know where Sandy ends up in the end....

Eventually it was May and the school term was winding down and Khail was graduating. Somehow at the very end, I managed to spend time alone with him when none of his housemates were around. Turns out, he was the first guy I ever got naked with. By the time we took our clothes off it was the wee hours of the morning, we were both so tired, and he couldn't easily get himself inside me because I was just too tight. I gave him a hand-job.—Of course I didn't really know what I was doing.

I remember the overall experience being a dream-come-true, in that this extremely appealing guy wanted to have sex with me, yet he didn't act like it was the most important thing and the only thing in the world. I knew him before we got naked, basically. I had a big crush on him for months.

A few years ago when Mikhail Baryshnikov was on some episodes of the TV show "Sex and the City," I couldn't help but think about Khail. —I wonder if anyone else sees the resemblance?

Throughout all my years in college, I always appreciated all of the fabulous, cute, gay guys in the theatre department. I agree with people who say, "Every girl should have a gay guy friend." As a matter of fact, the more the merrier! I also had a female friend who was gay as well, and she was nice, pretty, smart and so was her girlfriend. I like having friends! Straight, gay, whatever. I like people who really want to talk...and not just talk to "get something".

These were the first experiences I had....before I met the master manipulator Spring Semester 1984! Aggressive men I barely knew....a few make-out sessions ...some wonderful friends....and one naked night something almost happened. I felt like I spent a lot of time "up

in my head" thinking about all the things I wish would/could happen...
but weren't.

You don't own me........!
(A cautionary tale: Girls ...Guys...be smarter than I was!)

There is THIS little situation I would definitely like to forget. But,
I'll put it in this book, because I think if I were talking to Dr. Phil, he
would ask me what I am avoiding. Yes, my <u>imaginary</u> conversation
with Dr. Phil is compelling me to include this story now. Then I want
to release the negativity and never mention it again...period!

**I am electing to use a code name for the man in this story because
of the circumstances and because I don't even like to say his name!**

When I/Michele was 19, a man who I had <u>absolutely no attraction to</u> began pestering me. He was 12 years older and one of my
teachers, the second half of my sophomore year. I guess he had my
phone number because I was his student. He was NOT in the theatre
department, however he was teaching a class I was looking forward to.
He called me Spring Semester 1984 when I was living in a dorm room
and had no voice mail or caller ID to screen calls.

I will call him "Mr. Cruise Control" because during the very first
phone conversation we had he went on at length about using it on the
highway. I have no idea why but he seemed to think that made him very
clever. I've never used it so maybe I'm missing something...?

He started out by saying, "I could tell you needed somebody to talk
to." I don't know what gave him that impression, because I certainly
didn't want to talk to him outside the classroom. However, I had been
doing poorly in school and desperately needed a good grade and I had
had high hopes that I could get one in that class. Looking back at it
now, I figure he probably used that line with other people too, to have
an excuse to call them. I feel like a lot of his personality was manipulative. But at that time I was trying to be cordial and survive academically.

Our first phone conversation was rather long, not because I wanted
it to be but because I was afraid of "being rude" to someone who was
my teacher. At the end of the conversation he seemed quite tickled

with how much we talked...and said so. I really don't remember any other topics of our conversation except for the parts about him cruising down the highway and also saying he had a degree in psychology and could "hang a shingle".

I look back on this and marvel at how little self-esteem I had. WHY didn't I make up some excuse after the first 10 minutes? Why didn't I just tell him my roommate needed to use the phone or I had an appointment to go some place? This is beyond me! I guess I thought lying was wrong.

My Mother was working on campus then and I remember telling her that my teacher had called me. At that point it was a one-time thing and I thought that that would be it. But then Mr. Cruise Control called me a couple days later and was sulking in an accusatory manner. He said that he had been called into the Office of The Dean in the college he was teaching for and told to stop calling students because it isn't appropriate. That seemed good to me. (**And I appreciate it to this day that that Dean did that, and probably would have done more if I had spoken up and asked for help.**)

However, in his passive aggressive way, Mr. Cruise Control managed to successfully manipulate me. He did it by making the comment, "You know how women are when they get together, they gossip...that's what they do. I hope I don't lose my job because of this. I hope you didn't cost me my job." I felt terrible and responsible. (I know now I wasn't. This was his fault not mine or anybody else's.)

He told me my Mother had said something in conversation to one of her co-workers and the co-worker said something to the Dean. I doubt my Mom was even tattling...although she had every right to. I assumed she was just mentioning it because maybe she thought it was interesting the teacher contacted me. I really don't know, I never asked her....ever.

All I know was, this man now had me feeling guilty as if his career was possibly on the line because of "a bunch of gossipy women and ME". I fell into line and tried to convince him that I was not against him and I hoped he wouldn't get canned. Why????!!!!!!

About Motives:

Mr. Cruise Control continued to call me. I ended up involved with him on a level I didn't wish. The way the whole situation went down is appalling to me even to this day. So is my stupidity. He kept calling and I would talk to him in sort of a jilted way and not really try to carry the conversation. I just wanted to hang up. **He kept saying that "some people have motives" about this or that.** He kept saying he didn't and that he just thought that we could "just be friends".

He said it's always good to have friends and he claimed that in Florida teachers could be friends outside the classroom with students because it is more laid back. I wanted to believe this idealistic concept even though it seemed suspect. I could see how teachers could be friends after the semester was over and the student wasn't their student anymore...possibly. But this was different.

I knew better and yet.....somehow in the way he would phrase things it was very effective in making me feel ashamed for even reading anything into whatever it was that was about to happen. It made me feel as if he was saying, "I am an innocent guy and you are pre-accusing me of doing bad things that I haven't done and never would do."

He had a way of twisting my mind! He invited me to his apartment to "just be friends" and eat dinner. I guess I went to prove I wasn't being judgmental. He also made being friends sound platonic. He pretended he liked my mind.

As I walked to Mr. Cruise Control's apartment I hoped that he was on the level about "just being friends". I hoped that he was actually pursuing a fellow faculty member closer to his own age for adult activities. I figured he could find a more sophisticated woman. I imagined them hanging out in a faculty lounge. I imagined him dating her and then talking about grading papers would be foreplay. I just plain didn't imagine him coming on to me. That was wishful thinking. I was naïve.

(And this is exactly why this segment is here. God forbid some young girl or guy reads this book, I want them to be smarter than I was...and tell someone if they are being pestered...before something happens or even after.)

When I arrived at Mr. Cruise Control's place, I noticed it was a small studio apartment where you can be staring at the bed when you are in the livingroom or kitchen. He made steak and something else but I don't remember what. The food was "ok"...I don't have any recollection about what we discussed. I don't recall being scared or interested or bored or anything. Then he said we should watch TV. That was by the bed. The bed was made and the TV was at the end of it. He liked to watch music videos. I tried not to read into things. I told myself he was nice and a gentleman. But I was completely wrong.

The weird thing was, Mr. Cruise Control never obviously looked at me in a way that indicated he was attracted to me...I really couldn't tell. He didn't compliment my appearance. He didn't flirt with me. I don't even know if he knew how to flirt...I never saw that trait in him. He was just a very dry matter-of-fact kind of personality. So I never got the impression anything was about to happen. It was also winter semester and I was wearing jeans and a heavy sweater top...nothing revealing or dressy or unusual or special...nothing. And I was wearing shoes to walk in snow.

As we were watching TV, he suddenly leaned over and kissed me. I was shocked... but my self-esteem was weak. He had a weird smile on his face and I felt guilty for lacking interest. I told myself I should be flattered. I told myself I shouldn't be rude. I felt that if I got up and left right then, that I better be ready to drop his class. But I really needed a good grade badly because I was so bad at certain other subjects.

At first I didn't respond. But then he kept kissing me ...and I kissed back....but I felt like I was on some alien planet, because I wasn't at all attracted to him and I didn't know what to do. I really think I was just so young and stupid that I probably also kissed back just to prove I was a good kisser...always worried about how I was being perceived.

Then, before I knew it...he had his pants off and was sticking himself in my face...full erection. It happened so fast and was possibly the single weirdest moment of my life. (Perhaps only rivaled by the odd moment that comes later in the book when I have an operation on my face that catches me off guard.) I had never had "actual sex" before. And I certainly didn't plan to be with someone I barely knew and didn't find attractive. And I was fully dressed, not in the least acting like I wanted more.

So there he was ...Mr. Cruise Control...in my face and I just looked at him. I literally felt like I was in a stand-off. I looked at him, he looked at me. Maybe 20 seconds later he backed off and lay down and held me as he breathed heavy and pouted. I felt horrible because I believed that this was all my fault for going to his apartment in the first place and kissing him back when he kissed me. And afterall I was 19...legal age to consent.

A million different things went through my head and I really was unable to imagine anything but complete and utter embarrassment. I even felt badly for him because he had to have realized he had made a big mistake. I kept thinking, "HOW are we going to get out of this?" The thought of confrontation seemed painful. I could barely imagine getting through the next 5 minutes or looking him in the eyes again.

So...unbelievably.....I slid down the bed and did what I did. It was my first time. I didn't know what I was doing and I am sure that had to be quite obvious. All I wanted to do was pretend I wasn't mortified ... and I wanted to give him an "out" so he didn't feel like a big fool either. —Then he came. In my mind, I thought, "This will be it, certainly he will move on." I figured I'd respectfully stay for another 10 minutes and then gracefully leave. I just laid there doing my time, but I didn't get up fast enough.

No...he insisted on pulling my pants off. And that was the first time *that* happened. But we didn't have intercourse. I really didn't feel anything. I just thought it was presumptuous of him to do that because I remember when he first began to tug at my jeans I pulled at them too as if to indicate I wanted to keep them on.—But he insisted. And then he spread my legs. I don't remember what I thought about, but I never imagined my first encounter with actual sex being like that. I was grateful that my first naked encounter the year earlier was a pleasant one. At least I had that much.

I guess he thought he was going to do something that would make me happy. It didn't. It was very personal and I barely knew him. I still wasn't attracted to him and if I had wanted sex, I would have chosen a cute boy a lot closer to my own age who turned me on...or even an older guy I liked. I definitely had other teachers who were more appealing. I swear my brain kind of turned itself half off just to cope with him.

He asked me if what he did felt good and I lied. Then I made some comment in a smart ass tone of voice, "I'm getting ALL this experience."

But what I really meant was, "Can't you tell I've never done any of this before?" I wanted him to just forget about me and I wanted to leave.

At that point in time my chest was fairly well developed because I was working out a lot at the campus gym. I remember seeing a lady on TV who had nice cleavage and I tried to divert his attention towards her and I commented that I was small in comparison. I guess I was hoping that I could convince him he should want some woman that is a different type than I was. For the first time in my life I wanted someone to think I was ugly.

But then Mr. Cruise Control spouted off something like, "Anything more than what you can fit into a champagne glass is excess." He claimed the French people say that. He further went on... "Or anything more than what you can fit into the palm of your hand is too much." OK! I got the point. I wasn't successful side-tracking him.—Damn-it!

Eventually I went home that night. I really didn't stay all that late, but it was still too long. And I figured, "Guys want one night stands, so I am safe, he'll be through with me now." But that was not the case. He called me again and I asked why he was calling. I know I didn't say it in a positive tone...more bewildered. You would think that it would matter that I was not happy to hear from him again. He seemed shocked I'd question him, but at the same time I could tell he knew I wasn't happy and he just didn't care.

He said, "Well I was feeling really comfortable the other night." He never bothered to ask me if I felt the same way. But I still didn't have the guts to just tell him to go fuck off. He wouldn't stop calling me. And I stupidly continued to see him because I didn't want to drop the class. I should have looked into whether or not anyone else was teaching that same topic but it never occurred to me. I'm not sure if I could have switched classes. And way back then getting enrolled in a class was a very tedious process, which fast technology hadn't made so easy yet. —I just felt trapped.

Somehow in this sick twisted situation, it actually seemed easier just to pretend I was able to deal with it all. I guess that is what hookers do. As time went on I watched more music videos with Mr. Cruise Control. That was the time of the colorful 1980's legwarmers, and I wore them.

My Mother had constantly preached "save your virginity until marriage." I was pretty sure I no longer believed in that for myself, but at the same time I used that notion to keep from doing anything more with Mr. Cruise Control than what I was already coerced into doing. And even though he got a bit perturbed, he actually never tried to force me to cross the line. The limitations of what I would do also didn't seem to deter him.

There had been one point when I was still in his classroom that I saw some really pretty girl approach him and seem very happy. She looked a few years older than I was. I told myself that he was probably hitting her up too so he was getting what he wanted with someone else anyway. And by the way she smiled at him, I imagined she must have actually liked him. I figured she was also closer to his age so maybe she "got him" in some way I didn't. Nevertheless, phone calls inviting me to his apartment continued. I remember one time he mentioned her to me as if he was trying to make me jealous. I wanted to say, "So...go!" But I was afraid to, I needed the class.

The thing is, I had to not think too much about what was going on. I told myself, "Michele, at least you are getting experience." Somehow that kind of seemed ok, and made me feel "more adult". I have heard it said that even if someone is being molested, it can end up feeling oddly and confusingly good. Well, that is kind of how this was. It was like, I was now dabbling in "the middle zone". Not out of the sex-game entirely anymore, yet still could say I hadn't given up my virginity which my Mother often mentioned to my sister and me. Sometimes this nonsensical situation seemed empowering and other times completely soul shredding...and disgusting.

I tried to make-believe that "the acquired experience" justified the weirdness of it all ...but it never did. I thought he was ugly and his personality was sarcastic and annoying. I have known guys before who I thought initially weren't very attractive but then ended up thinking they were sexy because of their personalities. So I am not saying guys have to be models, I'm saying I have to like who they are and enjoy their company to be glad I'm intimate with them. A person's personality really counts for something.

That year I had a roommate named Jessica. Her sister came over to visit and we gabbed a bit. Later I was told, "My sister Jeanette thinks you are really cool because you are your own person." I won't ever forget this. Jessica had no idea that I had been enslaved to my teacher and I was anything but "being my own person". I never told her he kept calling me, and she was out of the room enough not to notice. Jessica and Jeanette based everything off of my lighthearted humorous talk and my willingness to dress a bit flashy. But despite my demeanor, I was far from free. Not at all my own person.

Mr. Cruise Control would say things as if he thought he was tough, but I could tell that he was actually fragile. This really kind of did a number on me too, because I didn't want to be hurtful. He told me he used to work on the lighting crew of the Ice Capades and that he was up on a ladder and fell off and broke his back. He said his wife left him the same day. That made me feel even worse and responsible for not hurting him. He seemed sad, yet I recall another time he snidely referred to women as "ball and chains".

Mr. Cruise Control told me he was teased a lot as a kid and called "Icky". He didn't elaborate but I figured it was because of the way he looked. He wasn't very appealing and he had very strange green eyes which he said were sensitive to light, so he often wore dark glasses. Typically green eyes are exotic, but his were not.—To me, they were the eyes of a manipulator! However, knowing he was teased made me feel bad for him because I never felt "pretty enough". (Thankfully I only remember a little bullying in grade school and none in junior high or high school. What people said about me behind my back I didn't know and it didn't hurt me. And I'm grateful.)

But anyway... here is the part that really disturbs me so many years later. At some point in the middle of my involvement with Mr. Cruise Control, I was so disgusted with my submission that I began to imagine that I liked him. It was quite obviously a defense mechanism and my way of trying not to feel hurt. I tried to imagine he was wise... or a rebel who was cool... or that I was lucky and flattered to "be chosen". If only I could convince myself that he was actually appealing and there was any shred of attraction towards him. I used to wish that other pretty girl in his class would take him away! I imagined that she <u>must have</u> been doing better things with him. I figured she probably wasn't a virgin and he didn't really need me.

There was one point about 2/3 of the way through the semester when Mr. Cruise Control said he was having a party at his apartment for all his students. He asked me if I was going to come, but said it in a tone of voice that demanded that I do.—So I went. To make a long story short, about a dozen people showed and hung out with him for a couple hours. I don't remember what he served because I didn't have anything to eat or drink. I just recall sitting on a couch and some good looking guy named Bob talked to me. He was from some other class Mr. Cruise Control taught.

Bob seemed mighty interested in me despite the fact I thought one of my project partners, Jenny was much prettier. But I didn't feel able to encourage Bob at all. **I knew Mr. Cruise Control thought HE was my owner.** I just pointed out Jenny to Bob and he shook his head as if to say "no" and we continued to talk... but I didn't leave with him.

That was the first night Mr. Cruise Control and I didn't mess around and he even gave me a ride home. It felt odd that he didn't expect anything, but it was also good. He hugged me but that was it. And furthermore it was strange that he wasn't just dismissing me to go walk home many blocks alone in the dark as usual. He actually seemed rather OCD about cleaning up his apartment, so I guess he wanted me to be off and out of his way.

That was fine. I would have rather been with Bob then him anyway. I was never with Bob, but I would have preferred him for sure. This just confirmed in my mind that I wanted a cute boy my own age.

Then at the end of the semester, Mr. Cruise Control told me he was moving back to Florida where he was from. He said he had another job lined up. He made it sound like it was for good and he wasn't coming back. This was news to me but I was relieved. He said he already packed up his apartment and he wanted to pick me up to take me to a hotel so he could see me one last time. He said it had to be at a hotel because he had to vacate his place already.

I just assumed he knew how much to expect from me. I foolishly went along and we did "the usual things". He never actually said he wanted more, but then he just kind of motioned as if he did and put on a condom. Again I thought he was presumptuous. Without even thinking, I blurted out, "I'm saving my virginity." He sighed and told me to turn around and he laid on top of me and came just like that.

I was still a virgin when I left, he didn't push for more. He just looked bewildered and disappointed that I wouldn't give in, but then he also seemed sad to say goodbye as he drove me home. He said he loved me and he gave me his new mailing address. I didn't intend to keep in touch, but at the same time I again felt emotionally confused about the whole experience at the hotel. I felt constantly conflicted between wanting to get away from him, yet wanting to "prove I wasn't a drag"...or wanting to "prove I wasn't superficial". I just plain wish he would have left me alone to begin with.

Mr. Cruise Control seemed somewhat attached to me and yet he really liked Florida and he never said there was a chance of returning. I said good-bye feeling as if I dodged a bullet. Mr. Cruise Control was out of the state and I was glad. He seemed far far away. So in my immature mind, I told myself that I should send him a card and a picture and say something nice just to "leave things on a good note". I figured there was nothing wrong with just "giving him his fantasy" since he seemed to think there was more to things than there was. That was a big mistake!

Dear God! Noooooo! Mr. Cruise Control moved back to Pennsylvania. And he did it without calling me first and asking me if I wanted him to ....or at least telling me he was considering doing so. I realized this situation was now partially my fault...or more.

He simply called my parents' house and asked to talk to me. He said he had moved back to town. (My parents didn't realize who he was.) I was shocked! I also was at a loss for words but managed to say, "Well, I thought we were going to see other people since you left." He was quiet and I am sure hurt. But then again, what did he expect...he was 12 years older than I was and he had said he was moving away and Florida was great. I kept thinking, "I hear all the time about guys who just want one-night-stands, but here I am with someone I am not attracted to and he won't go away!"

The next semester soon began and Mr. Cruise Control figured out what dorm I moved into and how to call me. And so it started all over... the phone calls. He was no longer my teacher and yet I oddly felt bound to him. I told myself I had to "prove that in the past I hadn't just used him for a grade". This was laughable really because HE is the one who wouldn't leave me alone. And I am sure I would have gotten a good grade if he had been a "normal respectful teacher" and just let me take the class in peace.

This time he was no longer living in an apartment complex across town, but rather renting a room on the second floor of a house with a bunch of units. I only went there one time to watch a movie on his TV. And he came to my dorm a couple times. I was surprised he insisted on doing that because he claimed that he was still working for The University. I never knew how he managed to get his old job back so fast.

Winter Break, he went on vacation to Florida and brought me back an orange. He kind of made it seem like it was a big present. For some strange reason I kept the dried out navel part of the peel for quite a long time as if it was a memento. I have no idea why.

Finally I got to the point where I just thought it was crazy to be caught up in this awkward emotional bondage. We never went out in public together....and I didn't want to! I wasn't attracted to him even after a year of getting together here and there. And I wanted my freedom. I wanted out!

I don't actually recall what ended things, which is very odd. I think he just kept calling me and I seemed less and less enthusiastic. Not that I ever was, but I think it had become blatantly obvious ...even to him... that I was not interested in getting together. I remember things just trailing off.

I can't recall exactly when it was, but a couple years later he called my parents' house when I wasn't around and my Mom took a message and his new phone number. She gave it to me and asked who he was and I said, "Just some guy I'm not interested in." I never called him back. And I think he finally got the hint because I never heard from him again.

Long-lasting effects on me? Who can say for sure. But Mr. Cruise Control definitely ruined the word "climax" for me. He liked it more than "come". It sounds so hoity-toity. Bluck! He thought very highly of himself! Climax...whatever!

"A" is for Apple.....and "A" is for Awful.....

Now, you would think that would have been the absolute end of that right? No. This little messy sex-thing haunted me in a way you would have never suspected. Remember, I needed a good grade because I was struggling in college due to lack of focus and enjoying life (without alcohol or drugs). Well, I got an "A" in the class.—I earned it. I knew when I signed up for the class it was something I could do well in. It wasn't science or math.

For years my Mom would periodically bring up my "A"...because I was such a terrible student that that one damn "A" stuck out! She was proud of that "A" and I would just cringe...and feel guilty...very, very guilty.

Throughout the years... as far as Mr. Cruise Control is concerned...

Now, I must confess...this is going to sound terribly mean...but... over the years I have often thought to myself, "I don't ever want to be famous cause God help me if I am and HE comes out of the woodwork to say he knew me and we were lovers." I think I would die.

I have even gone as far as to think that I would never want to be a famous actress because I don't want him to SEE ME....even if he doesn't surface. Weird, right?

And even meaner...I have googled him a number of times to see if I could figure out where in the country he might be living...in hopes of finding an obituary instead. Terrible...I know. But that is how I feel. It isn't that I actually feel hate for him. I just don't ever want him to approach me in any way ever again.

I feel embarrassed that I ever allowed myself to get manipulated into spending time with him. And if he can watch M-TV and give me his judgmental takes on who is or isn't appealing, then I am allowed to say, "This is who I like and this is who I don't." And I don't like him! I never did. I tried. His personality was just way too dry and blah... and selfish.

And...NO WAY...I do not in any way count him when I think about "who I've had sex with". Yes, oral sex is sex, but I only count the people "I've gone all the way with" so I can exclude him. I simply refuse to count him in any way shape or form as significant.

The only way he is significant to me is as a segment in my book telling young inexperienced people that <u>"Sometimes people DO have motives!"</u>

One time when Norma Jeane was about 13, she/I was told to go upstairs and give some man his change from the grocery store. When I approached his room he was sitting in a chair. I stepped forward, reached out my hand and the man grabbed it, pulled me toward him, and tried to force me to touch him. I was morbidly shocked...shaking. I ran downstairs and stammered as I told someone. They asked if I was "sure".--Yes! Little-by-little, my sense of "choice" eroded.

So, there it is.....the beginning of my sex life during this Michele-lifetime after Marilyn Monroe's. Later in Chapter 9, I talk about some of my ups and downs negotiating "The World of Men" in my attempt to lose my virginity and beyond.

Marilyn was a major sex symbol who was murdered. She came back to the world pretty fast...as ME. However, things are different. Not nearly as pretty, having very strict parents, and not particularly photogenic, I can't pull the "usual tricks" Marilyn could. No one is going to bail me out of anything or think I'm "a real swell catch" because I look really great on film. Those days of being highly photogenic and constantly forgiven are over! But nevertheless, life goes on...and even though Marilyn never found Mr. Right, I certainly wasn't about to give up the search!

"SEX in the life.....after Marilyn Monroe".....

Chapter Six:

MICHELE: WHY DO I BELIEVE MY SOUL WAS MARILYN'S?

*S*ummer of 1983, I had a part-time job and also took a science and gym class on campus. It turns out that a really pretty girl named Carolyn was in the same classes. She had been the first runner up for the Miss Pennsylvania contest a couple years earlier. Her older sister Cheryl was working on campus. Anyway, I think between hanging out with Carolyn and theatre people a lot, it opened something up within my soul.

This was the summer I turned 19. One night I was sitting alone in my parents' house and I was talking out loud...going over a line or practicing my diction. It was about 11:30PM and my parents were already in bed. Oddly, I was in my Father's kitchen seat and not my own assigned one which I usually sat in. As I heard my voice spouting something, I suddenly felt a tingly energy go up the left side of my back. Then the energy hovered over my shoulder. And with a *whoosh* it went over the left side of my head. And there it was...I heard another voice...

mine had become one I recognized from TV. Marilyn Monroe's! I had never been overly into her movies, but her voice is very distinct. I was baffled.

The immediate dialogue in my head was this:
"Marilyn Monroe? Marilyn Monroe.
Yes, I was Marilyn. Huh, I was Marilyn?
Don't you remember you were Marilyn?
How could I have ever forgotten I was Marilyn?
That's a whole other lifetime! HOW did I forget?"

I had heard of movies like "The Reincarnation of Peter Proud" and "On A Clear Day You Can See Forever," but I had never given the concept much thought before. Now I had to. I asked God to let me know if this was true or if I was imagining things. I immediately saw my childhood as Norma Jeane in a flash. I knew. It wasn't up-close details....but the feeling was all there.

I proceeded to tell people about my past...while trying to process it myself.

Here are some of the people I told of my new revelation:

First I told my parents:
I said it very casually while at home. I just said it and they barely had a reaction. They probably figured I was just being my usual odd self.

A few weeks later, I recall mentioning it again. This was their response:

Dad: **"Huh....I always kind of preferred Jayne Mansfield."**
Mom: **"I remember seeing Marilyn sing happy birthday to the President, and I felt sorry for her and thought she seemed pathetic."**

OK, those were two ego-boosters—ha!

I told my favorite acting teacher Michael C., as we were both briskly walking down the hall after class. Michael was a few paces ahead of me. He glanced back and said:

Michael: "Then why are you here? Marilyn wouldn't want to be an actress again. She would get married, have a family and settle down."

Michele: "I want to be a serious dramatic actress!"
(I was also thinking, "And famous!")

I often think about what Michael said because I think he had the right idea.

I told Wayne and Michael H. who were co-teaching a director's class.

Wayne: "Well then I suggest you go watch all of Marilyn's movies and enjoy them." (I think he was thinking, "Yah, sure you were.)

Michele: "I can't....her movies seem like they will be dumb."

I told Peg, an acting teacher who I first met through community theatre, but also knew in college. A very lovely lady and accomplished actress.

Peg: "Well, Missy.....a while back I would have thought that was crazy. But now, I am more open-minded and believe anything could be true, because my sister and I saw a full body apparition of our mother in her bedroom after she died. We both saw her very clearly for a few seconds." (I felt so relieved she didn't just dismiss me as nutty.)

I told my friend/pal/buddy Bro Kenn, who was working on his masters degree in play writing.

Kenn: "Well, I was Shakespeare during my past life. So, now Marilyn is hanging out with Billy Shakespeare."

We used to walk around the theatre a lot together. One time I even left my lipstick kiss print on a glass wall and the janitors didn't clean it off for 10 months! Kenn and I laughed every time we walked past it.

I told my theatre advisor Helen. She was a very special woman who constantly encouraged me, even through very bad grades and my obviously confused and floundering college endeavors.

Helen: "You know, people really love Marilyn."
Michele: "Why?"
Helen: "Because she was a nice person."

I thought that was so sweet. She didn't say it was because Marilyn was pretty or sexy...she said she was a nice person. Helen was one of the nicest people in the world. I was lucky to have an advisor who was caring.

I told my friend Mark, who had bright red/orange hair and was a very sensitive person in an acting class with me.

Mark: "Yah, I know you were."

He said it without hesitation and it was very reassuring.

One time I told a woman...I can't recall who.....and she replied,

"You probably just want to believe you were Marilyn because she was prettier than you."

—I'm thinking her name might have been *BITCH* !

Clearly telling my theatre friends/mentors was part of my "coming out as Marilyn". It was just my way of dealing with what seemed so odd and unexpected. I've heard stories about small children who have had past life memories early. But for me, until age 19, I had no upfront conscious realization that Marilyn's lifetime or any other lifetime could be influencing, helping or interfering with my current lifetime.

I had so many good things to be thankful for during my childhood... yet I was often quite unhappy. Something always felt "off". By the time I was a teen, I often wished not to wake up in the morning. I would literally pray to God a silent prayer that I would just be taken and that would be it. I used to sometimes feel as if it would be "my last night" because I felt that way so strongly that I almost thought I could just will myself to cross over. It wasn't until I was 18 and majoring in theatre that I was suddenly thankful to be alive and I felt pure joy. There is a big difference between going to the theatre now and then versus being immersed in it 5-7 days a week and knowing that every single day you go to class you are going to encounter other people who love it too.

Here is something I tell people often, "Acting classes benefit you even if you choose another profession." Self-expression matters. Poise, eye contact, communication, vocal clarity, focus, objectives, enthusiasm, energy, overall self awareness...maybe even fierce ability to charm—ha!

I'm not sure how it is now, but back in the 1980's there were basically two main theatre buildings on the University campus that I attended. The one was theatre-in-the-round and the other had a proscenium stage. My very first acting class on campus was held in the building with the later. During my following years of college, my acting classes were held in a big classroom that didn't have desks. I had dance movement and diction classes in that same room with various instructors.

So, I said before that Michael C. was my favorite acting teacher. Why...?

Well, I had a few other really good acting teachers too, it is just that I had Michael for more acting classes than the others and also for an interesting theatre history class as well. Michael's eyes are very blue and he was rather dramatic. Michael had an edgy personality and he wasn't afraid to give the students the cold hard truth about things. This was both kind of scary and exciting. I appreciated his candor. Michael also had a heart too and when he critiqued he did it constructively, never harshly.

Year One: Class in the auditorium.

Know who you are!

One time in Michael C.'s class we each had to create and develop a well crafted character, and get up on stage and be interviewed as them. I was a cheeky British girl named Devereux Blake. I wore a tight white shirt, and jeans on which I had tied a colorful flowing scarf through a belt loop. Michael began asking questions.

Michael:	**"Is it alright if I call you Dev?"**
Michele:	**"No, Devereux."**

(I was being a smartass ...as I leaned back in my chair.)

I don't recall what Michael's next question was, but he mentioned some place in England (Wiltshire... perhaps)...and also the word "stodgy" and I drew a total blank. I knew he could tell I had no clue what that word meant...and it was obviously so-British!

My character was clearly only surface level, she lacked depth. I hadn't really studied up and thought about what such a person would know if she really existed. All I focused on was looking cute and I did an accent I had practiced many times. I didn't expand my horizon and try anything new...yet I still didn't have my character down. I probably blushed.

OK, he got me there! Damn! Acting is really about committing.

Year One continued...

This was still the year my class was in the proscenium style theatre. We students would sit down in the front two rows of seats and then go up to the stage when it was our turn to perform.

Ham Sandwich...

I remember a time when we had to perform a scene in pairs. I can't recall who my partner was or what the script, but we did something and I felt very distracted that day. Whatever we performed got some laughs and Michael gave me positive feedback. But then I proceeded to cut myself up...tearing down anything good that I had just done. Michael looked at me perplexed and asked why I didn't think it went well. I said that it was because what was going on inside my mind was really different than what it looked like.

I used to think that you <u>had to</u> feel every little thing the character did and that was the only way that the act would be good.

But Michael said to me, "Well, I thought it went alright and ultimately you can be up on stage thinking about a ham sandwich and as long as the audience enjoys the performance, it doesn't really matter."

The idea of thinking about a ham sandwich really cracked me up, and still does to this day. I also got the point. And I'm glad that that is true. Because Marilyn certainly had a lot going on in her head while she was acting. Marilyn didn't hallucinate because she took pills. Marilyn took pills because she hallucinated and that was very stressful.

Following Years: Class in the room down the hall.

Michael wasn't afraid to knock some of the stars out of our eyes and tell us things weren't going to be super easy. I think he knew each of us probably expected to be "the special discovered one," who gets carpal tunnel syndrome from signing thousands of autographs way before turning 30. I have never personally collected autographs, nor do I care about having any even from my favorite stars, but I did expect to **be a star.** It wasn't even a question in my mind. I thought about it every single day from about age 5–22. After that, I realized life was more complicated than expected.

I remember one time he said, "Folks, I know you want to think that show business is about 'show', but most of it is about 'business'. You have to be smart and understand that it is a tough BUSINESS."

Michael went on to say something about getting a small royalty check for some commercial from years earlier. He said that when you are struggling as a performer you can really look forward to and be dependent on those if you are lucky enough to even get them.

No pressure...

Sometimes right before we students would do a scene or monologue in class, Michael would sit back in his chair and say, "Entertain me" ... and then he would just look at you. —OK, that isn't intimidating at all!

He also said: **"People pay to be entertained! They want their money's worth."**

I think I got the point. I'm thinking....by the time you are in college majoring in theatre, you better not be there just to boost your ego and show off. You better be there because you have something to offer and are willing to work <u>darn hard</u> to get even better. Competition is out there! It's everywhere! If you aren't willing to work hard for it, then go fill out an application at your local coffee shop, where you can probably play the part of the good-natured chatty barista who stands next to the little tip jar.

Properly prepared...

So there we were, another mediocre acting student and myself. And we were going to do some kind of tragedy type scene. I don't even recall what it was... Greek, Roman, I don't know. We might have been playing brother and sister roles.

It was our turn to get up in front of the class and we brought no costumes, no props..... and it was time for another "Michael lecture" to the class. He nicely scolded my scene partner and me for not committing to the roles. Michael told us all that it is vital to have props to give us something to work with and be more convincing and carry-out the doings and beats in the scene. I knew he was right. Just because it's "just one scene" and "only for a class" doesn't mean we should be vague—-we had to COMMIT!

The next class, we had props. I think I borrowed some dull knives from my parents' kitchen. I made a hideous make-shift two piece outfit out of some ugly rough-fabric long skirt I cut up. I think our characters were supposed to be people fending for our survival after the deaths of our parents ...and we were supposed to be scared, dirty, on the run and fighting with each other. My character was a bit upset and hysterical.

I remember streaking brown eye shadow on my arms, face, legs, middle. I was attempting to look like I had just crawled out of the mud while on the run. There was just one problem. I never actually tried my costume on before going into the class. And then when I did, I wasn't sure how secure the top part of the outfit really was... I tied it closed with a knot.

I remember standing there, seconds before starting and mumbling something like, "My top might just fall off." —Turns out it didn't. I'm not sure how good at improvising I would have been had it fallen. But I definitely learned a lesson in props, costumes and dress rehearsals. They require EFFORT!

Theatre is fun....theatre is spectacular....there is nothing on earth as exciting as being in the theatre. But Michael was right. It really is "a business". The audience sees the performance...the actors lose sleep to make it perfect. So many times at both the local community theatre and in college theatre, actors or construction crew toiled into the night. And it is only through hard work that the illusion of "ease" is

85

created, so that the audience really can sit back and relax and believe the magic on stage.

And this is one of the things that is so exasperating about remembering my last past life, as Marilyn. To think about holding up other people who were giving their all to the show is embarrassing... and shameful.

I read that during the filming of "The Prince and the Showgirl" they kept a replica of each of Marilyn's costumes in an alternative size, because her weight fluctuated so much. So, maybe that is why I was on my own and making a costume for myself for class this lifetime around. So I would understand that it isn't something you just throw together quickly. There is some skill involved.

I remember one time I was in a scene at the community theater and I absolutely hated the brown over-sized dress they made me wear. But I was afraid to speak up and say so. Unlike Marilyn, no one is ever going to keep me around because my face ...or other parts...draw a big crowd. This time around, I definitely cannot afford to make demands and tax people's patience. I guess that is what people mean when they talk about karma.

I'm that type of girl.....a secretary!

By one of my later years in college, Michael C. began to require that we acting students read a new play each week and type up a "play report". We had to turn them in on Fridays. I think I was the only one who consistently did. The truth is, I was still in that "must be a good girl" mindset and I wanted to meet requirements. I think I was the only one who actually thought that the reports were part of our grades. Or possibly, the other kids were just more confident in their performance abilities and figured they could still pull off at least a "B" even if they never turned in a report.

Anyway, about halfway through the semester, Michael laid down the law! He told us that the play reports had to be done and that it was especially good if we managed to find some more obscure yet interesting works instead of always reading the popular plays that are standard production pieces which everyone has already heard of many times.

But here is the thing. Michael said, "I know you don't want to hear this, but most of you need to learn to type. A lot of actors end up typing for a living." —Now, to budding actors and actresses, the possibility of this sounds downright cruel!

But...I learned to type. And I learned on my parents' typewriter that had clunky keys, which stuck quite often. Not only that, but something was seriously wrong with their machine and it would start typing backwards over the line you just finished sometimes. I would get out the correction fluid and try not to lose my cool. (This was right before computers were in all the classrooms and homes.)

As it is, I do type for a living. I type letters, checks, office instructions, court documents, and.....you get the picture. I type! And I tell people this story quite often. My acting teacher Michael gave very good advice.

Not a triple threat...

I remember one time we had to sing a song in Michael's class. I began singing the "Sixteen Going On Seventeen" song from "The Sound of Music." Now there are some times I have a bit of a singing voice and other times not. This was not a good day for sure! To say I was making a fool of myself would be an understatement.

Mercifully when Michael heard that I was struggling, he took pity on me and said, "OK that's enough." —Thank God! Still to this day I am grateful he stopped my humiliating rendition of that amazing song.

What I wouldn't give to be able to sing like Marilyn could. Then again, I didn't think I was so great when I had that voice. You never know how you will come back in the next lifetime! That's why it is good to be humble.

Clearly, I failed at meeting the "Entertain me" request!

I can't sing... I can't dance...and acting was a "challenge".

I kept working on my typing skills.....

Now…Peg and Helen were wonderful ladies in the theatre department, and also two people who knew about my Marilyn-past.

One of the nicest things Helen said to me was that I could probably go into the field of make-up if things didn't work out with acting. OK, typically I'm told I wear my eyeliner "rather heavy" and it's said with a disapproving tone. And sometimes people say, "Oh, yah blue eye-shadow" as if they don't realize it's the coolest kind around! So, I really appreciated Helen's ability to see the good in me even if it was a bit far-fetched. She made me really feel special and supported. I told her I was pretty sure no one wanted me doing their make-up.

And Peg…she told me one time, "If you want to do something, you have as much time as you need…you work through the night." I got it. You don't put a time limit on your work or dreams…you just keep going. You decide when you're done…not the clock…not some other person …you. And this kind of makes me think about me writing this book. It may be late in the game, but I'm writing it anyway…because Marilyn expects me to.

Summer 1983, I hung out with my friend Carolyn….pretty girl with dark hair and green eyes. Carolyn said she and her sister considered themselves very spiritual. I couldn't wait to tell her my soul was Marilyn's.

Michele:	"Guess what. I was Marilyn Monroe during my last past life."
Carolyn:	"No you weren't. That's silly."
Michele:	"No I mean it. I really believe it. I had an experience, and I know it."
Carolyn:	"Let's go see what my sister thinks. Don't tell her who you think you were. We'll make her guess."

Cheryl was busy cooking and in no mood to talk to us.

Carolyn:	"Michele remembers a past life, so tell us who you think she was."
Cheryl:	"I don't have time to fool around."

Carolyn: **"Just guess."**

Cheryl reached her hands out in my direction, just short of touching me.

Cheryl: **"Marilyn Monroe, now get out of the way."**
Carolyn: **"How did you know?"**
Cheryl: **"I could tell by her energy, now stop pestering me."**

Carolyn and I were speechless.....but then why wouldn't
she say MM?

Dreams.....

During my college years I had very vivid dreams at night. I supposed it could be because I exercised a lot more than usual and had
better circulation. Or perhaps because I was pumped full of caffeine
once I began drinking coffee. Or maybe because I was horny....I don't
know!?! I used to dream about intercourse long before I actually had
it. –And that always perplexed me. And I used to dream about having
sex with some of the cute gay guys too, even though in real life they
never would have done it with me. Occasionally I had dreams where
I was about to walk on stage and star in a musical, but I would always
feel great inner conflict. The conflict was that I had a great voice, but
I knew I didn't have a voice. It was like I knew that what I had <u>in the
dream</u> wasn't what I had in real life. It was like a dream within a dream
kind of think.

Sometimes when I was back at my parents' house, I would sleep
downstairs in the den that they put a bed in. It was cooler there during
the summer months. One time I had a dream about seeing white flowers
falling from the sky, and I heard a narrator say, "This is a story about
death." I felt like I was watching some old news real. It was very odd.

Another time I had a dream where I was trying to open my eyes
and I could barely lift my lids. When I finally did, my eyes were closed
again. <u>It was like a dream within a dream</u>. Then I looked at the side of
my bed and saw a wispy white angel kneeling in prayer and I tried to

look into her eyes to see who she was but as I did I felt myself being sucked into them. I felt almost about to levitate, and as if I would have died if I had continued, but I then turned away out of fear. I don't feel that the angel was bad, but I think she could have taken me out of my body at that moment if she had wanted to or I had insisted on seeing her closer. I finally was able to wake up out of the dream. I didn't sleep in that room for at least week after that experience.

I cannot help but think I had the angel dream because I had discovered my past life as Marilyn and maybe being around theatre people in school was making me think a little bit more like she did. Maybe the angel thought I needed prayers. But this was not the first time I had a dream that I think I could attribute to Marilyn influence.

I remember disturbing dreams from childhood and I didn't know what to make of them at the time. I never thought "past life related" because I never thought about reincarnation then. When I was about 12, I had a dream about being with a lady and walking through the front door of an orphanage. —It was brief but vivid and full of instant fear and heartache all in a few panicked seconds. I began crying in the dream and woke up in tears also.

Then another time, I had a dream about a brick house which I quickly floated past in a very rapid motion. I cycled past it several times. I woke up feeling quite unnerved. I think it was the house I lived in when something terrible happened to a boy Norma Jeane knew during childhood.

The barn...

Here is a painful story I recall from Marilyn's lifetime, when she was about 6 and still called Norma Jeane. This was the worst incident of that whole entire life, and that is saying quite a lot. Norma Jeane was living with some people and they said that some other couple was coming over to the house and bringing their little boy. They said she had to play with him so the adults could visit. When the guests arrived, the two kids were running around the house playing cowboys.

When they almost knocked over a piece of furniture in the hallway, they were told, "Go play outside....but, don't go in the barn!"

I remember the boy and me running around outside and getting very out of breath. I walked into the barn. There on the ground was a big pile of spread-out hey. In the middle was a big sharp barn hook. I leaned up against a ladder at the end of the hey. The little boy sat nearby, but not too close to the barn hook. After about 5 minutes, I decided to leave.

The Boy: "Bang, you're dead!".
Norma Jeane: "Why did you do that?"
The Boy: "Cause you're a GIRL!." (Said meanly.)

It hurt my feelings but I continued walking out. As I walked toward the house I heard him calling, "Norma Jeane, Norma Jeane!" I went back and saw this horrific vision of the boy impaled in the stomach. I said I'd go get help. I have no idea how he fell on the hook, because I didn't think he was that close to it. I wonder if he got closer to take a better look and tripped?

Anyway, as I ran towards the house to summons a rescue, I suddenly became very afraid I would get into trouble and not have a place to live anymore. (This was all racing through the mind of a frightened child.) I went the other way! Yes, in that split second, I chose to flee.

I ran to a neighbor's barn and sat in their hey and cried and fell asleep. I have no idea how long afterwards I awoke to walk back to the house where I lived. But as I approached, the woman of the home yelled, "Norma Jeane, where were you?" I stammered and really didn't answer.

I went upstairs where a doctor and the other adults were standing around. The boy was in a bed. He cried, "Norma Jeane" but actually seemed happy to see me. I cannot recall if he said anything else, but he died shortly after I got there. I think he was two years younger than I was, very young. The whole time, I was selfishly wondering if he had said anything to incriminate me. I felt horrible. This incident became a well guarded secret.

Although I was young, I knew I had made the most horrible choice. He still probably would have died even if I had gotten faster help, but it was my fault for walking into the barn in the first place, and my fault he wasn't taken off of the hook sooner. He could have at least had people who loved him surrounding him longer. I remember the next day I was swinging on a swingset and crying and felt awful to the depth of my being. The boy I really didn't know very well was gone...and it was all because of me. Regret is a very sharp emotion. What if I had not gone into that barn.....if only.

This ordeal with the boy was one that haunted Norma Jeane/Marilyn throughout her life. I recall sitting on the set of "Bus Stop" and being in a pill induced stupor, exhausted. I was waiting to go before the camera. The memory of my "run from rescue" ran through my mind and I pushed it out as fast as I could. I felt such shame all those years later. I could never bear to actually face it, so it was always something I slammed the door of my conscious mind down on. I remember standing across the yard and watching the dreaded barn hook being removed by a pulley and I was crying. I don't believe I ever told another soul about it. And if I had, I am sure I left out the parts about my negligence. I/Michele wish I knew who the boy was.

This ordeal which I experienced during my past life followed me into this lifetime. I remembered it by my third year of college. I recall my friend Carolyn's sister Cheryl recommending I see a psychic medium named Dejawn. Unfortunately, I called him the day before he was going to be leaving the area. He agreed to come to my dorm room on campus and give me a reading for $40, before he caught a bus. My sister Chris who doesn't even believe in reincarnation, gave me the money to see him.

The next day, I told Dejawn about the incident and he asked for permission to read my soul. He sat across from me and appeared to go into a trance. I literally saw a white cloudy light appear above him during the minute or two his eyes were back in his head. He then told me he saw the same incident I had just described and that the boy's name was John and that I had to forgive myself for the decision I made when Marilyn/Norma Jeane was just a child. I told him I couldn't. I have no idea if the boy's name really was John because I have never remembered that detail on my own.

I ran away again!

And I must confess: I am really sure I/Marilyn was with Johnny Hyde when he had his fatal heart attack. We either just had sex or were just about to, because I remember running out of the building figuring I'd get blamed. I was such a coward! I feel terrible when I think about it. I know it is true.

Another memory I have about being Norma Jeane/Marilyn is my Mother telling me my Father was coming to take me out. I was very small, and I don't recall what the guy's name was. I think he brought another child along when he picked me up. I remember he took me out to eat and gave me a heart shaped locket. I was so very happy.

I thought I had a Daddy but he never contacted me again. I didn't know if he didn't like me or if someone else had told him that I was going to be too much responsibility. I'm not sure if my Mother had a final conversation with him...or a fight, perhaps. I just know that days went by and by and then my Mother said not to get up my hopes because he was never coming back. I was devastated. Years later I would think about that situation and wonder if it was real...but I knew it was. I just didn't know how someone could have actually met me and disappeared. Was my mother trying to pressure a random man to help her take care of me? Or did my real Father walk away? I would never know.

I recall one time in Marilyn's life when I was still Norma Jeane and a teenager. It was night time, and I was rummaging through kitchen cupboards to get some crackers to snack on. I suddenly realized that the people taking care of me didn't have to. I paused to think about that. Taking care of someone is an obligation sometimes, but still people make the choice to take care of others. Even in the middle of obligation, not everyone gives much. Every day we make a choice, and so do the people around us.

We shouldn't take things for granted in each other. For Norma Jeane, this was somewhat scary. She/I always felt like things could be just taken away. But many people were kind during that lifetime. We hear a lot about the abandonment in Marilyn/Norma Jeane's life, but many people were helpful.

Michele-life...

I went to college, for which I am grateful because I loved my college years. I have used many things I learned there both in classes and as a person who worked there after graduation. But....I was a terrible student who resisted going to college at first. Yep, sad to say. I think I thought I could just land in the movies after graduation... by osmosis or something

My grade point average was quite low. So low in fact that my parents were fretting I might not even graduate. When I finally talked to my advisor who assured me I would, I told my Dad. We were just starting out on a family trip to my Nunny and Papa's house. My Dad literally pulled over alongside the road and told me in a gruff voice, "Michele Marie, get out of the car." I got out and he did too and he hugged me. He even seemed a bit giddy. He was so relieved I was graduating. I love that moment in time. It makes me really happy and chuckle to myself.

I then opted not to attend the big formal graduation ceremony and my Mom was not happy about that. She said they spent a lot of money to send me to college and I better go and she wanted to watch me walk in a cap and gown. I told her I was simply going to pick up my diploma at the Bursar's office on the far side of campus.

Thankfully, my friend Meredith's Mom had attended a ceremony for a different discipline on campus and that was a week or two before the one for Arts and Architecture. When my Mom was told that that other ceremony was rather long and grueling, she suddenly said she was fine with me not going to mine! Yeah, I was off the hook! I know to some people it means a lot to attend...but as a gal with a small bladder, I avoid long productions as much as possible. It's just an ongoing fact of my life!

MY DADDY: Michele-lifetime.

A number of years later, my Dad got his PhD and that ceremony I happily went to. We were all so proud of him and he kept saying, "PhD at 53." My Dad actually began his PhD while working in one college discipline ....got laid off...moved to another college....and finished his degree. He really stuck with it despite stumbling blocks along the way.

One thing I will never forget is this story my Dad told me during the time his studies were in progress. He said he was feeling discouraged while working a full-time job, trying to complete his degree, and having to switch colleges for employment in the middle. My Dad is a positive, highly motivated man who is extremely brilliant and loves to learn new things. But a big part of the reason he had taken on a PhD was because some others at his first work place had encouraged him to. My Dad was somewhat questioning the purpose of getting it at his middle age in the first place.

I am not sure who he was speaking with this one day, but my Dad said he was talking to an older gentlemen about how he felt he would be old by the time he finally got this particular diploma. (My Dad had had a master's degree for decades at this point) My Dad said it might take him a whole 10 years before he finished up.

The other man said, "Well look at it this way. In 10 years you can either be 10 years older <u>without</u> a degree...or 10 years older <u>with</u> a degree...but in 10 years, you will be 10 years older no matter what. You just have to decide which it is going to be." —Smart!

My Dad graduated. "PhD at 53!" I'm so proud of him. And that is why I always address mail to him with the "Dr." on it. Not because I care about status, but because I am proud my Dad is so strong and smart and accomplished. He persevered.

I display a lovely framed picture of my Dad and Mom taken on his graduation day. It's in my spare room that has my 75 gallon goldfish tank.

Yes, I do believe I was Marilyn during my last past life. No doubt about it. I believe it...I know it. But during my Michele-life, I have a solid family. I have a Father who has always been around and reliable and who believed in giving his daughters an education and also constantly learning himself. So this is surely one big improvement over my last past life!

What if you lived a lifetime before the 20th Century?

Photography wasn't even possible prior to the 19th Century. Furthermore, initially it wasn't so accessible for the average person.

What if during your lifetime, you could only afford ONE picture? What if you blinked!?

What if you lived during an era where capturing your likeness was up to the interpretation of a painter?

I look more like the Mona Lisa than like Marilyn Monroe.

Chapter Seven

MICHELE: A PLETHORA OF PAST LIVES.

Life after life...after life...

*Y*es, I do remember other past lives...15 or so. I don't recall them all to the same degree. For some I just remember an event or two. But what I recall is typically profound. Some lifetimes I remember more but still don't get too involved. Then there are the few which still hold the power to pull me right back into that lost energy.... love, fear, despair, ambition...... it can be powerful.

Typically, I don't recall good memories from the past, mainly just traumatic events. It seems that if I do remember love, I typically remember a loss. I don't know if other people's past life memories are different and more positive.

I've had most of my past lives come to me during my early 20's. But even now as a woman in my mid-50's I've begun to remember a little bit more, with the help of a lot of meditation. There have been a number of lifetimes where I died at someone else's hand and it was very traumatizing.

So often on murder mystery shows family members of victims will tell the interviewer that they want their loved one to be remembered for their LIFE and not the tragic way they were lost. As a college age girl in my 20's, I would definitely become more upset by any unpleasant and unfair memories I would have from the past. I think I have learned to manage them a bit better now.

So now...I ask myself, "Who was I and did I like myself before that fateful day I was lost? What was that lifetime about?" I need to make peace with my past life deaths, but I need to focus on the days that proceeded it. Past lives....are about LIFE.

Charlotte Massey Hawthorne:
One of the lifetimes that I have grieved is that of a young woman named Charlotte..... I will tell her story in first person, although it is rather painful to do so.

I/Charlotte was 19 (maybe 20) when I died. I was burned at the stake for adultery. I believe I lived this lifetime between 1820-1842, somewhere in New England, but despite my best efforts, even after hypnosis I cannot recall what state or town. I don't know what year I was born or died.

Anyway, I was not a bad woman. When I was 13 I looked 19. I was well developed at a young age. One evening, when my parents fell asleep early, I didn't heed my Mother's warning to stay away from the town pub, and I snuck out of the house, walked to it, and I stood beside it...I was so curious. I didn't go in, as I was very young. I was there for maybe five minutes before I realized there was nothing for me to do, and I decided to go back home.

But just a fateful moment later, an intoxicated man stumbled out of the establishment's door and noticed me. I recognized the man as John Hawthorne, the general store's flirtatious owner...all the grown women loved him. He grabbed me, dragged me to the back of the building, and he raped me. It happened so fast and I wasn't quite sure what had actually happened, so I didn't tell anyone...especially not my Mother. Mr. Hawthorne was in his 30's. My life drastically changed.

I began getting sick each day, so my Mom took me to the doctor, who diagnosed me as pregnant. Then the church counsel made me wear a red dress for the duration of the pregnancy. The same red dress, every single day. It was a sign of shame to them, but amidst my loathing for it, I began to secretly love the color....I was tired of wearing the straight-laced black and white clothing that everyone else wore. Nevertheless, it was painful being stared at and scorned and my Mother's love towards me turned to embarrassment and hatred. Our bond was severed.

Then, John Hawthorne came to the family home and said he had been a very busy businessman and had not had time to take a wife yet. He proposed marrying me and raising the child "as his own". Around town, he was seen as a saint.....but the child was his! I had been a daddy's girl and my sweet Father hesitated to give me away. But my Mother only cared about getting me out of the house, because this unwed pregnancy was a disgrace in the town and might cost her good-standing and friendships. So, my parents married me off to that same man who attacked me, although they did not know he was the one. Once married, I never saw my parents again. I know it must have made my Father sad, but my Mother would not allow it. I grieved this loss the rest of my days. Mr. Hawthorne became "John" to me.

I moved into John's house. His furniture was very masculine, but truth be told, he had a much larger home than the one I grew up in...afterall he owned a store. Our wedding night was horrible, but I don't think he noticed. And once I was a married woman I somehow regained respectability, for the most part. Still, no one ever knew that the child I was carrying was in fact John's. For the rest of my days, I did my best to ignore the stigma the red dress months had signified.

I was befriended by a group of grandmotherly older women who taught me to bake pies, make stew and sew. I hated making stew...and even worse was trying to keep it from spoiling in the summertime.

I had wished to be a writer and was heartbroken when I had to drop out of school under condemned circumstances to raise my child. I loved math and history and reading. One of my favorite authors was Edgar Allan Poe. I was amazed at Presidential elections. And remembered the suspense of waiting to see who finally won the presidency after the big count. That was a classroom subject for months. I had had big dreams before Mr. Hawthorne had come along.

I increasingly saw myself as trapped. I was trapped by a man who came home at the end of the day for just two things....stew and sex. I supposed that most of the other women in the town thought I had a great life and even envied me. But that was not the case.

Jenny was born. And I did dearly love her. She was a pretty little baby who grew to be a blue-eyed, brown-haired girl with funny teeth and a lot of energy and humor. Her Father did spoil her too and could get nice things because he ran a store. Jenny had some special hair ribbons and dolls. I will admit John was good to our girl. Then, when she was four years old, Jenny was killed in a tragic accident. I wasn't with her at the time, but the friend who was watching her said that she ran out into the street and was struck by a reckless man driving a horse drawn wagon. I was devastated....and depressed for a long time. In my mind, the only thing that bound John and me together was Jenny. As time went on, I saw less and less of my husband who managed the store and then went to the pub. I felt isolated ...but at least I had my novels.

A year or two went by, and eventually I had a fling with a traveling salesmen. It meant nothing accept for a meager attempt to stop feeling so alone. A month later he came back and appeared at my house, and we were caught in the middle of an embrace. For some reason, John had come home in the middle of the afternoon that day.—This was something which he never did before. John nearly killed the guy. At first John seemed under the impression that I had been attacked. But when I begged him to stop beating the man, he realized that was not the case and he allowed him to run off.

Then John and I argued for the very first time. Up to that point, my life had been one of holding in resentments and never expressing true feelings. The louder we got, the bolder. And finally I blurted out that I had never loved John in the first place and was forced to marry him! I could see the grief in his eyes, but then that turned to anger! John was bitterly hurt and went to town to complain to the menfolk.

Hours later he returned with his buddies and had a document in hand. It was signed by some leader in the town and sealed my fate, to be burned at the stake at sun-up a couple days later. At first I thought it was a bluff, but was informed it indeed was not. John took cover in town with friends and I stayed in our home and waited. Quiet, quiet... alone...reading my books ...eating food...strolling around the woods in our back yard, looking at nature....waiting to die...just waiting...

I thought about running away, but knew I had nowhere to go. My hair was an unusual shade of white blond and I stood out in a crowd. On top of that, I had no money or horse of my own. And I recalled one time when a fugitive was hunted down and brought back to a nearby town for punishment. I simply refused to run and be brought back humiliated like a captured animal.

On my last night alive, I read part of a novel by candle light. I thought about how my dreams were all taken away from me because of this man, John. I also felt that seemingly bottomless moment when I realized I would never get to finish all the books that I had started. That night I slept with the rag doll that had belonged to my darling Jenny. The fancy doll had been buried in the ground with her.

The next morning I awoke before the sun rose. I only ate a couple bites of food. And I took off my wedding band and placed it on the dinner table. When the two men came to the door to walk me into town, they had rope, but I didn't resist. They lightly tied my wrists together anyway...I supposed they had to put on a show. The whole mile and a half I thought about what a beautiful sunny morning it was. It was like any other day....accept I knew I was going to die.

When I was brought to the grounds where the burnin' post was, I made up my mind, I refused to cry or look my husband in the eyes. As I walked forward, I could see my best friend was off to the left looking grief stricken and there for support. She had an anguished look on her face and her blue eyes filled with tears. I could see that John was standing off to the right. Then the nice old man who had always said good morning to me when I went to town, did so again. I thought it was odd that such a nice man, wanted to be in the front row of such a horrible event. I thought perhaps he wasn't so nice afterall.

I was walked up past the fire pit burning to the side. A tall gangly man with a scraggily beard was keeping it stoked and ready to go. I was tied with my hands behind my back at the burnin' post. The post and I were one. Kindling pile under foot. I could see John out of the corner of my left eye, but I just looked past him and into the distance at a branch on a tree. I noticed that someone had brought a couple German

Shepherds to the yard. I imagined that if I could attempt to escape, the dogs would stop me. It was just a passing notion...there was no way out.

Truth be told, I was relieved that only a small part of the town had shown up. I suppose not everyone had come to town in the last couple days and heard the gossip.... "whore to be burned at sun-up." I couldn't help but notice Elijah, the very attractive, blue-eyed, curly-haired boy was standing there looking drained. He was my age. I had always hoped that some day he would be mine. I imagined there had always been an unspoken thing between us. But those were during my school days. Those days were as dead as I was about to be. There was no telling if my parents knew of what was to become of me. They were not in attendance.

Then it was time......I was asked if I had anything I wanted to say, and I said, "No." Maybe John was waiting for an apology or for me to beg him to spare my life...but I didn't...I couldn't. I wanted out of that small minded town where most of the people were petty and gossipy and my dreams had all been killed.

The scraggily man tending the fire moved a piece of burning wood over to the pile beneath where I stoically stood. I kept my eyes fixated on that tree branch across the yard. A few seconds passed and the fire didn't seem to move as quickly as I expected, but then ...it was....there. The heat crawling up my right foot...up my leg...what a sickening weird sensation. Up my hip, groin......the pain was so strange and unexplainable. My muscles were contracting and I was having my first orgasm, but didn't know what it was. (I only understand now, because I relived this experience through memories and from the vantage point of my current lifetime.) It was accompanied by pain and terror. Then the unbearable heat...moved up towards my chest and up towards my neck and up the side of my face...to my ear and eye. Tears flowed as a reaction, but damn-it to John, I would not cry! That is when I went out of body....about a split second after I felt my insides explode.

My consciousness went way up in the sky...and felt free...I was liberated! I was happy to leave, free as a soaring bird. But then the sound of angry men pulled me back to the ground. It was a dark, heavy energy dragging me downward and I could not ignore it or escape it, though I did try.

My consciousness was on the ground level near the grass. People were still standing around. They had lit me back on fire because the flickering had gone out and the left side of my face and body had barely burned. The women were upset. Men were grumbling and beginning to argue. Soon they were blaming one another for what had happened. Apparently taking a life in such a hideous way wasn't the entertainment they expected. Elijah was still there....not saying a word. John was just locked in a stare as if in utter disbelief. He looked like an empty shell... but stubborn still.

Then one man came forward and told all the others that they would be a big disgrace if their neighboring communities discovered what they had done. He said that they must make a pact to never mention this ever again. Wipe it out of their minds, go home and never speak a word of it. That was the moment I knew I was destined to fade into the ashes without a trace... possibly not even a tombstone. But at least I was free to go. And perhaps...I would see Jenny on the other side.

And yes, I am saying this happened during the first half of the 1800's...not the 1600's or 1700's. The 1800's! Hard to believe perhaps...but true.

I want my picture back!

I remembered Charlotte's lifetime during the 1980's when I was in college and Julian Lennon's "Valotte" song was popular and often on the radio. It has a truly hauntingly beautiful sound. At the time, I admit I was feeling pretty sorry for Charlotte...which translates into feeling sorry for myself.

Now, I find this so odd. Charlotte was purposely killed in broad daylight in front of a group of spectators....yet I can't seem to find her in a census to prove she exists. Maybe I don't know what I'm doing in my search, or maybe her parents just never registered her. I can't find her husband either, but then again, maybe he was avoiding the law or something...I don't know!

I do know that Charlotte lived during a year when photography was possible. She was only ever in ONE photo, and that was taken at her husband's store. He and a few customers were in it as well. At the time, photography was a new invention and a real novelty and rare. The photo was framed and hung up in the store. Does it still exist? Did John destroy the photo so he wouldn't have to look at it anymore? The people in the photo were all wearing black and white. Charlotte was wearing a long black skirt and white blouse. That was the typical dress code in the area. And also the ugliest black walking shoes. I know that I, as Charlotte, was in this photo.

During that lifetime, I had white blond hair, brown eyes with really long eye-lashes, and a deviated septum in my nose. I was very well developed. I attributed my colorless hair to a terrible illness I had had as a child. I had also been blind for a little while as a toddler. And that is what was so sad, my Father adored me no matter what. I remember him holding me then.

It's ironic that Marilyn was pretty and talented, yet so insecure and terrified to be the center of attention. I can't help but wonder if her insecurities have anything to do with Charlotte being the center of attention when she was burned at the stake in front of the townspeople. At least Marilyn worked to overcome her fears.

When I/Michele got married during my 20's I didn't want to be the center of attention, so that is why I was happy to go to Las Vegas and avoid a big ceremony. Somehow the idea of being the center of a wedding was really too much to handle. Is that because Charlotte was forced to marry John? What exactly is Me-me...and what is someone else's influence having its way with me and directing my decisions?

What is strange fate is this: Charlotte's death was ignored and even covered up, and then my soul went on to live another lifetime which is beloved and remembered because of being accidentally killed.

I don't remember the names of most other non-famous people I've been, but Charlotte's name came to me right away.

Mary Virginia Wade: Historical figure from Pennsylvania

During my next lifetime, I was Mary Virginia Wade, born in 1843. I died, at age 20.

Mary Virginia Wade is better known as Ginnie Wade and even Jennie Wade. I read that she got called "Jennie" by a misprint in a paper... but it stuck. Although she was a good citizen and helped bake bread for Union troops, she is primarily famous because she was hit in the back by a stray bullet, and was the only civilian casualty in The Battle of Gettysburg.

This is nothing she brought on herself or did for attention. She didn't even know what hit her when she was shot. It isn't like I actually saw anyone pointing a gun at me, or that my death was even on purpose. The bullet went through the door of the house as I was in the kitchen. I remember being her and dying... instant fiery pain around the left shoulder blade....it ran down my spine...I was immediately nauseous, and threw-up as I hit the ground. I didn't know what happened. I briefly stayed near my body, as I was trying to figure out what had just occurred.

Oddly enough, during my current lifetime as Michele, my 5th grade class took a long bus trip to the Wade house in Gettysburg, and I practically had a nervous breakdown during the weeks that followed. I didn't know why. Neither did my parents. I just kept crying and re-evaluating my life (I was only 10!). My parents took me to a counselor for two years, until the doctor told my Mom and Dad there was nothing really wrong with me.

During college that lifetime finally came back to my memory. Then I understood. My soul had belonged to Ginnie Wade. (Also note that the "Wade House" is not really her house, it was her sister's home, where she was staying when she was killed.)

Ginnie Wade is a beloved public figure but it isn't as if she was trying to grab the spotlight or would want her private experiences detailed. I remember having some health issues during this lifetime, but because she is an historical figure, I won't talk about that.

During this lifetime:

-I had some freckles even though you can't tell from the photo.
-An old man used to bring me and a young boy colorful hard stick candy and we loved it.
-The man used to warn us that too much candy was bad for our teeth but our teeth were already a bit bad.
-Because of my health issues, I tried to passive-aggressively persuade the man who liked me to not feel obligated to come back to me after the war. But he wouldn't listen. Oddly, we both died anyway.

Mona Lisa: Painted by Leonardo daVinci

I do recall some details from this lifetime as the woman who posed for the Mona Lisa. However, I don't recall what my name was then. Lisa? I have no idea.

During this lifetime:

-I had amnesia as a teenager and got lost at a big fair.
-I was matched up with my husband, but thankfully loved him.
-My husband was out of the house a lot on business.
-Our baby son was killed in a house fire that mysteriously occurred in the middle of the night. I didn't know how it happened and my husband was away. I blamed myself and never got over it.
-I had some health issues later in my life and an operation.
-People came to visit me often and we would have tea and philosophical conversations in my home.
-I died by choking on some food and beverage, and I fell off my chair when it happened. No one else was in the house at the time.

Johann Sebastian Bach: Classical music composer

I do recall some details. However, this lifetime is hard for me to remember because Bach was a very manly-man. I recall some other male past lives but their energy is different. I feel uncomfortable dealing with Bach's lifetime during my own.

During this lifetime:

-I really grieved the loss of my Mother.
-I had a horrific temper and that was the worst part of being me.
-I once threw a book at a man and it hit him in the back of the head.
-My friends would constantly plead with me to get my temper under control. I would tell myself I would, but then relapse.
-I had affairs and hated all the long material petticoats women wore because I thought they got in the way. They were pretty but a nuisance.
-I knew I ate too much pasta but I delighted in over-indulging.
-I would sometimes stare into a big oval mirror at the landing of a staircase. I reveled in my genius but couldn't figure myself out.

Cleopatra: I like to think of her has "the mother of my incarnations".

I know it is cliché to claim to have been Cleopatra. Well, I claim her! And NO...despite the fact that many others have claimed her before me, I do NOT believe in the "split soul" theory. I think energy can spilt off, but not the soul itself. But I'm not God or The Master of The Universe, so I don't really know what can or can't happen.

During this lifetime:

-As a child I often went to a market where pottery was sold.
-I had green eyes and was slender. I walked very straight and proud so as to give the illusion of a little more height and complete control.
-An Uncle tried to rape me in the family home when I was first an adult. I never wanted to return.

-As a young adult, I had some gaudy gold rings I didn't really like, but I wore them because they symbolized prosperity.

-I hated my brother and even felt grossed-out towards him.

-I sometimes put stuff in my hair that gave me red highlights.

-I got very aromatic perfume-oil delivered to me from afar.

-Once I was over-looking a battle and panicked and fled like a shameful coward. It took a long time to get over it because internally it hurt.

-I thought Marc Anthony had a great body, but I was smarter than he was. I liked feeling superior, because I always had to fight for respect.

-When I was pregnant I felt the most vulnerable and yet most powerful and beautiful. I thought about this when I was alone at sunset.

-One time I attended an orgy and made some demands on men who were considered lower rank than I was. It felt wrong, although it was really commonplace for others. I believed in making men come to me.

I, as Michele, felt extremely depressed when I first had memories of Cleopatra's lifetime during my 3rd year of college. It was winter semester and I began re-experiencing things through my dream state at night while I was asleep in the dorms. Most memories come to me when my eyes are open....but not Cleopatra's. It was odd to recall a lifetime that took place in a dry heat setting, while in the middle of a snowy Pennsylvania season.

What was so hard to deal with about her lifetime was how suppressed I was in it. Cleopatra had to always present an exterior that was much stronger than she felt. It was a constant internal struggle. I remember that I often just wanted to cry, but dared not to. This was a "might makes right world"... "a man's world"... and in order to survive and thrive, I/Cleopatra had to present myself, manipulate others, and always keep up a brave front. I also traveled expansive distances often by foot and alone during the first part of adulthood.—I became very introspective. I could tell the time by the way the sky looked. This solitude made me feel stronger, although lonely.

My true death...relinquishing the struggle.

People have different ideas about how Cleopatra died. Here is what happened. I remember I was on the ground in a little contoured drift. I had just finished eating something like a picnic. I believe there was some fruit on the ground still. I saw the snake (asp) and it was far enough away from me that I could have gotten up off the ground and avoided it. But I was exhausted by life. <u>I chose to pause</u> and it slithered nearer and bit my left leg. The sickening poison rapidly spread throughout my body and went to my head. It was utterly revolting... and for a moment I regretted my decision. <u>This seemed like such a small way to end a life I tried so hard to live in grandeur.</u> It was kind of like taking syrup of ipecac.....nauseating. I died within minutes, but it was disgusting. There was nothing dignified about it. Still to this day, I remember exactly what it felt like and tasted like in my mouth...the poison. Parts of that lifetime were amazing, other parts were torture. So....yes, it was suicide. (I do not recommend this to anyone.)

But, there was just one snake not multiple ones which I picked up and forced to bite me, like some people report. And it was also not a toxic ointment or a sharp implement that caused my death. <u>I knowingly paused and the snake came to me.</u> My exhaustion took over my thinking, and I made that choice.

Why famous.....?

Now is a good time to broach the subject of the saying, "Why do people always recall famous past lives?"
Some skeptics say that as if everyone is just out for attention. I remember non-famous lifetimes as well as famous ones. Non-famous lifetimes matter too. Non-famous lifetimes have joys, sorrows, love, loss...and every lifetime ends the same...by dying.

The thing is if you are constantly bombarded with hearing your name in a history book or seeing your image on things then you are more likely to remember being a former President, or an inventor, or a well-known painter or whatever. Being subject to hearing about yourself might jog your memory, whereas with non-famous lifetimes you aren't going to hear anything specific to remind you of that former self. Repetitious reminders may open up the door to the past. This is what I believe.

Imagine how many things Marilyn's face is on these days. Honestly, it's a wonder it took me 19 years to realize I had lived my last past life. How did the memories not come to me sooner?

Some people hypothesize that people who think they were a famous person during another lifetime most likely were not. But rather, they may have just lived during that same era and heard about that famous person or been in contact with that famous person. I don't agree or disagree with that concept.

Completely overlooking things…

It's funny to me. During the 1970's, shows like "Happy Days" and "Laverne and Shirley" were popular on TV. "Grease" was also a hit movie. People seemed to look back fondly on the decade of the 50's . I would try to imagine what it felt like to live during that time of sock hops and poodle skirts. All those things seemed rather charming, and also foreign.

After I remembered Marilyn's lifetime, I realized I just never related to those things. During the 1950's I was too busy wearing next to nothing or fancy costumes. I was caught up working the Hollywood system, because I had no childhood home to go back to, and being a "sexy bombshell" was somewhat controversial. I was busy trying to prove I wasn't "dumb" (stupid). I was busy fighting for respect. My memories of the 50's were different than the idealized Hollywood version 20 years later. I didn't even recognize my own (Marilyn's) era when I saw it.

Chapter Eight:

MICHELE: THE SHOW BIZ DROPOUT.

Well, I'm somewhat shocked myself that I am not in the arts for my paycheck. I love the arts! I did get a degree in theatre.

I honestly wasn't in any big productions. I helped build sets, I helped change sets between acts, and one time I did some brief, experimental theatre thing that a grad student wrote. There was this concept/event called "Midnight at 6". At midnight, you go see a short performance in room 6, which was in the theatre basement on campus. The room was the size of a small classroom, and the stage was just an elevated area in the floor more like a platform. I played a girl who was OCD and having a breakdown. I wore a ton of make-up. I was asked to play the part, there was no audition. It was just attended by a handful of other theatre majors. The whole thing was very artsy-fartsy and fun. Theatre people are fabulous! Love them!

I admit, I only remember auditioning for one play on campus my whole college career. The shy part of me would just put off trying to get out-front. The craziest part of that is this, my only audition was for "Children of a Lesser God".....and I knew absolutely no sign language. Needless to say, I was clueless. One summer, I did do one community theatre play in a park while I was still college age.

It is interesting to me that Marilyn wanted a solid family foundation very badly. And having one is certainly a blessing...no doubt about that! But what comes along with having a family is also sometimes worrying about how they will judge the things you do, especially if you look at the world differently. A family also can instill values.

I remember working a play in college, where I was doing scene changes. The F-word was used quite a bit in the dialogue, and I felt mortified. I'm not going to say that I don't ever use that word now, but I remember thinking that my parents would NOT want me in that play! For some reason I always overly cared about what my parents thought and I used to think that it would be hard to find scripts that I thought they would "approve of". Just look at the movies these days!

Now I know this is an over exaggeration, but kind of true. But my Nunny used to often say, "All people care about these days is someone else's arse." I truly do miss the charm and less blatant nature of movies from decades ago. Sex was certainly out there even then, but it was presented in a different way. People knew how to be alluring with their clothes on. People knew how to be sexy without throwing themselves at each other right away. Audiences didn't have to see a character screw someone else to know that that is what they wanted to do and probably would do. I just saw a movie with Kim Novak called "Bell Book and Candle." Just looking at her face and hearing the way she talked was so much more powerful and classier than watching people rip each other's clothes off. And Elizabeth Montgomery and Barbara Eden never talked dirty or got naked in their sitcoms, yet they are two of the prettiest and sexiest women on film....ever. And look at the gals from the old TV show "Petticoat Junction". Mostly they just wore nice but not overly revealing dresses, and they were certainly appealing. I don't think people need to be prudish, but I wish more new films were classier. (Yah, I know...seems hypocritical coming from MM.)

Most sitcoms these days also seem to exploit very crude ways to get a laugh. There must be writers who can write jokes without stooping low. Why do we need to hear about farts, poop, and body parts? I know some sitcoms have achieved hilarity without that. I'm amazed at how fabulously written some shows are. So why are so many programs on film crude these days? It's actually quite hard for me to think of a movie where I would even want to play a part even if I were qualified. There are a few. But the good ones are outnumbered I think. The show "Friends" had a lot of love and also maintained its innocence. That's probably why it had a long run.

And what about actors or actresses who might have very attractive or interesting faces, and might be really great performers, but just not "camera ready" to go nude on film. If the nudity aspect of films wasn't so big, the pool of people we might see in starring roles could be broader. I'd still rather see a guy whose face gets me hot and bothered than a bunch of chest or butt shots... or simulated penetration. And what about the actresses who maybe are considered "a few pounds" over-weight. Can they only aspire to playing second lead roles in dramas?

One of my favorite movies in the world is Jacqueline Susann's "Valley of the Dolls". There is all kinds of implied stuff in that movie but it stops short of going too far to demonstrate what the audience knows is happening in it.

I first saw that movie over a very snowy Thanksgiving break at my Nunny and Papa's house, when I was in 8th grade.— Best memory ever. Nunny and I watched it together late at night. I think my sister Chris did too. Watching late night movies together was "a thing" with Nunny and me. And that Thanksgiving weekend with that particular movie was really a very eerily significant happening in my life. I feel like it was a big influence. Maybe it warned me to never start pills, so I never have to get off of them...? Dionne Warwick's rendition of the theme song to that movie is beautifully haunting and one I listen to often to this day. It takes me back in time.

Another thing, a lot of movies these days are sci-fi and I am not into so many special effects. Just good acting! I love the simple and charming "Lost in Space" 1960's TV series though. Guy Williams plays the father in that show. His face is beautiful and he makes his pajama styled space uniform look hot! My good friend Tara and I used to watch the show all the time...and then act it out at our swing set my Dad built. We even had pretend stage names. Hers was "Ann Marie" and mine was "Marie Ann".

I could go on and on about how much I don't like movies that rely too heavily on "shock value" either. Suspense...yes. Graphic visuals, no!

Yes it is true, I am not beautiful and I don't have any real talent for the biz this time around. Maybe I sound like I'm talking sour grapes. But I swear, if I did have talent, I would be out there touring around singing Rodgers and Hammerstein musicals. Even if I had the looks and talent, I'm not sure where I would fit into films these days.

Yes, there is also another reason..... a practical aspect.... to why I never pursued a career in show biz.

As I said earlier in the book, I have always had bladder issues. It dawned on me that it might be hard to have the lead in a three-hour play which has lots of costume changes, and have to pee just 40 minutes into the show....20 if I was really nervous. Actors also need to drink water to hydrate themselves and keep their speaking voices clear.—My bladder would surely punish me for that! Often restrooms are also a long way from the stage.

Well, I figured maybe I could be in film instead of plays, right?

I thought about doing movies instead, so I could just perform one scene at a time, and take breaks more often if necessary...plus I love film. But today costumes seem so elaborate. I figured I would irritate a lot of people if I were being intricately costumed for a movie and had to get up and go. And this time around, no one is going to wait for me to be ready on the set. I am not Marilyn Monroe...I'm me...my soul was Marilyn's before mine.

An interesting thing...when I first went for hypnosis in June of 2018, my hypnotist Toni said that maybe the reason I have to go to the bathroom so often is because of my memories of being Norma Jeane/Marilyn. I remember being molested by a doctor boyfriend of my Mother's during that lifetime. When Toni was trying to hypnotize me to another memory, I kept getting stuck on that one. I remember thinking, "Don't pee Norma Jeane, don't pee." But I/Norma Jeane peed my pants. I was a very small child then.

Toni tried to put suggestions into my head about this in order to solve my problem....but unfortunately, nothing has changed. We only tried one time. We both laughed because it felt more like she was trying to make me go during my session, instead of stop me. Thankfully the bathroom was right across the hall.

An actor's nightmare!

Alas, there is also a male incarnation that has influenced my current career path greatly. I remembered this one while in college. It was hundreds of years ago and I was in an all-male acting troupe going into a big performance. I don't know what my name was, but I had brown hair and blue eyes. We thought we had the acting competition clinched! I was known for being the best at memorizing difficult material. But as I stepped on stage, I choked ...nothing came to mind or out of my mouth ...I had lost my very first line and all the rest! I couldn't remember anything and I was completely humiliated. I ran off of the stage...out into the street...and was hit by a wagon. I remember seeing my blood-streaked face as I was a bit crumpled up where my body had been thrown by force to the side. I was about 18.

Since my college days, I/Michele have often felt that I no longer have the capacity to remember things... I'm deathly afraid of blanking-out like my former actor self did. Maybe I have just talked myself into that mindset...?

So, I've basically stated that I dropped out of show biz for lack of much talent, fear of memory lapse, over-active bladder issues, questionably high standards, dislike of various types of movies.....so then what could I do!?

If not show biz, then in what profession would I land?

When I first looked for a job post-college, I went for an interview in the Dean's Office of Earth and Mineral Sciences. At the time, my Dad was working in mineral engineering. During my last semester of college, Spring 1987, I had changed my naturally brown hair to blond and then right before finals I went red. My Mom was concerned I might not get hired because of my hair color and she said I might "appear to be a floozy." On top of that, I had managed to give myself a scratch on the cheek with my fake diamond ring...must have been while I was sleeping, because I just woke up with it. Thankfully, I interviewed with a very nice man named Everett and I got hired on the spot. I don't think he thought I was cheap. His daughter was just one year older and went to the same high school. He treated me somewhat fatherly. He was kind. I kept my red hair for quite some time.

I continued to work for The University from age 23 to 38. I went from the College of EMS, to the College of Science, to the main Campus Library, to the Campus Assistance Center, Off-Campus Living, and then Research and Assessment (surveys). At some point the Legal Office that gave free legal advice to students also got added into the mix. I was a secretary for 15 years before I moved to San Diego, CA for a while. I just got used to the hustle and bustle of clerical work. I guess I got used to the regular hours. I also liked various people in different office environments. Quite frankly, it was just easy to continue secretarial type work in my home town, even if it was often demanding and not glamorous. Plus I got a great apartment very close to all my jobs. My landlord didn't raise the rent for 11 years.

And no, no one has to refer to me as "An Administrative Assistant". People whine about silly things. I'm a Secretary...I'm fine with that! I know what I bring to the table. And I don't mind making coffee either, as long as I don't have to wash someone else's coffee cup. I make coffee all the time.

But anyway...during my very first clerical job, I entered a Marilyn Monroe look-alike contest and won, much to the shock of myself and my friends who jokingly supported my entry.

It was October 1987 and the bookstore on campus was having a contest because there was some book about Marilyn coming out and it was also the 25th year since her death. I told the girls at my job that I was Marilyn during my last past life. They laughed. Then Sue challenged me. She said, "OK, prove it. Join the contest and win." I told her it was pointless because I have a pointy nose and my hair was colored red at the time. She taunted me and then I gave in. She said she would bring in her camera the next day. I went downtown during lunch hour and bought a very tight fitting, blond Halloween wig....and it had bangs—-ugh! It was all I could find quickly. I felt I had to go through with this contest!

The next day we took some photos during lunch hour. The Dean was out of town and the office manager was gone too. Sue had a key to the Dean's office, so at noon we quickly scampered in there and she took my photo as I was posing on the Dean's couch. I was wearing a skirt and heels....and I took off my top so the photo was really showing the top of a slip above my waist. I submitted one picture and threw away the rest because they were horrible. The wig...the damned wig! Nasty. I actually had hopes that some girl would really look Marilyn-like and win...I wanted to see her!

Surprise, surprise! I won the contest. How is beyond me. I got a call from a guy who gave me the news, and I blurted out, "I can't. How? Didn't anyone else enter?" He seemed taken aback by my response. He said other people entered but I won. Of course I was happy...but slightly bewildered as well. How on earth could I be the best candidate for a Marilyn contest! I know what I look like. My face is angular and not cutesy-roundish.

I must confess, I had worked two summers in a row in the back of that bookstore on campus while still in college. I priced books and inserted brochures into them. I helped inventory merchandise. One semester I worked at the cash register during rush sales week, and that was when people had to process credit cards on carbon copy papers. A part of me has always wondered, "Who judged the contest...someone I know?" I seriously thought that living in a college town with so many pretty girls surely someone else would have come forward and been so convincing that the bookstore would have had no choice but to choose them. Then again, maybe the girls submitted photos that were too scanty for the campus paper. I have no idea what the deal was. But, I figured I should point that out. Maybe I just got chosen because I had worked there before. They say in show biz, "It's who you know!" It was a fun moment in time anyway.

Anyway......then there was the ordeal of it all. My photo was in the campus newspaper, in black and white. I was happy...at first. There were several old women working in the accounting department of the same college I worked in. They were in the building across the street, but I saw them often because I had to walk over there to deliver paperwork. They had been with the college for decades and recognized the piece of artwork in the background of my photo. They called the office manager and asked, "What is Michele doing on the Dean's couch? We recognize the picture in the photo."

The office manger was all twitchy and nervous and thought there might be a big scandal. (He was actually the man who had hired me.) Sue was not only the photographer of my photo, but she and her husband were also good friends with the Dean. So, she explained to him what happened. "Michele joined the contest....I took the photo....it was like a joke to us, cause we never imagined she would actually win....we are sorry." The Dean roared with laughter ...case closed.

I still keep a yellowed copy of the newspaper in a photo album. The day the paper came out, my Dad drove me to a pick-up sight and I grabbed 16 copies! I told the man on the phone that I spell my name "Michele"....with one "L". It was spelled wrong. Boo!

I was both extremely flattered but also perplexed that I could win this contest. What is funny is the line in the article that says that the judges looked for an entry which portrayed the All-American girl closest. I must not have read the contest rules too carefully...or at all. I think I look more like Jane Russell did in the "Gentlemen Prefer Blonds" courtroom scene where she wears a blond wig pretending to be Marilyn's character. Funny.

Chapter Nine:

MICHELE: ALL THOSE MARVELOUS MEN: WHO PUT ME IN CRAZY POSITIONS.

Take Two:
Michele: All those CRAZY men:
Who put me in MARVELOUS positions.

Sexalysis....

I am electing to change the names of the main men and women in this chapter's stories because some of the subject matter is sensitive. Maybe it is "TMI"? But, Marilyn only lived to be 36, and these are my years leading up to that age. So I really didn't see how I could leave them out of this book.

I suppose I do a lot of "sexalysis". But then again, Marilyn was a sex symbol and also lived a crazy lifestyle...if I do say so myself. So I do tend to analyze my relationships with men. Afterall, Marilyn had three failed marriages, so many lovers she couldn't keep count, and she died while one of her last lovers stood in the same room. Somehow this Michele-life has to be better than that!

Earlier:

In Chapter Five I explain my upbringing and also some of the situations that influenced me and rather pulled me in different directions. I began to ask myself, "What do I really want?" And as I was trying to figure that out, I was forced to figure out, "Why do I care more about what someone else wants than what I do?"

Later:

In Chapter Twelve I confess to a couple flings with married men. They each lasted a bit longer than a year. I guess they were a "friends with benefits" type thing.....but we didn't even have deep friendships. I'm not really sure why I bring them up, other than I suppose it is because I wish that Marilyn had been smarter and gotten herself out of her situations with the Kennedys instead of trying to hold on. To me it was pretty obvious early on that getting involved with someone else's spouse is not only selfish but also just plain STUPID!

So....here goes...the last part of the puzzle that entertained, confused and side-tracked me from pursuing a career in film: MEN...Sex... Relationships...and the chaos that comes with all that! Marilyn was/is a major sex symbol. I am not. And on top of that with each new lifetime there is a new struggle to find real love.

When I was 21:

A handsome blue-eyed Portuguese grad student named Franche was my math teacher my 4th year of college and I had a big crush on him. He was mid 20's. I loved his facial bone structure and his innocent, discombobulated demeanor.—He was constantly wiping chalk all over his black pants and face. I flirted with Franche at the chalk board and he told me we could go out after I wasn't his student anymore.—We did.

Franche was quite cerebral... into classical music including Bach... liked strawberry ice-cream... and was still pining away over his ex-girl-friend who had cheated on him. Franche came to The USA to get his PhD in math and said he owed it to his country to return after graduating. He felt he had to teach for a while there. I realized my time with him was going to be limited. But I did my best to beckon him towards the bedroom. He was so "my type" physically. I really wanted to lose my virginity with him.

Turns out Franche was raised Catholic and a virgin too. He was also quite hung-up about being uncircumcised, because he heard some girls on a bus say they don't like that status. It didn't bother me. I thought that he was beautiful.

Sometimes we would actually romp around naked and kiss but we never had sex. Every time we would get close to doing anything it seemed like his phone would ring. And, unfortunately, Franche seemed more interested in figuring out equations in his head than in me. Fellow mathematicians would call and he would get caught-up in intricate math-speak...and then the rest of the day he couldn't turn his brain off and he would be preoccupied. A friend of mine suggested that maybe it wasn't "the math" Franche liked, but maybe "the guys". I didn't know. Maybe it was just me...or maybe me being "an American girl".

At the time we were together Prince Andrew and Sarah Ferguson were about to get married and I remember us both talking about that. Franche seemed as happy about the event as I did. I loved Fergie's beautiful natural red hair. We loved that she was down-to-earth and very outgoing, and didn't seem like she would take any guff. Another royal wedding seemed exciting. When the wedding day came, I thought her dress was very pretty. I still like Sarah Ferguson to this day.

One time as Franche and I were walking up to his floor in the apartment complex, there was a girl with a very big over-bite standing in the stairwell. She really stood out. **By the time we got to his unit, Franche commented, "Did you see that girl we walked past? For some reason, I find her ugliness very attractive."**

I took that to mean he was probably not attracted to me. I had had braces in high school. But not only that, I didn't look anything like that girl, and for some reason he thought he needed to point her out to me. I felt like I wasn't his cup-of-tea. Or maybe that was just his way of telling me he wasn't ready for sex afterall. I have no idea.

Oddly enough I had a big overbite two lifetimes ago. It was the lifetime right before Marilyn's and I was a young opera singer with blond hair and blue eyes. I was involved with a married doctor who came to town now and then but didn't treat me well. My family tried to push me into the arms of a handsome family friend who lived in a big estate with beautiful gardens and ivy growing up stone walls. But the friend and I always laughed at the match-making, did our time chatting and roaming the grounds, and knew from the beginning that we were never going to marry. Franche actually reminded me quite a bit of that young man from two lifetimes ago.

Although he never said so, maybe Franche actually thought pre-marital sex was a sin ...or it should be saved for marriage. If so, I wish he would have told me. Or, maybe he was afraid I would get pregnant and trap him into staying in The States. It could even be that he ended up forgiving the Portuguese girl he loved and hoped to reconcile. I got the impression his parents expected him to be with a girl from his own country...and that I could never be. I just didn't feel like we had much in common, so that was it. I didn't have an over-bite, I wasn't overly intellectual, I wasn't Portuguese, and I didn't plan to wait for marriage to have sex anymore. We seemed mis-matched. I really didn't figure Franche would even miss me if things ended. If I had thought he merely wanted to wait, of course I would have stayed with him. I would have never given him an ultimatum about sex like I felt so many men had given me a few years earlier.

On our last day together, I remember walking from Franche's apartment to the library with him. He said, "I have the feeling something is going to happen". It was like he knew I was thinking of breaking things off, even though I was being very calm and not obvious, I think. But at the same time, he didn't say anything to change my mind. I never said a thing, I just never called him again. I didn't hear from him anytime soon either. Neither one of us picked up the phone to make plans.

A couple years later my Mom said he called but I never returned the call. I figured Franche was leaving the country and, although I considered throwing myself at him before he did, I refrained. I think when we were still going out, I had given him a strip of photo booth pictures to use as a bookmark. I'm pretty sure I wasn't wearing much. So maybe he still remembers me. I haven't forgotten him! He was very attractive.

When I was 22: January 1987, a cute brown-eyed New Yorker named Adam was in the same film analysis class. He talked to me one day and asked me out the next. He was only 18, but seemed confident and assertive and had a nice low mature sounding voice. We went to lunch. It was my last semester in college and I just felt long over-due to experience what most of my friends had several years earlier. At this point, I was rushing to meet a deadline. I wanted to have sex before graduation so I could say it was "a college thing". I had him show me his driver's license so I was certain he was at the very least "legal age".

I really didn't get to know him very well and there was no pro-longed flirtation. It was more like, "This is what we are going to do." Adam told me to come over and I knew just what he meant. He also told me he was curious about girls who were "shaved"... and I got the not-so-subtle hint. When I met Adam I was a brunette, when I saw him next I was blond.

About two weeks after Adam and I met, we got together in his very messy dorm room, but we simply couldn't manage to get him inside of me, although we tried and tried. We gave up after a couple hours. Then we got together a second time, and I finally lost my virginity a short time later with the help of some strawberry lube.

My very first time was while I was sitting on his lap and we were making out. I remember opening my eyes and admiring his curly hair, but I had no idea he was inside me! When it was done, Adam strutted across the room, wiped himself off and asked me how I liked it. —I was more than a little perplexed. Then I saw the disappointment register on his face. Needless to say, he wasn't happy with my questioning look, but I couldn't back-track and tell him it was fantastic. He already knew I wasn't going to brag to my friends about how great my first time had been and that's what he probably wanted. I had heard that sometimes the first time hurts, but I felt ***nothing***.

Whatever the issue was, of course I felt like it must have all been my fault, and I felt terrible that Adam looked hurt. Nevermind my own shock. The truth is he could have made it so much better if he had just laughed it off and said that it would get better with practice... something like that. But despite the fact "he came off mature" he was, afterall, only 18. Eventually, I just concluded that I was over-lubed and so I figured the answer was using less.

Adam was well endowed, but that still didn't mean I was overly sensitive, especially since I was just sitting on him while he was up against the side-bed-cabinet. We did-it again later that same day. He was young and studly and eager. It was a little better, but still on the messy side of the room. I wondered who his roommate was, who made his bed so neatly and had a collection of small stuffed animals. Adam introduced me to some hip guy with long dark hair who was a friend from down the hall. I felt like he was pointing out, "Pssst...she's the one who lost it."

We got together another day as well. Adam was cool. He was the experienced one and I could tell he aimed to please. But, I must admit, I really expected sex to be different. Again, I noticed his roommate's side of the room was very neat in contrast with the messiness we were lounging amidst. I somewhat felt is if we were having sex on the wrong-side-of-town in the middle of a shelter that had been hit by a powerful bomb. I told myself it didn't matter, but in some odd way it kind of did. Text books and trash surrounded us and it wasn't overly sexy.

So after such a long wait, was this experience what I imagined it to be? Well...I guess I thought I'd see fireworks and be enthralled by instant, uncontrollable passion that sent me over-the-edge. And at one point Adam was mad at me because it was obvious to him that I wasn't all hot-n-bothered. We weren't the perfect match. I'm sure the opinion was mutual.

Then of all the truly stupid things, Valentine's Day came. I sent Adam some candy and a little stuffed bear. But I put the wrong last name on the package because I had never seen it in writing and had only heard him say it once. When I first met him, he was sitting in front of me in an auditorium, and he turned around and quickly introduced himself. I heard something similar, but wrong. I guess when I saw his driver's license I hadn't noticed the spelling, because I was busy looking at the birth date and photo.

Anyway, I am sure he felt that added insult to injury, and he never contacted me again. Again, Adam could have laughed it off and teased me about it. But he was only 18 and it didn't seem like our chemistry was all that good anyway...so that ended that. I can't recall how I finally found out what his last name really was, but I felt very stupid when I did. I could see how I heard it wrong, but still, he was the first man inside of me and I didn't even know his real name! Life is weird sometimes.

We barely knew each other, so we didn't know how to talk to each other. And sometimes....just sometimes....talking is very important, even with sex. I just hoped sex would get better in the future. But at last.... I no longer had to pretend that I was a chaste, pure, virtuous untouchable being! I did, however, have to wait to get back to my natural "unshaved" look...and feel.

Adam began to attend film class at a different time, with his long-haired buddy. Nevertheless, I still maintained a crush on him for a while...from afar. To this day, every February 6th I think of Adam... because HE is the one who said I should look at the calendar and remember the date forever. I lost my virginity on a sunny, snowy, winter day and I didn't even know it!

I confided in my bro Kenn (Billy Shakespeare) from the theatre department. He gave me a photo of Adam that was from his actor's file in the office. Adam had had his picture taken because he played a guard in a Shakespeare production later that semester. This exempted him from doing set crew.

One time I saw Adam across a cafeteria not far from the theatre buildings. He was with some friends, one of which was a girl much prettier than I. He looked cute. I was so nervous I broke out in big red hives, and left abruptly before he could spot me.

I admit, the rest of the semester I was rather emotional. My Great Aunt Babe listened to me cry over Spring Break which I spent at Nunny's house. Of course I let out a few details because she is so religious. I am not sure how much of my torment was depression over the whole confusing sex-thing...or maybe it was partly because college was about to end. I tried sex again with another guy before I graduated... and that was a bit reassuring.

When I was 22: Lover number two was a guy named Dan who had a way of making me blush. I met him a couple years earlier when he visited a costume class, and I was a bit standoffish. However, he won me over with his adorable smile, bright blue-eyes ...and his persistence which was turned up a notch. I began to consider the possibility and I suddenly realized how sexy he was. I don't know why I never noticed before.

Dan was a guy I will never forget for this. He never really had a class with me or was in charge of a crew I was on. But one time he was hanging out in the hallway after I was done with work. He was being adversarial with me and telling me how hard it is to make it as an actress. He said in a demanding tone, "What makes you think you can act for a living and get anywhere in this business?"

I looked him straight in the eye and said, "Oh, I <u>know</u> I will. There is no doubt in my mind, I will be famous in the business. I've known since I was a kid. <u>You'll see</u>."

Dan straightened up and said, " Maybe you will. I think I believe you. You actually make me believe."

The look on Dan's face was rather sober. (But now, I of course, look like a fool.) Thankfully most of my friends aren't as good at remembering conversations as I am...so maybe he has forgotten our little exchange. (But I want to know, <u>who</u> was talking? Was it me...all ME.... or was Marilyn in there somewhere asserting herself?)

During the final weeks of the semester, Dan began hanging around the construction crew I was working on. One night as things were finishing up, he took me by the hand to a darkened classroom... pulled down my pants... had me lay over a desk...and licked me several times. Then we returned to the set before anyone came down the hall because they noticed we were missing. I went home all turned-on, not knowing if it would happen again.

One Spring evening while it was still light out, Dan said he would drive me home from crew. I got into his truck and he parked in what he thought was a secluded wooded area... it was just him and me. I tossed my pants but kept on my top, which had bold bright-pink and white stripes. Dan grabbed up under my bra and I got on top of him in the front seat, and I began to push as he was inside me. It was very, very exciting...until some other vehicle came along while we were in the middle of the act. We immediately pulled ourselves apart and sped out of the woods laughing.

The mission was incomplete...yet it completely changed my view. It was definitely more exciting, doing-it "on the edge" instead of "in a total mess". The thought of possibly getting caught didn't even bother me, but Dan said that we didn't know what the other vehicle was up to and their intentions might be bad. He smiled at me the rest of the way home, and dropped me off at my parents'. Of course I had to tell my Bro Kenn.

Nevertheless, I went back to being somewhat depressed about how things ended with Adam. —I guess in some way virginity was more important than I thought. Either that or I was still unsettled about how over-rated "the sacred first time" seemed. I didn't want to feel like "I just threw it away." Afterall, I had passed up many opportunities in order to keep myself in such a "condition". **And my "virginity story" was stupid!** I felt like I must have been the only person in the history of the world who didn't know it when I lost-it. I still wanted a better story for this pivotal point in my life.

I colored my hair red right before finals. I graduated college and moped around a few months afterward. I put off getting a job all summer long, but then got one in the fall when my parents confronted me about my lack of ambition. Of course, I couldn't explain the reason for my depression to them. I told myself it was all about "the Adam-thing," and my Mother finally guessed. But then... maybe afterall, it was about something more than that rattling around in my psyche.

Remembered:

Something horrible happened my last semester in college. A lovely young lady named Dana (who I never met) was murdered in her apartment a block from campus. It happened over Spring Break '87 and that was the same week I was crying over sex and men. I remember going back to school, and hearing about the tragedy. It was in all the papers for a very long time and people came forward to say nice things about this fellow student who had so much to live for. It was hard for me to dismiss as "just another crime". Because crimes involve people, so there is no such thing. Plus this young woman seemed so loved.

The case was highly publicized, yet decades later it remains an unsolved cold case, which greatly bothers me.—I hate injustice. I cannot help but wonder if part of the reason this disturbs me so much is because Marilyn's murder wasn't solved and no one paid. Solemnly, I think about Dana every March 5th...just as I think about Marilyn August 5th. Dana is always remembered.

When I was 23: I was already out of college but my sister was still finishing up. One day I went with her to a fraternity where she was a "little sister". It was a very nice, large building with bigger-than-life fancy architecture...and sweaty occupants who clearly didn't clean up after themselves. The smell of stale beer was everywhere. Yet there was something rather intriguing about this place...there were lots of energetic young men....all under one roof!

Chris had left me in a TV room for a few minutes and a couple guys were sitting on chairs in front of me. They turned around and said something and somehow they brought up the topic of cleavage. Not to shy away from such a conversation, I pulled my sweater tighter on my chest and the boys giggled and someone made a funny comment.— I can't recall what. Soon after, one boy, Blake, asked me out. He had blue eyes, blondish hair and was a little stout.

So a few nights later we went to see "Fatal Attraction." It was cold out and I wore jeans and a fashionable short coat with some fancy boots. I am not really a boot type gal, but these were sort of sexy. Sexy... until I fell in them...and cracked my elbow!

A few blocks from the movie theatre, Blake had wanted to quickly run across a busy intersection and he grabbed my arm and pulled me and I fell. I had jarred my left arm when I put it down to catch myself. Then we walked to the movie a few blocks away.

The whole time I sat in the theatre I could tell my arm was not right. But not wanting to ruin the date, I just sat through the whole film.... There was even a point when something startling happened on screen and Blake, who was holding my hand, yanked it really hard. That was not good! But I was so happy to be on a date!

The movie was a suspenseful success and then we went back to the fraternity afterwards. We began to watch "Top Gun". But Blake couldn't figure out why I hadn't taken my heavy little coat off yet. He had asked me if I wanted to in the theatre as well. I confessed to him that my arm felt "stuck in place" ever since the fall. He didn't understand and he decided to undress me.

By then I could barely get the coat off and when we pulled up my sweater sleeve my arm was purple and much bigger than it should have been. Needless to say we went to the Emergency Room. I got some painkillers and a sling which I had to wear for the next month. Blake was very patient and nice the whole night.

Despite my handicap, I still managed to keep my day job in a Dean's Office, although it involved some typing.

Then there was some formal at the fraternity and Blake asked me to go. My sister had a date who was a "brother" there as well. Chris said the guys had all been teasing Blake, "How rough were you? You broke Michele's arm...you must have been really giving-it-to-her." Chris didn't seem amused...I was.

My Mom took me shopping to get something fancy to wear with my red skirt and my sister did my hair. Against doctor's advisement, I ditched the sling. My sequined top was long sleeved and I kept a glass of wine in my left hand most of the night because my arm was still in the bent-up position. Blake and I made-out a bit on his bed and he went up my shirt a little, but that was it. My sister said she hoped I hadn't had sex with him because she thought that he was "childish like a lot of the guys at the house".

A week or so later, Blake and I got together in the evening. A buddy let us use his room because Blake had only a small bunkbed. We began rocking with the motion of the waterbed...but then much to my surprise, I was practically as tight as I was when I was a virgin. Blake struggled quite a bit to enter me and flustered I apologized. I definitely did not expect that, but I hadn't had sex for about 6 months and I didn't know that could happen.

Blake found some lube and didn't give up, and when we were done he had a big grin. As I pulled my pants up I saw a little blood and was feeling slightly embarrassed. I buttoned my jeans and hoped he hadn't noticed. I don't even remember bleeding the day I lost my virginity...then again, strawberry lube is red...nevermind. I probably just didn't see it.

I don't know if Blake believed me when I said it wasn't my first time. But despite the fact it didn't go smoothly...it was fun. I almost felt like I got a "do-over". It felt like I lost my virginity a second time but with a guy who was older, in a bigger bed, and the fraternity was much more naughty and exciting than the dorm room during daylight. It was awkwardly nice.

Blake graduated and left town. I never saw him again. Chris asked me if I had gone to bed with him and I said "No" ...but a couple decades later I finally told her the truth when we were reminiscing. Blake was actually pretty nice to me...really a gentleman. I liked him.

Thankfully when Blake moved on, I had a job in a building where lots of men paid attention to me and acted like I was a goddess. There were cute construction guys working on the basement level at the time, and I had to go down there to pick up the mail every day. Soon I met someone hot!

When I was 23: A sexy dark haired guy named Adrian was introduced to me by the friendly guy who sorted the mail in the building where I worked. He had nice cheekbones and brown eyes. Adrian and I began dating. He said his family fled Cuba from Castro when he was a baby. (This is interesting since some conspiracy theories about Marilyn include being killed because she was threatening to divulge Bobby's plan to kill Castro.)

Anyway, Adrian rode a motorcycle and I was very attracted to him, but not the idea of riding a bike. I immediately got my driver's license since he didn't have a car. My parents were kind enough to let me use one of theirs. —Yes, I was that old when I finally started driving. I was 23. Prior to that I took the bus a lot because there was a good transportation system in our area and I was also a bit afraid to learn to drive, although I am not sure why. Often my friends seemed shocked it took so long for me to get on the road, so I'd tell them, "I learned to drive so I could get laid." –We'd laugh.

Adrian was the first guy I had sex with many times and I really liked it. I thought he was the perfect body type for me because he was the same height I was and I liked how we "matched up". When I wore heels out in public, I was taller, but at the time Billy Joel was with Christie Brinkley so I just figured that made me more like a "super model" girl.—-Ha!

Adrian was hot! Typically we hung out at his place and watched a movie. He made me dinner and I sent him flowers. Then we had sex. One time I couldn't remember if I had taken my pill, so I took one... and I'm sure it must have actually been the second one in the same day. I had my period for three weeks straight!—What a delicate balance the whole thing is!

However, as embarrassing as it was to explain this, Adrian didn't let it stop him. Nope! Not at all. I have no idea if he had good laundry detergent or just threw out his sheets, but that was fine with me. It looked like someone had been murdered in his room. Then we got together again...and again.

One time my parents invited him for dinner and he met my sister and a guy who she was dating. I kind of think Adrian was attracted to her. Not that he said anything, but I think he was. My sister and I are very different and she is really cute. I imagined he might have thought he was with the wrong sister. She lived out-of-state by then though and she was just in town visiting, so I didn't let my insecurity get the best of me. She was leaving town.

Adrian and I were together for 10 months but it was still really only as deep as a fling. He was working on a PhD in one of the sciences and the more stressed out he got the less he talked to me even if we were side by side. While it was respectable he was working hard, his unhappy look and quiet demeanor was intense. I liked sex, but ...I had no control over the politics at the science lab...and the situation was getting extremely uncomfortable. Cute guy...silence...sex...go home. I couldn't help him with his studies.

I switched jobs because I needed a higher paying one. I moved across campus and met someone new...his name was Trevor. I saw Adrian right before Christmas and we exchanged gifts, but I told him I was starting to like someone else. He had no response at all, so I figured it didn't matter. Maybe he was just hurt. I don't know since he didn't react...and that was the end of that! I once saw Adrian from a distance downtown. As he was wearing his brown leather jacket and getting off his bike, I thought he was appealing as ever. (So this is the year I basically gave two different men Christmas gifts...the old boyfriend and the new one I ended up marrying.)

When I was 24: A quirky well-dressed man named Trevor came into my life. I met him October 27, 1988 on my first day of work at a new job. I worked across the hall from him five days a week and he was hard to miss. My manager told me he had wanted to interview for the job I got, but she turned him down because he had such a strong personality.

Trevor had an air of confidence and was very outgoing and gabby. His necktie collection was stylish and he seemed quite ambitious and hardworking. He was a runner and prided himself on moving fast. Trevor was 31 when I met him. He had been engaged a few years earlier but never married. His family lived in the area, as did mine.

While working in close proximity, I recall a day Trevor proudly served me some buttered banana bread. I think someone else had brought it in to share with everyone, but he made sure he served me some. That was cute.

Two months after we met, I gave Trevor a small Christmas present and he sent me flowers. We began dating. We went out to brunch and then to a friend's place where he was house-sitting and watching their pets. He had a very nice body and knew how to use it. Unfortunately he also had a big ego, but he made me laugh so much I overlooked how much he talked to himself in the mirror.—He was constantly telling himself <u>outloud</u> that he had "a full thick healthy head of hair" and he often called himself "fresh" and bragged that he had "swagger". He and the mirror were in love.

One day while we were "in the middle of things" he said something and I thought he told me he loved me. So, I said "I love you." He claimed he told me "You're a lovely lady" but I misheard. Soon after that he insisted we get married. This was only about five months into our relationship and seemed way too soon. On top of that, because I never planned to have kids, I never really felt I had to get married...it was never a necessity in my mind. But Trevor insisted that "if you love somebody you marry them."

I had mixed feelings because I didn't want to rush a big decision like that. On the other hand, at that time, he was also the most fun guy I had ever dated. Trevor liked jewelry so we exchanged engagement rings. I got him a band with a fancy setting and a small diamond in the middle. He got me a small ruby, which was the birthstone of both of us July babies.

At first Trevor acted like he was all into me, and he insisted we had to make a commitment. But then once we were engaged I began getting the hint that he might not be the most focused guy around. I would ask him if he was sure we should marry. He would constantly buy me little cute things or leave me notes or tell me I was pretty. My Mom warned me that those were manipulative tactics, and she was probably right.

My parents began to question some things but because they came on incredibly strong with their opinions I went into emotional overdrive, feeling that I had to protect my relationship with Trevor because I wasn't ready to throw it all away. Of course looking back I realize I should have tried to distance myself from their heavy-handed opinions and also Trevor's pushiness and made a decision on my own based on what I really wanted. But I was just 24, acting like 15.

The following December 26th we said "I do" in Las Vegas while on our paid Christmas vacation The University gave us as full-time employees. We had planned the wedding, it was not an impulse thing. While in Vegas we never gambled at the machines, but we did go on a search down the strip for which bar had the best Bloody Marys. We had quite a few drinks but we were getting around on foot. It was the first Christmas I had ever spent without cold weather. It was about 70 degrees the whole time we were there. Unfortunately all the big name entertainment acts had left town.

Caesar's Palace had my favorite ambiance. The first couple days in Vegas I only saw it from the outside, but I longed to go inside.

My dress…

I had always thought if I ever got married, I would get married in a red dress. It just seemed like a splashy good idea. But I procrastinated so long before getting something, that I ended up buying a white toga style dress off of a co-worker. She had bought it to impress a boyfriend and then he broke up with her before she wore it. Then she met her husband and just kept the dress in storage because it reminded her of the other guy. It was unworn. So, this co-worker, Diane said she would sell me the dress for $30. That is the crazy way I procured my wedding dress. I also bought pasties because I couldn't wear a bra with it. The day of the wedding, I couldn't figure out how to get the pasties on smoothly, so I ditched them and went without.

I wore shoes that came from a wedding shop. A year or so later I got a small part in a play and had them dyed aqua to match a fancy dress I wore on stage. Closing night I went to a cast party after the performance and it was slightly raining out…at that point I was carrying my shoes, which proceeded to bleed all over my hands and the shoe box. Needless to say, those aqua shoes were not seen again. But aqua is a favorite color of mine now.

Our wedding day came and went. I really wish I could say that the next four years were filled with wedded bliss…but I can't. Life with Trevor could be extremely fun and we laughed a lot. But Trevor played mind-games. Trevor used sob stories of various kinds to manipulate me into overlooking his problematic behaviors. These stories could range anywhere from sad things such as "My Mother died when I was young"… to unfair things such as "My ex-girlfriend Valerie cheated on me so I can't help how I treat you now."

Trevor was also still mad at the world because the second half of his childhood he had to move to the town his Step-mother was in. While it's understandably upsetting to move out of the home where you lived with your real Mother, it had nothing to do with me or my actions! I often experienced the fall-out for things outside my control.

Trevor pointed out that his ex-girlfriend Valerie was a very hip African-American woman and that he wanted "to be more cool like Black people." He constantly implied or outright said I wasn't dressed "cool enough". <u>Did he not know I was white when he met me?</u> How could I live up to being something I wasn't and was never going to be?

One time we were standing in a high-end men's clothing store and I dared to call him Trev instead of Trevor. As soon as the salesman was out of sight, Trevor snapped at me and said that I should always call him by his full name because his ex-girlfriend said that full-names are cooler.

The bloody train trip...

One time we were taking a train trip to Boston and the bar was a distance away from our seats, so Trevor kept plying me with drinks and getting them for himself...walking up and down the aisle flirting with everyone. The more he drank and got up-and-down, the more careless he was.

I was wearing light gray jeans and Trevor began dripping his drink on me. Then he got me on the thigh.—It felt really gross. I told him he had to sit down and be steady. Of course, he was too afraid of missing something on some other part of the train. He got up again and I ended up even messier. I am talking bright red thick Bloody Mary messy!

Finally, I couldn't take it anymore. Enough! Trevor swaggered down the isle and came back with another glass apiece. I took my full drink and threw it directly on his crouch! —This was not revenge... this was "education". I asked him how he liked it. He had a fit and went on and on about his good dress pants. I didn't feel sorry for him. We got them cleaned at the hotel...where he proceeded to flirt with a cute punk-style girl in the diner.

Of course, my Nunny's opinion always mattered to me. She seemed to get a kick out of Trevor. She said he always walked into a room as if he was making a grand entrance. She said he was "a real show boater" and amusing. She told me he was with the wrong girl. Nunny said that Trevor craved attention so much that he should have married a very plain girl, so that everyone would always be looking at him. (Of course, she was my Grandmother, so she was biased and said I was pretty.)

Trevor said he had also previously been engaged to a girl whose parents supplemented her minimum wage income with a couple thousand dollars a month.—Supposedly they were some filthy rich business people in Germany. So Trevor acted like nothing we ever had was good enough and therefore he had the right to act out. He began asking me if I would inherit any money. This disgusted me to the core. I'd rather have my loved ones than money.

In the beginning Trevor pretended to be so nice and interested in me, but over time not so much. He would say things like, "You are too pretty to clean" because I didn't like vacuuming the apartment as much as I should have. But yet he would constantly tell me I didn't wear fancy enough jewelry, and he would make that sound of paramount importance. The way he talked sometimes you would have thought he was brought up in a palace and used gold leaf toilet paper. More and more he seemed very materialistic.

Trevor would tell me to "look stylish and hot." But if I did and I got attention from males then he would be ticked. It was like I got the mixed messages, "Go out and impress people but don't get noticed"… "Be sexy, but I'll be mad if a guy tries to speak to you then."

Trevor steadily worked in a good position the first few years I was with him. But when he became jealous of a co-worker he began to hassle his office manager and that got him canned. This is where everything derailed. I was used to him picking on me, but suddenly his employment was a big issue and our last year together was very strained and uncertain. From there he floundered around to get work and would get a job, quit a job, get a job, quit a job. He would start them each with heightened enthusiasm and then for no apparent reason stop going. My mind was in a whirl.

There was one job he seemed to really like, but about two months into it, he got into trouble for underhandedly taking something from the employer. A visit to the police station and a court date followed. And even crazier to me was that he had insisted I accompany him to some company event just days before he stole from these people. So I had met them, been welcomed and told what an asset he was to their office and then bam! He stole from them!

Then on the home-front, Trevor wrote a bad check. He took it out of my checkbook and forged my name. He disappeared for the Netherlands without telling me, and then called me collect so I could Western Union him money so he could get something to eat and buy a train ticket to the airport to fly back home. There he was...crying on the phone.....ugh!

Trevor would sometimes come home with a bunch of second hand, well maintained designer clothes. He implied he might have had a little fling with a local hair dresser who gave them to him.—A bit of a shock.

Trevor also told me that in the past one of his friends in Boston had tried to pull him into the swinging world and he was interested. But he said he never had a girlfriend who would do that with him. That was not my idea of what a "real couple" does. But he whined as if my saying "no" would shatter all his dreams...and I decided to be open-minded. Big mistake!

While I was with him, Trevor found a place a few hours away that masqueraded as a "swim club" but was really an "adult swing club". Trevor would constantly claim he wasn't interested in doing swinging "too often" but this type of situation seemed to be on his mind constantly. He was pushy and I felt I had to "prove myself as open-minded"... although I'm not sure why. The more he pushed me into the arms of strangers, the less I wanted to have sex with *him*.

We met a handful of couples through some swinging magazines as well. I felt Trevor was forever searching for my replacement. But one time I met an extremely beautiful woman at a club and she said her husband treated her the same way...always searching for the next stranger to screw. I felt badly for her, but a little better for myself. I realized it wasn't necessarily my inadequacies that drove Trevor, but rather something else inside of him that was there before we met. I was just too stupid to walk away at the get-go.

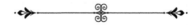

The sick thing was, Trevor was only happy if HE was happy. He never wanted me to be because then he was afraid I might *like* someone. He seemed to constantly want to meet people where the woman was attractive and the man was not. I would put up a fuss and decline. There was a whole variety of situations we encountered, and several of them still crack me up now.

Story One:

One story was when a slightly younger, really cute couple came to our apartment. The woman was petite and blond and Trevor was very eager. Turns out, she was more interested in me than him.—She outright said so. I like men...that I know....but these swinging situations typically seemed to come with a certain amount of pressure.

The lady's husband was adorable but he was still upset about getting his feelings hurt during another encounter. Apparently it happened with some long-time swing partner. He told us about his bad experience but his wife seemed to have no sympathy, nor was there a pause in the action. He just sat on the couch looking sad and I only half heartedly attempted to pull him into the fray, because he had the right to protect his feelings and abstain. The lady beckoned me into the next room and Trevor followed.

Trevor of course roped me into a threesome so he could get next to the cute girl who wanted to get next to me. It was so stupid really. A very good example of no one being on the same page...primarily because no one really knew each other before we took our clothes off.

Soon after the couple left, I got very sick on the homemade White Russians I had been drinking out of very large glasses. I spent a good bit of time on the bathroom floor and vowed to never get drunk again. I learned my lesson. I just made up my mind, "Never again." Drinking is no big deal! I don't have to have alcohol. It is not a "need".

The cute girl seemed to want to come back, but we never got together again. When Trevor called the couple a few days later I refused to get on the phone. What was the point? I liked the guy and he was still upset with someone else and pouting. I wasn't about to pretend to be something I wasn't long term. It's one thing to *try* something, it's another thing to pretend that it is "your thing" if it isn't. The girl could be cute as can be and not my cup of tea! There is nothing wrong with girls being together, it's just not for me. I got the impression the husband just came to our place to make his wife happy. Her need for variety seemed to be the driving force in their relationship, based on the way she talked.

And what was it that actually disturbed the cute guy so much? He and his wife had been in a 2-year-long swinging situation with another couple, only to find out the lady got pushed into it and never wanted to do it in the first place. Of course he was hurt! This lifestyle seemed to sell the idea of carefree and fun but it sure didn't live up to that really. This was also a real eye-opener. It isn't just the girls who sometimes get hurt. Guys do too.

Story Two:

Another time, we drove to Pittsburgh and Trevor was with this really slim out-going lady who I thought that he would be thrilled with. (We had previously met them at a "club" held in a home.) She even showed us some magazine she had posed for. She looked quite lithe and glamorous.

But Trevor was so annoyed because her husband was a really big flirt and wanted to see me again. The guy was probably twice my age and had dazzling blue eyes. (Trevor' eyes are hazel kind of like mine.) It's amazing how Trevor could go on and on about various women's body parts in graphic detail on a daily basis...but if I mentioned another guy had nice eyes...jealousy!

Trevor proclaimed we could never get together with that couple again because "the woman didn't wear make-up for the encounter." This seemed awfully silly because her lack of make-up didn't seem to keep him from getting a hard-on while he was with her. Was he really looking at her eyes when she was naked? She was in great shape and cute. I think Trevor couldn't stand it that the guy was flirting with me and the guy and I actually seemed to have a connection after the sex was over. Oh well...

The dopiest thing about this whole encounter was the couple were self-proclaimed hard-core swingers and proud of it! They were rather big braggarts actually. They had so many stories and were full of advice. Well ...I thought advice was supposed to make sense...right? I swear it burned my ears to hear the stupidity I heard there. They were very pleasant and I liked the guy....and I think they were even well meaning. However, when they told us "there is no need to use condoms because peeing immediately after sex eliminates the chance of getting STDs" I was baffled. —Huh? Say what? Disagree! Strongly disagree!

Story Three:

One time Trevor arranged for us to meet some girl after work. I wasn't happy since there wasn't going to be another guy in the mix and I was going to be really tired from working.—I used to work an extremely tedious job at a library where books had spine labels put on them and cards needed typed up for a catalogue drawer. (Pre-techno improvements)

Anyway, Trevor insisted the three of us rendezvous. We met the lady downtown at an historical restaurant. Trevor thought this would be a great evening because the girl's ad said she was a serious oboe player. Translation: Trevor thought that meant "good at oral endeavors".

Turns out the girl looked like she had just walked off an old west prairie, very conservative with long skirt, long braid. She also talked incessantly. On top of that, the girl said, "I might faint or scream if I take off my clothes in front of anyone." She confessed her husband had been pushing her into swinging too and had encouraged her to go see us alone. Trevor could not wait to get away from her!

Story Four:

Another time we drove to Johnstown to meet a couple who said they had a hot tub. Trevor said the woman "looked kind of wild and savage." He had her photo from their ad with him in the car. As he pulled up to their home, he stopped at the end of their drive way, took a deep breath, giggled and seemed very excited.

When we met the pair, it turns out they looked about 10 years older than their photos and the woman's boob job had gone awry and one of her breast implants kept popping out of place in her chest. She compared her boobs to mine and sulked. I tried to reassure her. I told her that her butt was much cuter than mine...and that was true.

Nevertheless, Trevor told me we should go through with things because the woman literally had a huge trunk full of sex toys. I remember feeling trapped in a steamy hot tub with a guy I wasn't attracted to, although he seemed like a nice person.

Suddenly the woman seemed out of control and running around with handcuffs and other erotic paraphernalia. The man rolled his eyes. A number of things occurred... (let's just leave it at that) ...I think the four of us covered every room in the house. Apparently the woman's favorite phrase, "Give-it-to-me, Give-it-to-me, Give-it-to-me."

The next morning after coffee, we were all saying goodbye and the guy kept hugging me and they both were asking me to come back. Trevor asked me, "What did I miss?" Well... let's just say... "I guess you shouldn't drink so much you pass out!" I still look at that whole experience as an odd and interesting encounter.

Then when we got back home, Trevor had an idea which he thought was hysterically clever. He decided we should write the couple some kinky thank-you note on toilet paper! So with magic marker I wrote as he dictated. It was beyond stupid and I don't recall what it said but it was all about how we wished to get together again. He was trying to impress the wife. We then got a call a few days later, after the note was received. Trevor said the woman was so happy she was crying. But we never followed through. We both had had enough.

And the harsh reality of it all was, the couple seemed to be struggling in their own way, despite what they portrayed as a hard-core love of swinging. They repeatedly said that they had to keep their lifestyle a big secret from their daughter who was 19 at the time. And the man often rolled his eyes as if he was overwhelmed by his wife's need to make everything over-the-top. He was a marathon runner so I don't think he lacked energy. It seemed that things had simply become too convoluted...not actually relaxing or exciting for him anymore.

Story Five:

And last but not least, was the couple a few hours away who Trevor insisted we spend a torrid overnight with. The man was huge ... I mean HUGE. He was pretty good looking but more generously endowed than I prefer. Anyway, he was very polite and kind of fun really. I didn't pay much attention to what Trevor was doing with the man's wife.

What I do recall was the guy filming something that we did and then later running the video for us. I fell asleep with my colored contacts in, and woke up in a bed with a diploma hanging over it. It turns out the man's last name was COX.

When we got back home, Trevor seemed a slight bit perturbed. Although the woman was a very petite attractive blond, apparently she showed more interest in her dildo than in Trevor. What I do remember is, she mentioned to me that she wanted to stop swinging because she was hoping to get pregnant soon... but it was hard trying to coax Mr. Cox to go along with that. Clearly it was time for them to rethink their lifestyle. I certainly had second thoughts. And mine began from the get-go!

I really was never into the lifestyle and constantly pleading to stop. And therefore we really only had a handful of mostly odd ...and laughable....experiences. There were more "almost did something" times than sexcapades. I like sex....but I wanted a LOVE RELATIONSHIP. And people who say they never get jealous are liars!

Strangely, Marilyn is known for the musical number about diamonds being a girl's best friend. But I can't get a diamond ring from a man to save my life during this lifetime! I get them if I buy them for myself...and I just have two non-flashy vintage rings....one of them from the 1950's.

Anyway....Trevor bought me a very tiny ruby ring. The ruby was shaped like a heart and set on an angle, so people never could quite tell what it was at first. My friends would tease me and not believe me when I said it was my engagement ring. And the lady I worked for at the time asked me if it came out of a Cracker Jack box. I tried not to be superficial and focus on "love" and not material possessions.

Then one night, I came home from a meditation meeting that I went to with a friend. As I got up to our apartment door, I heard Trevor talking on the phone with someone who he was arranging to meet. I opened the door and he said he was setting up a date for us to travel to "meet some people in West Virginia."

I was so sick of it! I went into the bathroom and flushed the ruby ring down the toilet. I told him I did it and he didn't believe me. The truth was I was glad it was gone. I was tired of pretending I liked it. And who knows, I might have liked it a little if he had behaved differently... cause it would have reminded me of someone loving and devoted. But, really, it was a disappointing ring that reminded me of a guy who didn't even buy me a Christmas present the day before we got married.

That is how I actually got my bouquet for my wedding. Because Trevor didn't get me anything for Christmas, I told him he should get me flowers for the wedding. He had bought the wedding package before we left Pennsylvania and flew to Las Vegas and he didn't even get the package with flowers! (OK, I'm the dummy who said "I do.")

Wedding night.....

As December 26th wound down, Trevor thought it made sense to pick up another lady at Caesar's Palace, so the three of us could celebrate. (I don't think he paid attention to the wedding vows.)

Yep, that happened. I remember the woman was a very spiffy full-figured African-American woman in a long dress. Her name was Fawne. I'm guessing she was late 30's or early 40's. She was sitting alone and drinking ...all depressed because she had just lost $300 and also come to Vegas on her own. Trevor made a proposal that we three go back to our hotel room. He gave me the evil-eye as if to say, "Do NOT ruin this for me."

Even Fawne was confused because she kept saying, "You just got married...are you sure? This is your wife, you should be alone."

I could tell she was a caring person. Again I got the evil-eye from Trevor. Eventually, we three managed to mingle and she seemed a whole lot happier. But then Fawne had to go back to her own hotel to call her daughter. She put her sparkly dress back on.

Fawne was afraid to walk alone and said she didn't have any cash on her. Trevor was ready to boot her out the door.— I thought he was rude! I handed her some money and told him to walk her out and wait for her to get a cab so he knew that she was safe.—He did. Fawne seemed like a nice lady.

A few minutes later I was bawling my eyes out. My new husband was an ASS! When Trevor got back to the room and saw how upset I was, he actually seemed sorry. I took a hot steamy shower alone and noticed that there was a heart-shaped swirl in the marble wall of the shower stall. It seemed rather ironic since I didn't feel very loved and cherished at that particular moment. But it was one of those little things that I'll never forget.

It always seemed like "in the moment" Trevor never cared about "me" or "us". He was always too busy corralling a pretty stranger. When we got back to Pennsylvania, his family took us out to a fancy New Year's celebration and also held a party to celebrate our wedding. They were always very good to "him", "me" and "us".

Somewhere in the middle of all of this lustful lifestyle, I did get my tubes tied. I never intended to get pregnant, and Trevor was paranoid that I would...he badgered me. It was July 18, 1990...I had just turned 26 on the 10th. Thank God I never had a baby with him.

I suppose if I had to pinpoint the biggest reason I would put up with so much from Trevor, it was probably because I didn't feel "pretty enough" to really hold anyone's interest. Years later my hypnotist suggested that I didn't feel "pretty enough" because I remembered being Marilyn and compared myself to her. I really don't know if that is true or not. There was plenty in the current media during this lifetime to make a young woman feel "not enough". I also heard a lot of college boys talk about girls as if they were "pieces of meat." On top of that, I grew up with a sister much cuter than I am...so I always knew ..."pretty wouldn't be my-thing".

Revising the resume...

Here is something Trevor would do often during our years together. He would constantly be tweaking his resume. He would add things that seemed silly. One time he said that he "streamlines procedures". He asked a co-worker to look over his resume and tell him what she thought of that addition. The co-worker asked him what he did to "streamline" things. He said, "I collate documents." She smirked and said, "Uh, Trevor...all you have to do is press a button on the copier to collate." He deleted that line.

Then he put his marital status at the top of his resume. **He would say, "It makes me look more respectable if I am married."** I would say, "WHY do you need to be made more respectable? Aren't you already?" The resume was in constant flux.

Anyway...several years into our marriage, Trevor said he needed a counselor...his idea. We found one. At first he really seemed enthusiastic about getting help. But after just a few sessions he said he gave up on counseling because, "The doctor doesn't wear designer jeans or have very cool artwork on his walls." —Really? I lost hope. We all need hope, but you can't force people to help themselves. You can only control yourself. His actions were out of my control.

The final straw was when I went to my parents' house and we were going to go out of town to Nunny's for most of the day. I suddenly realized I had forgotten my purse at Trevor's and my apartment. That very moment it hit me like a ton of bricks. I had completely lost trust in Trevor. I literally was terrified he would rifle through my wallet and take money or write another bad check. I just couldn't live like that. I knew immediately I was getting a divorce! My parents were completely behind that decision and helped me.

I filed for divorce around late October 1993, and three months later it was final. Trevor said he needed a car to move away, so he took the 1970 Green Dodge Dart which my Papa had given me. It did not have a lot of miles on it, despite its age. It still had the Pirates baseball sticker on the bumper as Trevor drove away and headed towards Boston to work with an old friend. I was sad, but also relieved he had somewhere to go....good riddance! That relationship really didn't do much for my self-esteem. Jumbled confusion!

Despite having a very fast-paced job, I was allowed to take a week off work because at the time I decided to divorce I was pretty frazzled. I went to my Nunny's house where I felt genuine love. And I still fondly remember climbing up on a ladder to pick apples off her tree so Nunny could bake a pie. I was wearing a long flowered skirt.

That old red-brick house in Hollidaysburg, PA was so "home". My parents house was nice too, but perhaps I related so well to Nunny because she could talk about all the decades....the 1920's, 30's, 40's, 50's. Afterall, I was alive then.....right? Whenever I would leave there, Papa would hug me and say, "Come back again and see us, ok?" I always wanted to.

Counseling...

At age 29, I had finally realized a divorce was necessary, and I had to cut ties with Trevor. I was certain...yet, it was still a big decision. I went to a counselor twice. She was a very nice lady and also the Mother of a boy I had had a crush on years earlier. She was also good friends with my boss.

Anyway, somehow in the middle of one of the sessions, I ended up telling this doctor that I had been Marilyn during my last past life. She asked me how I had died then. I told her Edward smothered me. She said that that couldn't be true because the autopsy report would have shown that I had died that way. She said people would have known if it happened like I told her because there would be specific signs for that type of death. I responded, "All I know is that it is true." (My consciousness left my body for the first time when he smothered me with my pillow.)

I actually remembered that part of my murder a few years before I remembered the rest with the hitman. But still, even if I did die by some other means in conjunction with that, I still feel that that was the moment I began to die. I still feel Edward is the person most responsible. Not the only one, but the one who made the decision to go through with my murder. After that there was no turning back. I've told people about this for years....decades...it didn't just start with this book. (More about Marilyn's murder in the chapter coming up about that.)

I can just imagine some people will think I'm just making this up about Edward. Possibly thinking I'm just piggy-backing on the fact that a lot of people suspect him of foul play concerning a lovely young woman a few years after Marilyn died. No! Edward helped kill Marilyn...I was there. If I'm guilty of anything, it's have a really embarrassingly messy bedroom which has been photographed and put on display. But not lying. As God is my witness...I know that Edward smothered me...when I was Marilyn.

Of course, this is nothing I can prove. I have no evidence to support it.

Back to Gettysburg...

While married, we spent a significant amount of time with Trevor' sister's family and babysitting her kids. Trevor had Dawn up on a pedestal because she reminded him so much of their beautiful Mother. I went on a woman's religious retreat with Dawn and her church friends and it was very nice and relaxing and I felt like God was present. But as she was dropping me off back at the apartment, I ended up blurting out many of the marital problems I had had with her brother. So by the time we split, Dawn understood why.

Trevor's sister Dawn is a lovely person and she knew I would be sad about breaking up with her brother. Within a day or two of his leaving town, she and her daughter took me off on an adventure. They decided we should go to the "Jennie Wade house" in Gettysburg. It was not my idea, it was theirs. I don't think they even knew about my past life beliefs.

By that time I was 29 years old, and I realized I had been Ginnie Wade several lifetimes ago. This time, I went and enjoyed the historical site, and I didn't have any emotional meltdowns afterward, as I did 19 years earlier.

Come again....?

Now, you would have thought that after all the time Trevor spent trying to pawn me off on other guys so that he could get to other girls, that he would be glad to be down the road and done with me...right? Wrong! Our interactions didn't end as abruptly as that afterall.

About two months after our split, Trevor called me to say that he was coming home to visit his family for Christmas and he wanted to get together. I told him I was already with someone new. He said he wanted to see me and he wanted me to spend time with his family too because he said I "made him look better." I got together with Trevor but there was no messing around because I had a new boyfriend (Demetri).

Trevor said he knew our issues were all his fault and that some day we would get back together again. He claimed he "just knew it." Of course I was flattered, but "I just knew differently." Reuniting was never an option in my mind, not even for a second.

Trevor and I went out to our favorite breakfast restaurant and I remember writing something on a paper placemat that had a Christmas motif on it. It seemed kind of sad. There we were, spending our 4th year anniversary together but divorce proceedings were already in the works. Nevertheless, I was not about to back-track given our lifestyle together. I was still very fond of him but I wasn't about to jeopardize my new relationship.

Trevor was the first guy I ever went out to eat with a lot... the first guy who liked hanging out at cheese and coffee shops... the first guy who ever went on vacations with me ... and the first guy who ever introduced me to his family. There were reasons I liked him. Trevor sometimes referred to us as "The Twins" which made it seem like we were close.

But I knew that I was moving forward and not going backward. Trevor was all too wrapped up in other girls already anyway. As time went on there was the really loud, sweaty blond girl, who he was fighting with but banging. And there was the young hairy, brunette secretary, who he claimed would "take it up the butt". And there was the much older German woman whose sons were older than he was. He met her one cold day when she was walking through the park in a fur coat and he complimented her. He moved into her apartment and he said she was falling in love with him. He actually bragged to me that he was giving her "the best sex of her life". —I shook my head. His buddies all teased him.

Trevor was always working-it with somebody. And he was always kiss-and-telling me more than I cared to know. He never slowed down. He didn't need me. He pretty much operated as if he was a super-stud and "God's Gift To Women". I think he tried to pick-up 90% of all the women he met. I wasn't sure if he really loved women, or was trying to convince himself he was completely straight. I have nothing against people being gay or bi, they just shouldn't hide that information from a potential spouse.

On top of that, when he got into a major fight with his German lover, she sent me a letter and photos of herself in tight flowered pants. I got the impression the woman thought I would confront him and tell him to behave for her. Or, who knows, maybe she was afraid he was going to leave her and come back to me. But why did he give her my address?!? I dimly recall having a phone conversation with her also, which truly was awkward!

Trevor said he gave away the couple gold rings I had given him. So in my mind, I felt that that was a definite sign things had ended. You would think all the women would have been "the sign" but it was the jewelry! I knew he really liked the fancy gold ring with the big garnet in it, so if he got rid of that, I felt it mattered. I knew I was never-ever going back to him!

Then one day...he showed up on my doorstep! A bunch of months had passed and I don't recall the date. Trevor said he had taken a bus and was back in town. I told him I was still with the same boyfriend and so he couldn't stay in my apartment.

He checked-in at a shelter down the road. They had all kinds of rules there and a curfew. For a month or so, Trevor would come to see me after work and have ice-cream or cookies at my place. We would talk and then he would go back down the street. Then one day I called the shelter and was told that he had left. I was baffled...no good-bye.

Trevor finally emailed me a couple weeks later and said he was in South Dakota because he had read that the employment rate was really good there. It still seemed odd. At the time a mutual professional friend of ours asked me why she was constantly getting calls to be a job reference for him, and why in so many different states. She said she couldn't continue.

Eventually Trevor called me and said that he was in California. One time he called from a train station to say he still loved me. I informed him I was still with the same boyfriend. He ended up living in several different parts of the state and finally met his second wife and said he was going to try hard to make things work because she was so cute. I hope he is better to her.

Now and then Trevor would still email me. He said his wife could see all of his emails and he was being open about our correspondence. I did actually meet her one time when they came back to town for something. She said he had been upfront with her about all the trouble he put me through. She was very poised, lovely...and obviously the mature one of the two. I hoped she would get the better version of him than I got. I hope she is a strong woman.

Trevor continued to email me once or twice a year. Typically he would tell me about some hobby he had or a trip they were planning. He sent me a photo to inform me that he had been seriously lifting weights and had really bulked up. This was just further proof that we were not a good match because he was so much more attractive without the gigantic muscles.

The Year 2011:

Then down the road, my hometown was rocked by a bunch of bad publicity and Trevor launched into his usual put-downs about The State of Pennsylvania, my hometown, and The University where we met. (He had done this for years...this was nothing new.) I knew it was time to put a bullet in this nonsense. I fired back an email that I knew would end things abruptly... I hit his Achilles heel. Over! Done! The End for Sure! Yep!

I love my home state. I love my home town. My college years were the best years of my life overall...I love The University I attended, period! In my mind, there is a reason "Happy Valley" is called that. I love it!

Thanks to all the great teachers...and friends...

I think back on my college days as probably the most overall exciting time of my life. I made some really great friends ...some of whom are my facebook friends decades later. I think back on all of the wonderful experiences I had in the theatre department, especially the acting classes which were the most fun. I remember so many times I had teachers who said something that made me laugh, made me think, made me feel supported. I had great teachers in many subjects.

My first year of college, my French teacher Nancy said part of our final was describing something to her fluently in French. We had to go to her office to do that one-on-one. She showed me a picture and I pulled out all of the words I knew and strung them all together as best I could...and apparently I was longwinded.

Nancy laughed and told me I had "verbal diarrhea". I still love her comment, it cracks me up!

It takes a special kind of person to inform, entertain, critique with kindness, enforce discipline....and still come out well liked...and remembered. I had some of the most amazing college teachers. I don't need to be told everything I do is great, I just need to be given instruction that makes sense and in a kind manner.

As for that one teacher who snared me into the world of his neediness...well, there are people like that all over...not just in one place. I'm not letting that one bad apple ruin the whole darn thing for me.

As far as the new "Me Too Movement goes," I think it is great people are becoming more aware...as long as due process overrides jumping to conclusions. Just because someone is accused of something, doesn't mean they did it. And just because someone takes

a long time to come forward with their story of betrayal doesn't mean they are lying.

When I was 29: You would think as I headed toward age 30, I would get smarter about picking a match. Nope...not really. On the cusp of my divorce, I began dating Demetri, a man 15 years older. Demetri is a brown-eyed computer guy who I first met a couple years earlier down the hall from my office. He used to smile at me in a lingering way that made me blush. I wore mini-skirts and higher heels quite often back then.

At the time I really didn't think about any attraction to him because I was still with Trevor, and Demetri made me nervous. He was ruggedly handsome but he looked at me as if I was a piece of candy. I'd think, "You can't have me" and move on. When he said "Hi" to me, I'd just say "Hi" back, but I don't recall any real conversation with him then. I always had to rush back to my office, which was very busy.

Initially, I was married and Demetri was engaged so neither of us was available. But by the time I filed for divorce, he was single again and he asked me out one day when he came to my office to fix a computer. (He used to work down the hall, but at this point he worked in another building.) I thought it was convenient he also worked for The University and only lived about 10 minutes from where I did. I said I'd go out with him.

Demetri was nice and smart but I was pretty much operating under the misconception that quickly dating someone else was "proof" I was desirable, and I thought I would feel less anguish over the end of my marriage and how screwed-up most of that relationship had been.

Oddly I don't have any recollection of what Demetri and I did on our first date...none. I don't remember any of our first handful of dates. I don't even recall if we first slept at his place or mine...and I have a pretty good memory. I think it was cold and rainy though. I just remember waking up in his room one morning and he had a Monet water lilies painting on his wall. But I can't recall anything else that we did, yet I'm sure we went out somewhere. It is just a blur. I remember thinking, "He seemed to want me when I wasn't available. I hope he isn't disappointed."

Seems to me I got really sick after our first couple dates too...like sore throat. I think we had begun dating in early November when it was getting bitter out. I remember Demetri came back to my office another time to fix the computer and he seemed wary of me...stand-offish. But, he was at my desk, so he was in close proximity. Maybe he figured I was 29 and heard my biological clock ticking and was going to try to latch on to him...who knows. But then he asked me out again after a bunch of small talk. A couple of friends at my job seemed happy to see me start dating him

Early in our relationship, Demetri made sure I knew that he thought children are annoying. He also said kids are expensive. He said this often, especially when we were out in public. So I went on the pill again...despite already having my tubes tied at age 26. I was scared to death I might get pregnant despite having had the operation. My Dad's side of the family is pretty fertile so I was afraid something flukey would happen with me. I was double-prepared to have sex without fertility for several years. I felt I was "doing my duty" to hold up my end of the bargain, so to say.

It wasn't until a few years later, he told me his ex-fiancee's parents had been constantly talking about wanting grandkids. So Demetri felt a lot of pressure to make babies right away, even though he wasn't sure he wanted any.

At the time I was dating Demetri, I had a friend who was 10 years younger than I was and she said she grew up with Cabbage Patch Dolls. I then bought one just for the fun of it. I don't know what possessed me, but I took it over to Demetri's house once...just once. He glared at it as if it was a real newborn human child who he would have to pay child support for. I get it that he didn't like kids and probably thought dolls were stupid too. But, I like dolls. So this was a sign that perhaps we weren't a perfect match.

Demetri and I enjoyed renting crazy movies, drinking lots of wine, eating cheese and olives...and his own special salsa recipe with chips. His secret ingredient was blending avocado into the tomato, which made the stuff look brown and weird, but taste absolutely amazing.

On weekends, we occasionally took drives around Pennsylvania and ate lunch in quaint little towns. We took hikes in the woods among colorful fall leaves. We spent time with his family and they were all extremely nice. His Dad was a very sweet man who sat in the livingroom and had long talks with me. His Mom was a great cook who constantly loaded us up with leftovers.

I got "Demetri" tattooed in purple above my derriere. A few years later...about two months before our break-up... I had it covered over with an aquatic scene. Surely he must have suspected that that "meant something"...yes...no? The tattoo meant something to me...and so did its disappearance. At the time I got it, I thought I would have it forever.

I love trolls and Demetri got me a green-haired Christmas troll I named Kipper Andrew. I was touched. However, he informed me a couple days later that it was on clearance and one of his sisters told him he should get it for me. It wasn't his own idea.

Early in our relationship, I saw Demetri's high school yearbook picture and thought he was so adorable. I remember printing off a copy of it and putting it in a locket. So maybe I was in love with his face...? Yes, I know. It sounds weird. I was about 30 and printed off a picture of him at high school age...17 or 18. (Just don't think about it. He was 44 when I actually began dating him. He was "legal".) Anyway, I liked this photo a lot. When my attraction would wane, I would think about this handsome photo.

One horrible snowy winter during the 1990's, it was below 20 degrees for a good stretch. Batteries were conking out in cars. Demetri and I decided to be daring...we stripped down, accept for wearing sneakers...ran out on his back snow-covered porch...and took a full length selfie. We were both a bit chubby, but it was a novelty. We both had a copy. Naked full bodied photo! We joked that the freezing cold made my boobs look bigger and his "Elvis" look smaller. I framed my copy and put it on my nightstand.

Then, I went on vacation one time, and my Mom decided that she and my Dad would "be nice" and clean my apartment when they were there to feed my goldfish. I had no idea they would go into the bedroom. My Mom's face was priceless as she told me they had seen "the picture". I know I did not get high approval ratings for that! More and more my sister became "the perfect child" I'm sure. But the photo was memorable to us... Demetri and me.....""Elvis and Ginger." Seems so corny to name your "areas". But that was one relationship where I did, because he did.

Leave *The Leaf*...

Demetri was a good guy who worked pretty hard, but often seemed cynical, unhappy and moody...and this seemed to increase with time. He didn't like his job anymore and he used to sit and stew and smoke pot out of a purple bong.—I would sit on the opposite side of the room because I didn't want second-hand smoke. I wanted <u>nothing</u> to do with it. I basically tolerated it because I was trying to be open-minded and not critical. And he would do it while we were watching TV in his livingroom.

Medical marijuana is one thing, but that was not what this was. And it didn't seem to make Demetri any less negative. I always thought pot was supposed to make a person mellow and induce "happiness". I called my friend Kris who told me that smoking regularly can do just the opposite.

Holiday dread...

A big problem I had was, Demetri didn't seem to like holidays....not any of them....he hated being required to give anyone a gift and didn't keep that a secret. I don't know which Demetri hated more...Valentine's Day... or Christmas ...or birthdays. They all made him frown.

One Christmas Demetri bought "a pile of clothing" at an outlet mall where things are on sale because of slight manufacturer flaws.—These were presents. He threw them on the floor to show me what he got. I didn't want any of it. I didn't mind the hard-to-see flaws, it was the impersonal approach of it all...and the "let's get this over with" attitude. Plus, one of the items was an ugly sack-like brown dress. I don't think I had a necklace in my jewelry box that would have dressed that thing up enough! Thankfully someone else got that. Maybe she liked it...?

A couple years into our relationship, we were lying in bed. And Demetri said, "Well your birthday is next week. I guess I <u>have to</u> go shopping. What should I get you?" He said it as if the idea was vile. I gave him an idea but made sure it wasn't expensive. I felt terrible for saying anything, but I did so so we could change the topic. He got me what I asked for. I liked the gift, but I felt like guilt was attached to it.

Another birthday he gave me a gold band with little emeralds in it. He had bought it a few years earlier when he was trying to get over his old girlfriend ...and probably was hoping she was the one he could give it to. It was a nice gesture overall. But then again, I thought he gave it to me because he hated shopping so much. I told myself to be thankful and grateful.

He also printed off a bunch of colorful abstract computer designs and laminated them and gave them out as placemats. He said he didn't have to go shopping for events for quite a while because he had a big supply. My Nunny liked one of them and framed it. There was one with a lot of aqua on it that I liked and used at dinnertime. But still... I wanted a guy who enjoyed holidays and birthdays and gifts. I like light-hearted celebrations.

Sometimes Demetri liked to analyze the cost of things <u>while we were in the middle of eating</u>. One time I remember eating a 40 cent yogurt and he was talking about coupons.—He wasn't even the one who bought the yogurt, I did. (I just wanted to enjoy what I was eating.)

One time Demetri was breaking down the cost of a pizza he had bought. He figured he could make tomato sauce cheaper and a whole pizza for less money than the pizzeria charged. So, Demetri did try making his own tomato sauce one day. Conclusion: It was too much work! I began picking up a pizza on the way over to his house on many weekends...green peppers, pepperoni, anchovies.—He got me into eating that combo. I hoped if I paid for it, he wouldn't complain about the price. He shut up about it.

Each hunting season Demetri would go out and come back with a deer. I was happy for him from the perspective that that satisfied him. It saved him money. But I honestly am not crazy about venison and would kind of hold my breath and pretend to like it. I had not had it since I was a small child. I ate it our first few years together but finally confessed I wasn't crazy about it. **Demetri got all irritated and** said, "Oh, so you are all upset because you think I'm killing Bambi, right?" Well, <u>that was part of it</u>.

I admit that during the years with Demetri, I went on a lot of spending sprees. I am sure he must have noticed I constantly was wearing some new piece of jewelry. It was mostly silver artsy stuff, but sometimes sub-quality gold stuff from a big discount store type place. I was just trying to feel pretty. I had issues to begin with, but being around cynicism just felt "ugly".

I probably needed a counselor more than baubles, because I think I went into my relationship with Demetri as a very "wounded bird". The ups and downs of my marriage were very emotional, contradictory and confusing...and then I immediately went into my relationship with Demetri...which was a mixture of fun and dismal. My chipped-up self-image was definitely not getting better in the new relationship. In some ways I think it was getting worse.

The "other woman"...

I am sure Demetri must have cringed to see my spend-thriftiness, being that he was so financially frugal. I am sure I was hoping for Demetri to "be what I needed him to be" and that isn't fair. He was himself. I really wanted a guy who thought I was special and not one who still seemed trapped in the past and ticked off his previous relationship didn't work out. I wanted a guy who spoiled me a little bit, enjoyed holidays, and was glad to be with ME. I can't help but feel he liked me but always was thinking about "her".

I even remember thinking, "I'm 15 years younger than Demetri is...and people compliment my legs and eyes all the time....doesn't he feel lucky to be with me?"

Then I found out his previous girlfriend/fiancé was 2 years younger than I was...and had been in a few beauty pageants! Apparently she didn't like being in them and was pushed into them by her parents, and didn't win any. But still, <u>that</u> put me in my place. I knew I could never even be in a pageant to begin with. Any ego or arrogance I had about "being some prize" on his arm was nixed right then and there.

Demetri told me that one time his ex had drank so much alcohol she had to go to the emergency room to get her stomach pumped. I imagined that even then she must have seemed more appealing to him than I was. HOW could I compete with a beauty pageant gal? It's ridiculous to try to compete with others but at the time I was so insecure.

I suppose I was really too needy. I don't think I ever actually <u>acted</u> needy, as I had a firm idea in my mind that "that scares guys away." But I'm pretty sure I was. Maybe I find it hard to show people I need something because during Marilyn's lifetime I was the "Queen of Need". Oddly Demetri's ex's name is "Tiffani". Funny because Marilyn sings that song about diamonds she is so well known for.

Fairly odd at the fair:

One day Demetri said there was a special fair in a nearby town and we were going to it. It was called "An Indian Pow-wow". We were also taking his good friend Joan who he met at one of his jobs. She was very pretty in a natural earthy intellectual no-frills way, and I really liked her.

Unfortunately it was two days before my monthly paycheck deposit into my account and I only had about $20 to my name. While at the fair there were many booths of silver and turquoise jewelry made by Native Americans. It was gorgeous and I wanted a ring or necklace or bracelet, but couldn't afford any of them. Demetri kept asking me why I wasn't buying any and I explained...but he never offered to get me a piece or float me a loan.

Then his friend Joan, who had somewhat long-ish blond hair, was fascinated by some fancy feather hair clips and she kept trying them on and debating which to get. Demetri told me he would get me one of those. I was so mind-boggled. He would rather get a $25 clip for a girl with short hair than a $40 piece of jewelry for a girl who loved jewelry and he had been with a couple of years? I didn't take him up on his offer...I wouldn't have worn it.

I suppose I could have asked him to loan me the money, but I really wanted a guy who just stepped-in and thought I was worth spoiling a little bit. I kept my mouth shut. But I didn't feel very special at the time. I still shake my head to this day when I think about it. I guess he meant well.

Scents and Common Sense:

There was the one time...surprisingly just for the heck of it... Demetri brought me back two nice bottles of perfume from a business trip to New York—Vanilla and jasmine knock-offs. And about two minutes later he told me about some gorgeous girl who got into the elevator at the hotel. I didn't need to hear that then... I felt like saying, "Just let me enjoy this moment... I'm pretending that you care."

Our last Valentine's Day... Valentine's Day 1998...a Saturday...

I went over to Demetri's house and gave him a bag of goodies and a card for the occasion. I can't remember what I gave him, but I think it was a bunch of stuff he could use. Even if I couldn't get anything fancy or didn't know what to get, I wanted to give him something ... just something....because he was "my man". Off-and-on I thought I was in love with him.

Demetri immediately looked nervous and said, "Well, I have something for you too but I will give it to you later...tonight....after you go back to your place and put on a dress to go out for dinner."

I knew he probably hadn't gone shopping and I didn't expect much. It was 4 years into our relationship and I knew how he felt about spending money. It didn't matter if we went places together, I got along with his family, we laughed over goofy movies, took hikes in the woods, had a couple different pet names for each other, or had sex on a regular basis. Nothing was going to make him think I was worth shopping for...nothing!

Later that day, Demetri came to pick me up at my apartment and gave me a nice 18k gold, sapphire ring for Valentine's Day. I am not into blue sapphires, but it was nice. The thing is, he told me he had bought it while in Thailand at the time he was trying to get over his previous relationship. It was a long vacation someone told him to take while he was depressed over the break-up. So basically he had it in storage, and it took him four years to decide I deserved it, and then by the time he gave it to me he already realized I didn't like sapphires.

He even said to me, "I'm glad you like it because I know you recently said you aren't crazy about sapphires." I had told him that just a few weeks earlier when we were discussing stones.

I tried to make the best of it, and tell myself not to be petty and over-think things. The ring was pretty nice and he even gave me a certificate from a jewelry store. Demetri had had it appraised when he got back to The States to make sure he hadn't been gypped out of a lot of money. It turns out, the ring was worth more than expected.

But a co-worker repeatedly said that Demetri obviously didn't love me because he would rather give me a ring he probably bought for another girl, should she come back, then to spend the effort or money to buy something specifically for me. I saw her more days a week than him, so that was stuck in my head. And I also knew it was true. But I kept trying to convince myself that Demetri's intentions were all good and I was being superficial.

Soon after, a really cute guy also began flirting with me. And then another one. One night I went out after work with the same co-worker and her cute guy friend was very forward. I told him that after that happy hour I was going to drive over to my boyfriend Demetri's house.

He said, "If I were your boyfriend I would be with you *right now*." I began to think, "How happy am I really?" I knew I wasn't very happy... but I was trying to be.

Cracks...in stones...and self-esteem...

I remember that after we were together a few years Demetri told me he had gotten a high school ring with a big red stone in it. At that moment, I really wished he would give it to me to wear, since I never experienced that when I was in high school. I also like red stones and it would have felt cool wearing "his ring". So, I inquired for more information about it and he said that while still in school he had given it to some girl to wear and it got damaged. I think he said they were fighting and she threw it against a wall and the stone cracked.—That ended that conversation. Yes, clearly I was still emotionally trying to make up for stuff I missed during high school. And also I was probably wanting a commitment too...which is sooo hard for me to admit! I always thought love relationships "just happen". NO!

I feel baldy he inherited the damaged me. But then again, I think I inherited the damaged him.

I remember him referring to some girls in high school as "high ass" ...he said they were the cheerleaders and popular ones.—I could hear the angry smirk in his voice as he explained that. I think Demetri had a real fear of women controlling him. He seemed to have some resentments.

For instance he said his Mom used to refer to "doctors" as if they were so much better than other men. (It might have been a generational thing.) And Demetri pointed out that his Father was not a doctor. I think maybe Demetri had a fear of not meeting expectations women had of him. —Just my guess. He actually seemed quite bitter and brought up the "doctor" story a few times. But I never said anything about one profession making a man better or worse. Heck I had a degree in theatre but was doing secretarial work. Who was I to judge someone's career choice? As long as it is honest work, it is good. I never said I thought Demetri's profession was lacking. I'm with a computer guy now! It seemed to me that passing comments his Mother had made many years earlier had put a chink in his self-esteem.

Ultimately there were a couple other things that were messing up our dynamic. The end was just inevitable.

Thing One:

For example, one time Demetri was getting something together to ship in the mail. He was trying to seal it up and the packing tape kept sticking to itself. So he told me to hold the box down while he toiled with the roll and covered the opening on top. But he was so ticked off at that point, that as he was applying the tape he was really yanking it hard. The box kept moving and he snapped at me, "HOLD the box still!" He looked mean. Well, I'm sorry, he is a big strong man and as much as I tried I couldn't hold the box still with him being so rough. Was this tantrum a one-time thing, or would it occur on a regular basis if we ever lived together?

I said to myself, "Could you live with that temper, Michele? Why would you want to?"

Thing Two:

There was also the time it was very cold out and I had stayed a Sunday night at his house. We had work the next day. I went out to my car first. My car battery was dead and he snapped at me. He was accusing me of letting my car door ajar and therefore draining my battery. He was mad because I was parked behind him in his narrow driveway, so he couldn't get out. As you can imagine, his wrath hurt my feelings...so I could barely contain my smirk when he then realized <u>his</u> car battery was dead also! His father came over and jumped both the cars.

But, I thought, "Michele, do you really want a guy who jumps to conclusions so fast? He didn't pause before accusing."

Thing Three:

Then one night, about 6 months before our break-up, Demetri suddenly stumbled around the words and asked me, "Uh...do you think.... we could....maybe....ever ...live together?" It was out-of-the-blue and while we were just standing in his kitchen. **I paused and said, "I don't think so. I think we have some issues in our relationship."** (Silence.)

Then a few minutes later he quietly took my hand, led me back to the bedroom, and we had sex. **When we were done he said, "Well, at least we have *that*...good sex."**

I remember thinking, "So you would really rather just do *that* than ask me WHAT our issues are that might be getting in the way of furthering our relationship....really?"

But at the same time, at that point I didn't care to press the matter. It was kind of like stale bread. Like, you can still eat it and it won't kill you, but it's past expiration. You know how products will say, "best if sold by" on them. I didn't want to be something Demetri was resigned to because a certain amount of time had passed. I wanted to be someone he actually <u>wanted.</u> I started to stop wanting him. I did... but I didn't.

Broken forever... June 1998...

When I finally broke up with Demetri, it was over the phone. I had just had sex with someone else the day before. I had known the guy for a while and the fact is I intended to see him again. Demetri called me and I immediately told him...there was no beating-around-the-bush. I simply couldn't deal with our relationship anymore and I wanted so much more for myself.

He blurted out, "I love you with all my heart." I could tell he was deflated but I really didn't believe him. I didn't think he loved me, I think he just didn't like losing control of "his predictable girlfriend". We hung up.

When we were still together, Demetri mentioned many times that his ex-fiancee "talked him into" buying her a diamond engagement ring at a jewelry store, and then talked him into allowing her to keep it when she broke things off. That really bothered him. He seemed fixated on the money and I think he kind of felt swindled too.

When I finally broke up with Demetri, he kept contacting me in what I perceived as an effort to get back together. **He said, "I should have asked you to marry me. I could have gotten an inexpensive ring if I looked through the classified ads in the paper. People are always selling diamond rings cheap."**

I told him I would want a ring that was all mine and not someone else's. I said I didn't want negative energy. I could tell he didn't like that response. But, he got the other gal a nice ring, so.....? It was really a moot point though. I felt bad but couldn't do anything to make things better for him without betraying my own happiness. I was happy to be unattached again. I was ready to explore other options.

I am sorry, but don't blame me because another girl broke your heart. Demetri could have looked at his break-up with the other girl as a "fate thing" allowing him to end up with me. If he loved me, he would have felt that their break-up was for the best in the long run. He must not have been in love with me.

Seriously, don't treat me "less than" because some other girl hurt you. That has happened to me in various relationships both before and after the one with Demetri. I get the attitude and the downgrade because the man still hasn't released his anger or mistrust built-up in a previous relationship. It's quite ...maddening.

Then one day I received flowers at my office. Demetri emailed me and informed me that he had heard someone say that "Doing something nice for someone else can make you feel good too." But he told me that sending me flowers didn't make him feel good or better at all. He seemed grouchy. I thanked him for the flowers but I had no intention of back-tracking.

As the months passed, I got a couple odd care packages in the mail. Demetri would send me gag gifts... colorful pipe cleaners bent like flowers... a goofy hand puppet ...a pocket knife. I didn't know how to respond. I believe I emailed him a weak "thank you." I didn't want to get caught up in discussing the items because honestly I was speechless. This was reminiscent of the Christmas when he gave me a weird book about a peasant girl being smacked for a long time on her ass by some guy who had a wooden paddle. I guess it was supposed to be sexy...I guess.... Uck!

He then pulled out all the stops. Knowing I like troll dolls, he sent me a picture of a troll that he just got. He said the troll was named Horatio and he wondered where his Mommy was. I sent him back another troll to keep Horatio company. But I could not help him raise them. –Ha-ha!

I felt badly, but we had been together 4 and a half years, and that was plenty of time for him to act like he really wanted ME. He never even got mushy and explained to me how happy he would be if we lived together...nothing. I concluded he just wanted my portion of rent for

his house. He never asked me what I thought we should work on.—
NOTHING! In my 30's I was still looking for passion, excitement, to
be swept off my feet! Damn-it, I wasn't ready to bury the fairytale and
accept "mundane". And his often grouchy look made me afraid to bring
anything up first. I don't want to live with someone I'm afraid to talk
to...unless of course, I'm agreeing with him.

**I am a big believer that "If you don't know you want me when
you have me, then don't act like you can't live without me when
I'm gone."** I think Demetri simply didn't want to be alone, it wasn't
about ME. Sending me a pocket knife alone pretty much shows "he
didn't know me". Some girls might find one useful, but I just stuck it
in a drawer. At one point he finally revealed that he had sent it to me
because he had two.

**The final straw...that broke the mattress...and sealed the
deal forever!**

**Shortly after we broke up Demetri said, "Well, I know how you
are ... you move on as soon as you bed-down some new guy."**
He made it sound like I was just living on a mattress! I suppose
that was his way of making me seem like a girl with no rules. That way
he could figure I was at fault for everything and he wouldn't have to
face his own quirks...nor would he have to entertain the thought that
maybe I just didn't want HIM anymore. It was easier for Demetri to
believe that I was just flawed. WHO the hell was he to judge me!?
Demetri literally used the term "bed-down" in regards to ME?!?
One time, while we were still together, Demetri told me he used to
go to "the working girls" occasionally when he was overseas a couple
years after college. **He said, " I figured they didn't really want to have
sex with me and probably just wanted to get it over with. But I had
the money and they needed it. I just wanted sex."**
Hmmm....so he had sex with girls he figured were unhappy
spreading their legs for him...yet...he was judging me...? He can do
that....by himself!

Down the line years after the break-up, Demetri still contacted me now and then. I tried to sway the conversation on to other women. I asked if he was dating. Demetri told me that he had dated some ladies after me.

But he said, "The problem is, they all have children and they want to talk about their kids or their grandkids."

Really, do you think maybe they <u>love</u> them? That still makes me shake my head. Sooo...that still doesn't mean he likes ME. It just means he doesn't want a woman who has used her reproductive organs! I think he liked me by default. I'm childless.

Demetri emailed me a number of times throughout the years ... our conversations were cordial, neutral, and then we would break contact. It was kind of nice to hear from him, but I also watched what I said. I think overall Demetri is a good guy. I did have some fun with him and at times I really did think I wanted something permanent with him. I admit I thought about marrying now and then. Sex was fairly good.

Probably one of the best times I ever had with Demetri was when his Mom sent home some really good homemade nut strudel. We were in the middle of a "compromising position" at about 3:00AM.... and then we began talking about strudel. Things went on and on... Demetri and I were working off the calories and suddenly starving. **Sex and strudel...good combination. We had both.**

<u>Fast forward to 2019:</u>

As I was in the middle of writing this book, Demetri emailed me out of the blue. I hadn't heard from him for a couple of years. I responded in a cordial manner. But obviously I live in a different state and have been with another man (Jay) for well over a decade.

As Demetri and I exchanged emails, I mentioned that I was writing my book. I am sure I told Demetri my past life beliefs years earlier, as he knew me during a time when I had life size cardboard Marilyn Monroe figures in my apartment. I believe I also told him I had been Cleopatra, because one Christmas he did buy me a couple silver Egyptian figure charms. (I had to buy the chains to wear them.)

After some email exchanges, it was obvious Demetri is cynical about reincarnation. He was very patronizing about the book too. I didn't expect him to agree with it, but spare the cynical thoughts and talk about something else then. Demetri has the right to be skeptical. I have the right not to write! It's 20 years later anyway. We broke up in June 1998. I'm done! I wish him well...with someone else. Hopefully his right match exists.

I know without a shadow of a doubt, that reincarnation is real. There is no question in my mind about that. REINCARNATION IS REAL!

I wish everyone could remember at least one of their past lives just so they could understand...and also so those of us who already do remember aren't looked upon as nutcases. But....alas...it is what it is. And I would rather tell the truth and be looked upon as crazy, than pretend I don't know what I know.

Brief Interlude From Relationships

Age: 33-36: The truth is, between breaking up with Demetri in June of 1998 and meeting a guy named Kyle in June of 2001, I had had a very weird sex life and not at all a love life. It was just so hard to find anyone around my own age who wasn't already married or newly divorced and bitter...there was plenty of "bitter" out there! I lived near a college campus. What's a girl to do?

I messed around with a handful of guys in their 20's who seemed to have the "Mrs. Robinson fantasy" in their heads. I resisted that for a while but then just gave in. Younger guys can be really appealing ...persistent as hell ...sweet ...and have a lot of energy. It kind of seemed like 35 year old men wanted 25 year old girls ... and 25 year old boys wanted 35 year old women. Odd. Strange. Funny. Interesting. I stopped fighting it. I went with it.

There were also a couple guys close to my age but they didn't turn out to be the best choices. Ultimately I ended up on a sexual roller-coaster that rivaled my swinging excursions a few years earlier...and

I couldn't even blame it on a pushy husband. Every single day is a new chance to make new decisions. And I am the one responsible for ME.

THAT is something I remember about being Marilyn, however. When she knew she was making bad decisions, she would take the "oh well, I'm hurt, I can't help it" attitude. I can't do that now. I may realize I am actually doing something motivated by hurt or fear, but then I know I have to change. Once I understand I am doing something for those reasons, I realize it's time to get smarter. No one's hanging around the corner to rescue me. I'm not that pretty!

Personal Ads, Part 1:

My younger friend Mary worked part-time in my office for several years, and she introduced me to the personal ads. She said she was answering some and recommended that I should too. I told her that that seemed like pure desperation and she threatened to answer an ad "under my identity" if I didn't at least give it a try.—So I did. I even set up my own profile. This sent me down a spiral of odd experiences.

I'll skip over the many miscellaneous dating experiences that resulted…they were really mostly odd. Here are just a few.

The Darlin:

One pleasant experience was with Donny, a 22 year old blond guy. He was a college student. We had sex a couple times, he took me to a rock concert on campus…and I gave him a bunch of my favorite men's colognes because he said he wasn't sure how to buy one. Donny was the kind of guy I seriously felt lucky to be with because there was something extra cute about him…looks-wise and also personality. Then summer came. We had planned to see each other the following school year, and talked about "doing something with whipped cream".

But there was just one thing…more and more Donny's emails were about beer and being hungover. It began to feel as if starting his day unable to function had become the norm. He would feel sick but then go out and drink in excess another night. I'm sure he was just trying to fit in with his friends. Donny mentioned our plan to get together, however I thought I just had to say something. I told him "the plan" was still on, but I was tired of hearing about his obsession with drinking.— That abruptly ended that!

I'm not quite sure what kind of reaction I expected. He never responded and I figured he had no intention of cutting back. It surprisingly really didn't affect me…I just understood. We never saw each other again.

However, sometimes I have thought I should have just shut up, because maybe Donny was sensitive and I probably hurt his feelings. I was just being honest though… hangovers aren't cool and more importantly haphazard things people do while they are drunk can be fatal. More and more I would hear about college students drinking way too much and some even dying from alcohol poisoning. It was hard to be in my 30's and just keep quiet. And when you care about someone that is what you do, you say something.

Donny was sweet and 20 years later I still think of our brief time together fondly. I hope he has been happy. I have often wondered where he went after college. If I had been younger I might have made an effort to work things out. I would have done my best to distract him from the bottle.

The Smart One:

Another memorable youngster was a guy named Scotty. He was quite cute, brown-eyes, brown hair and a tall, strapping lad with a baby face. Scotty answered my personal ad but something about him made me suspicious. Turns out he was trying to pass himself off as older than he was… he was only 19. I kept telling Scotty that our age difference was too big, but he kept insisting that it wasn't and continued to pursue me...and kind of talk tough. Eventually we got together at my place and he did in fact talk less forward than his bold email personality.

We sat on the couch and talked...and talked....and talked. Finally he asked me if I would take off my top and I did. He looked at me as if I had just walked on water. He also seemed quite nervous. Scotty told me I was beautiful and he touched me for about 5 seconds...his hand was shaking.

He said he had been with high school girls but said, "They didn't look like YOU." (I used to lift weights a lot and was often told my chest was nice.) I really think he suddenly realized I truly was significantly older than he was though.

I told him to just go think about it and we could see each other at another time. He nervously said he would and he left a bit flustered. I would have gladly gotten together with Scotty, but because of the age difference I really felt he had to decide that that was what he wanted. I have no idea how much prior experience he actually did or didn't have, because he started off lying to me about his age, so he could have been making up other things too. He was so appealing I am sure some attractive college girl scooped him up soon after. He could have had his pick.

Some time down the road, Scotty emailed me again and asked me if I could send him a picture of myself. I did. It was me reading a book in just my panties.... I think they were red. A year or two later when I had moved out of town, a friend told me she had just met him through the personal ads and somehow they realized they both knew me. She said he asked about me and said he liked me. I thought that was sweet. (My friend didn't date him, she is even older than I am but used to lie about her age.)

One of the things that really struck me about Scotty was part of our conversation at my place. Scotty proceeded to launch into what sounded like a sex-ed class lecture. In fact, he mentioned a high school class and said he would never have casual sex without using condoms. I thought he was pretty darn smart. I began buying condoms on a regular basis after his little spiel. Prior to then it always made me feel embarrassed and using them was hit-and-miss. But after that night, I realized that that young man had taught me to just do the smart thing.

I had always heard about guys who whine about using them and who try to talk girls into ditching them, but with cute guys like Scotty around who are willing to be safe, a girl really has no excuse to risk her wellbeing messing around with men who are reckless. **No one "likes them"…but…I am grateful I never had to be treated for catching anything. I would rather be embarrassed buying condoms than be embarrassed buying penicillin.** And explaining to someone that they have to use condoms couldn't possibly be as difficult as explaining a disease.

But Donny and Scotty were the exceptions. Most of my online dating conversations ended before we actually met. And a few I wish would have never happened at all, because the experiences were yukky.

The Nightmare:

There was a guy named Dante, who I will never understand. Dante, was around my age, had dark brown hair and was pleasantly average looking. I was happy to be talking to a peer and ready to mingle. We made plans to meet at a popular downtown restaurant, on a rather blustery fall evening. As usual, I went in a little dress with my legs exposed. However I did have a coat on and so did he.

We met outside the establishment and sat down on a bench, although I'm not sure why. I assumed after a few minutes of preliminary chit-chat we would go inside for a hot drink if nothing else. However, Dante never actually suggested doing that. The wind was getting worse. At some point I mentioned going into the building, but Dante just smiled and really didn't respond. So our "date" consisted of sitting in the cold and both of us shivering through an hour of conversation until I left with a sore throat. –I have no idea what we even talked about. The whole thing was baffling.

Finally we said good-bye and I was so happy to be free. I couldn't walk home fast enough. But suddenly with every step I took, a bizarre feeling descended upon me. Despite the fact we never touched at all, I literally felt disgusting and gross. It seemed the closer I got to home the more this feeling overtook me.—I just couldn't shake it off.

I took a long hot shower and tossed and turned all night long. I literally felt as though an evil presence had followed me home and invaded my dreams. I remember dreaming some man was after me, although he didn't resemble Dante at all. I have never felt that creepy way before or since and I have no idea what that was all about. I could understand being annoyed with Dante, but I am not sure what the feeling of utter repulsion was from.

Now, I would have thought Dante wasn't attracted to me...just as I was not attracted to him. But the very next day his email suggested "performing something" on me, and I was never going to let that happen! I have no idea how I responded, but I am sure I was afraid of hurting his feelings and replied in a manner that placed all the blame on me.—Done!

Well, so much for thinking that finding a guy close to my own age was going to be an easy fix for my loneliness. I think I found the only man in that whole darn town who preferred shivering outside in the cold to sitting inside with the food. Maybe he was broke...I have no idea. I would have paid for us to have something if I had been attracted to him, but I didn't want to give mixed messages, so that is why I didn't offer. At least I wasn't obligated to hug him since he didn't spend a dime on me. I have the feeling I might have felt really strange about it all even if we had gotten out of the cold. There was definitely something else at play going on...it was weird.

The Hunk:

Maurice, Maurice, Maurice. This guy was quite...hmmmmmm. He was looking for company while in school far from his home state. He said he really liked some girl back home but couldn't "hold-out" all semester. I got the impression she was a girlfriend who might have disapproved of his "personal-ads life".

He made that cliché kind of comment ..."What I do in Pennsylvania, stays in Pennsylvania."

Nevertheless, Maurice had a very nice face and obviously worked out with weights, but not too much. He was 30 years old...I was then 35. We exchanged emails...**met for coffee**...exchanged more emails... and he called me about a trip he was taking. He said something about going away on business for the weekend. It was a two hour drive with an overnight hotel stay. He seemed to be hinting around, but he never outright asked if I would go with him. And I didn't.

Between our various emails, Maurice told me he was used to dating girls who were blond and looked like models. He also spoke about being with girls who had breast implants and he seemed to continually be hinting that he was used to women generally looking a certain level of perfection. At the time my hair was dyed red, but he told me he liked Grace from "Will and Grace," so I figured he was open-minded about various types of looks. Grace is very, very pretty but not "the blond stacked type".

I continued to assume Maurice was flexible, yet I increasingly began to question that and really didn't know why Maurice was even talking to me. We had already had coffee together so he met me in person. He certainly already knew I wasn't his ideal type, or even close.

Maurice would also say things which seemed to indicate he had a very high opinion of his own appearance...but then he would do what seemed like a "fake modesty thing" as well. I really wasn't sure where he was coming from but I would say I met Maurice during a period of being somewhat depressed so I was looking for a thrill and going to see where this led.

I admit, at age 35, I had a bit of an attitude. Marilyn died at age 36, and I was getting close to that point in my own life. I was trying to live it up. My job was also extremely stressful, as my boss was brilliant and quite ambitious. So I really wanted a more exciting personal life.

Anyway, I got together with Maurice a couple weeks after we began emailing. He came to my place and we had sex. This was stupid on my part because I should have surmised from previous email conversations that he probably wouldn't think I was "good enough" for him. We got together that one time, and that was it. **WHAM-BAM-ThankYou-M'am!** I think I emailed him once after that and I think he emailed me once as well. It is really kind of a blur. All I know is things ended.

From MY experience...Maurice was good looking and that is all I can really say. He grabbed me and started kissing me very fast and we had sex but it was very impersonal. When Maurice was emailing me he made a very precise point of making sure I knew other girls thought he was "on the large side".—And he was. But when I mentioned to him that he was right about that, he seemed very embarrassed.

Maybe the truth is, some people can say whatever they want in an email but in person things get tricky. People get shy or suddenly feel guilty, or just decide they only imagined an attraction. The internet has made it very easy to talk way too candidly way too quickly.

I am not going to lie...my feelings were hurt. I knew he was better looking than I was and he judged me. But it is also amusing to me that it is natural for a person to care about the opinion of someone else even if they weren't all that ideal either. I think most people are psychologically delicate when it comes to sex. **Nobody wants to be rejected and everybody wants to be the first to say good-bye. It's kind of like saying, "I don't really want you either, but how dare you not want me."**

Shamefully, I was a catfish!

So, I did the only thing a girl in my position could do. (Just kidding.) I answered Maurice's personal ad and pretended I was a 19 year-old, blond girl named "Vanessa."

We exchanged emails for a week or so and then I sent him pictures of myself. Yes, they were pictures of ME...in a blond wig that I bought specifically for the shots for him. My friend Mary took the photos and for some reason they were slightly blurry. I think I was wearing black/green panties with fishnet stockings....and a black bra.

"Vanessa" sent the pictures to Maurice and furthermore boldly told him that she "worked part-time with Michele." I held my breath and figured he would surely catch on to the fact the photos were really ME (Michele). But he didn't seem to realize! Maybe into the blurry part of the photos, he was able to project a lot of imagination and make them out to be whatever he wanted them to be. Who knows!

Maurice told "Vanessa" that her photos were nice and then he proceeded to tell "Vanessa" ...."Michele is nice but not my type."

I remember staring and staring at the pictures, and of course, I could tell they were me. —But I knew. What I couldn't figure out was how he didn't know. Did he just want someone young and "controllable"? Perhaps this charade was really a joke on me! Was I being punked?

Maurice's interest seemed turned up a notch, so "Vanessa" told Maurice that she had a boyfriend. Maurice didn't seem at all phased by that. It almost seemed like he suddenly began playing the part of the "wiser older guy" who thought he should advise "Vanessa" on relationship matters.

As things continued, "Vanessa" mentioned Michele a few more times and mentioned her own fictitious boyfriend constantly. I realized I was having a bit too much fun. I was beginning to feel great concern that I had gone too far, although I wasn't ready to just give the whole thing up yet. "Vanessa" would constantly ask Maurice questions and play dumb and he would give her his opinion about this or that. "Vanessa" would often mention something the boyfriend and she were doing or planning to do. Maurice seemed undeterred and possibly took that as a challenge.

I speculated that quite possibly Maurice liked the idea of winning "Vanessa" over. And he may have also felt more secure thinking that since she had another guy in the picture she wouldn't get too attached and expect too much of him. I don't know.

But, eventually it all got boring because I was still ME and not some fantasy blond girl. I had to face the fact that sometimes people just aren't interested in whatever I am. Does that hurt, of course it does!

After a while, I kind of think Maurice just got sick of "Vanessa" going on and on about another guy and never making plans with him as he sometimes hinted towards. Things just ended after about a month.

Years later I saw the show "Catfish" on TV and was shocked there was a name for playing a fictitious role... as I did. I see people who get hurt, and it makes me sick. I don't understand how anyone can string someone along for more than an extremely short time. And I don't understand how anyone can cultivate a love interest without meeting in person early on. A friendship, yes. A love interest, no. I don't think deceit is a good thing. I think it is wrong. And I feel a bit ashamed to say I did that myself.

The only thing I can say to defend myself is that I, as "Vanessa", didn't make plans with or promises to Maurice. And I mentioned Michele and a boyfriend numerous times. So, I was essentially glaringly saying, "I know Michele, and also I am not really available." Hurting Maurice was not the intention, although what exactly it was is now unclear even to me. Marilyn was beautiful...I am not...and my ego got hurt. That I know.

The odd thing is, it was this very situation with sending Maurice photos and <u>gaining a grain of approval</u> that sent me back into a phase where I wanted to be photographed. I had gone through such a phase for a short time during my 20's but then quit. However, the whole "Maurice/Vanessa-experience" opened up that can of worms all over again. My friends and I began photographing each other.

Amusingly, before Maurice and I actually met in person for coffee, he had sent me a couple photos of himself. I had shown his picture to my friend Karen at work and this lead to many future laughs.

She razzed me about him until I left that job. "Michele, do you remember that time.... when you called Maurice A GOD?"

I had made my assessment from his photo and his nice arm muscles and bare back, and not from a place of knowing his character or our compatibility at all. At least my dear friend and I both got plenty of laughs out of that situation.

Maurice is probably a really nice guy who just thought he was slumming it with me. But, things aren't even always about the quality of each person individually...it's about the <u>combination</u> of the two people together. It's literally about the chemistry and fit...communication or lack there-of.

Even if I wasn't up to par in Maurice's mind, that is ok. I had plenty of flings with other guys who were more fun and a couple of them even better looking. And that was all coming up...because my mid-life crisis sexcapades had just begun!

Personal Ads, Part 2:

I don't recall who answered whose personal ad...I think he answered mine... but somehow I ended up sending a couple photos to a guy named Chase who was friends with another college student named Seth. (I sent him the same photos that "Vanessa" sent Maurice.)

I was told that Chase passed my scantily clad photos along because Seth was into photography. And so this interesting little saga in my life began... and because my email address at the time came up "MM" on the screen, often that is what these two guys called me.

Seth was about 22. At one point he invited me to come over to Chase's apartment for a photo session. (It was just us two.) There was a mattress on the floor between the livingroom and kitchen and Seth took photos of me, but I couldn't figure out what was taking so long to develop them.

Then several weeks later he claimed that they weren't even good enough to show me. He said the lighting was bad and created too many shadows. Bummer! I do know his hands were <u>really shaking</u> when he was taking the first set of shots.—Then we had sex.

Even though I don't recall Seth having a beard at the time, I do remember he had slightly long hair and nice features. I said something to him about how he sort of looked like Jesus. I told him we should take a picture of me looking like Marilyn and him looking like Jesus. He said that might be too sacrilegious. He was probably right.

Seth then took some weird naked photos of me with a paper mache bird mask on instead. It was so freaky, strange. I resisted at first, but I guess I just went along with it because he convinced me it was artsy... and he was sexy. I remember telling my co-worker Karen about that and she teased me for some time to come. "Remember that weird bird mask…?" Seth definitely had some interesting work at the time I knew him…"outside the box artsy".

Chase was 25 and a real interesting character. He bragged he could give any girl multiple orgasms…he was pretty cocky. Chase had curly dark brown hair and a wicked spunky personality. He had been in-and-out of college, not going straight through, so that is why he was older than most of his friends. He seemed like a real partier…totally wild…but with a sweet side too. His eyes were jade green and intense.

Anyway, at one point I got together at my place with both Chase and Seth. Once I met Chase, we were always pushing limits. Again Chase launched into his boast about orgasms. The three of us started out on the bed together, but the truth is, both guys were kind of strong personalities and pulling me in opposite directions.—Things were getting bumpy! The whole mish-mash was awkward and within a couple minutes we laughed it off and did things in separate twos afterall. Chase insisted, "I'm always first."

At some point, I guess Chase decided it would make him popular to bring his other friends over to my place to mess around. He just began doing it and I'd typically have very short notice. We never really discussed such a situation either…it all just began. So there was a year or two in my 30's I was with a handful of guys. I have to say, Chase had some really attractive friends: Matt, Jon, Steve, Alan, Jaron.

I was only with these friends, but I saw Matt and Jaron multiple times at my place. Jaron was 30, while the other guys were early 20's. I kept a stash of condoms in a fancy dish on my nightstand. This time period in my life seemed exciting *at first*. But, as time went on things just seemed more "iffy" in general.

Matt wanted me to get together with him and also his cousin who would be in town visiting over Christmas. I was hesitant, but I did so because Matt said it would mean a lot to him and he had become my favorite guy I was messing around with at the time.—I remember leaving my family's holiday gathering faster than normal to see the two men back at my place. Matt was down-to-earth and talked to me a lot. I liked having sex with him.

Then, Jaron started causing some problems.—Turns out he was grappling with a drug addiction relapse. Interesting thing is, my Mom had met Jaron at a community event and told me that there was a very attractive man, not far from my age and he would be a very polite guy for me to date. I asked what his name was and I was amazed The Universe put him in her path and she came to that conclusion.—What were the odds?! I informed her I already knew him and he was definitely not my match. I never fully explained the situation but over time she realized I was right, as she continued to see him in town and could tell that he had some issues. We still mention this "odd fate thing" to each other now and then ...20 years later. Well, at least my Mom picked out someone handsome.

At one point Chase said he had a friend and he wanted me to help him lose his virginity. He pointed him out to me in a store. I told Chase that I didn't think that that was a good idea because the guy looked about 18-19 and really timid. He told me his friend was older, but that was beside the point. The guy looked very bashful. I said he shouldn't be pushed into sex and should probably wait until he had a real girlfriend and not a 35 year old woman giving him his introduction.

I could deal with the guys who had desire and attitude, but I wasn't so sure I wanted to risk getting involved with someone who might actually take all of this casual nonsense to heart and get hurt in the process. I don't know who that young man ended up with, but I hope his first encounter was with the right, age-appropriate girl...it wasn't with me. Men shouldn't be pushed into sex any more than women should.

At this point I began questioning things. I had been married the later half of my 20's to a man who had kept pushing me into situations I didn't want to get involved in. But I could no longer put the blame on anyone else but myself! Life is a series of new decisions every single day. I lived with my husband, was legally bound to him, and felt I had public appearances to keep up. But I could walk away from Chase if I wanted to. And I didn't publically date any of his friends. I guess I just wasn't ready to quit the sex-circus quite yet. But several different things happened... and the time to get out was soon coming.

Situation One:

I think perhaps the whole situation involving limits came to a head the night Chase asked me to come to his apartment for a party.

I went to his place with no preconceived notions about what kind of party he would throw. It turns out four of his cute friends showed up.—-I was with them all before, and with them all that night...Jon, Matt, Alan and Jaron. I went into the bedroom and stayed until I went home. What went on in the livingroom....I have no idea. I left because I had work the next day.

I was drinking water, I was totally sober, and this was the only time I ever did this. I knew all the men from previous encounters, I was attracted to each of them, and honestly it was fun. Let me say, four hot guys are not a bad thing...but, I really just wanted to find that ONE good guy who was closer to my age and worth all of them put together.

I remember it being very windy and cold out that night, and by the time I left the party and walked in drizzling rain a bunch of blocks back to my place, I had a sore throat and ear ache that lasted a couple weeks. I admit, I wasn't dressed very warmly. I had some short black dress with those tacky fishnet stockings that you put on each leg separately. And the band at the top of each leg feels funny and they keep inching down and you have to hike them back up. Those stockings were so weird and were part of a phase which I ditched. They may look good in movies but they feel funny in real life.

Situation Two:

This situation was the ultimate mess. I had been with Chase's friend Jaron a handful of times and he typically acted really respectful. But one night he showed up at my apartment complex and called me from the lobby and I buzzed him in. By the time he was standing at my door he had three friends with him and was expecting me to mess around. Jaron confessed he had hidden the guys out of the sight of the lobby camera when he called me. I had never met the other guys before and was not interested but admit I went along anyway. I was with 2 out of three friends that night.

Jaron told me one of the guys had seen me before and wanted to meet me. While crawling into bed, that guy looked around my room and said he knew what to get me for my birthday already.—That was rather sweet but also felt odd. It felt funny too that the guy himself claimed he had "seen me around a few times" but I didn't recall ever seeing him.

The second guy started pouting about some family problems while we were "doing-it". And the third guy got mad his friends were taking so long and said he just wanted to go home and flicked a cigarette butt into my fishtank. (The fish was fine but I was ticked-off.)

Jaron shoo'd his friends away then and came back to my place. I read him the riot act about how I did not want him bringing anyone else around and how not telling me and giving me a choice felt weird. The truth is I only went along with it because of a deep inner fear of being forced if I wouldn't comply. To me a choice is not something you have to make under pressure. Or at least in a situation like this, there is no reason to have to.

Eventually, Jaron burned his bridges with me on two other occasions when he was loopy and acting very strange. He became egotistical, illogical, whiney, two-faced and rude when he was taking something. There is nothing appealing at all about that. And naïve me, I didn't realize he even had a problem until someone else told me. I do NOT want to be with guys on drugs.

At one point Jaron actually had my apartment key because after sleeping overnight he couldn't get up in the morning and I had to go to work. So he stayed in bed and locked up my apartment with the spare. But for some reason, Jaron would never return the key. I got tired of asking for it. Chase is the one who actually helped me get the key back. HOW did he do it?

It just so happened, on one really weird night Jaron came to my apartment and insisted on posing in his undies while acting like a fool...I had my Polaroid camera! I can't recall exactly what all he did but he ate cereal and catsup and a couple other things all mixed up... and was just flailing around and being dramatic and rough. He left his photos behind. So...when Jaron wouldn't give me my key back, Chase used the pictures as leverage to get him into returning it. Thankfully it worked. I was grateful! Chase really came through for me on that one.

Situation Three:

Now this one is hard to swallow. Ok...maybe that is a bad way to word it. There is a double-standard for men and women still. I was spending time with all these studly guys and they seemed to think they were pretty cool. I genuinely liked the handful Chase introduced me to and I chose to spend time with. But one day I heard my friend Chase refer to someone as "a cum bucket". I remember saying, "What?!?" He repeated himself with a giggle. I suddenly woke up. That was the worst thing I ever heard!

If he was calling some other girl that, I am sure he was calling me that behind my back. As crude and insulting as it was, I was glad I heard it. It stopped me in my tracks and I was done!—Well, nothing quite that dramatic. I still liked Matt and saw him until the end of the semester. But then the semester ended ...and that was when I quit! I never saw Chase or any of his friends ever again once summer came. I told Chase I was busy and I was. Soon...A new man came along and derailed me for a while.

During the same years I knew Chase and his friends, I also had a couple gal pals and we took Polaroids of each other in cheesecakey poses. One friend gave her photos to her husband. Another friend used hers to motivate her to work out more. I gave mine away to several different guys. **This whole time period was a fun time when I experimented...sort of like a consolation prize because I wasn't finding Mr. Right.**

How do I look back at this time in my life? Brief. Desperate. Fun. Quite amusing. Foolish. Somewhat regretful...but not too regretful. Good I got out when I did. Grateful that I was lucky, because so many things could have gone very badly and I could have regretted a whole lot more. **Did I say FUN? It was!**

<u>Caution:</u> **I think it is important to realize I was in my 30's and NOT a teen when I did the things just previously mentioned.**

These types of experiences all require good communication, common sense, birth control, condoms for protection, and enough

self-esteem to walk away or deal with things if something goes terribly wrong.

Risky behavior!

Nunny said....

I had never confided in my Nunny about anything going on in my sex life. But yet...she began telling me I reminded her of her Aunt Rose. This is a lady I never met or saw a photo of. Nunny said that Aunt Rose (who was my Great Aunt) slept with various men and it was rumored that some of the men she knew may have even been mobsters. Nunny said Aunt Rose mysteriously drown one night when she and some others were taking a boat across a lake to some big party on the other side. The boat tipped over and Aunt Rose couldn't swim (neither can I). Some people suspected her death might not have been an accident. I think Nunny told me this story about 5 times. I have no idea how she drew the conclusion that I was similar to the woman. I wish I could have met her. I guess Nunny just kinda knew me.

I think telling me about my Aunt was Nunny's way of saying, "I know you aren't staying at home praying on Friday nights."

When I was 36: I met Kyle less than a month before I turned 37. I was on my way to work and walking through the student union building on campus. **He approached me with the silly line, "WHAT did you do to your hair?"**

My hair was colored light red and needed touching up. I couldn't figure out why he was in my face. He was cute and obviously a few years younger (8 to be exact). He asked me for my phone number and I just giggled...declined.... and went to work.

But later that same day, during the lunch hour, I ran into him again at a convenience store.—That was odd. I was a captive audience because I was waiting in a long line to get a drink and chips. Kyle was dressed up and claimed he had just been in some final for a scene acting class. He wasn't a theatre major but said he had taken such a class. By the end of our conversation, I broke down and gave him my phone number.

He called and called that night and I never picked up. I thought he was too young for me...I wanted a relationship! But the next day he called again and I answered. I figured, "What the hell." Kyle and I began dating.

I was all dolled up and met him in the lobby of my apartment building. I remember him literally picking me up...lifting me high above his head...as I was screaming and laughing. I was shocked at how strong he was. He came back the following night too. That night we had sex while watching a video on my bed. Kyle quickly moved from "let's get together" to giving me puppy-dog eyes and acting like he was going to perish at the thought of leaving me.

It was after the second time Kyle left my place that I had the most odd experience. I had just said good-bye to him and then returned to lay down on the bed where he had just been. **As soon as I made contact with the mattress it felt like a ball of energy moved across the bed and went right into me.** It was so peculiar and like nothing I ever felt before. I didn't actually SEE the energy but in my mind I always thought of it as gold. I have no idea what it was or how maybe it has affected me. But sometimes I thought it was the reason I had a hard time breaking off our relationship sooner. For the following two years I was too emotional to be logical.

I found myself in a very odd situation because Kyle immediately threw around the "love-word". We ended up living together pretty quickly. I was hesitant... it was *his* idea and he wouldn't take no for an answer. He moved into my small apartment. **He said I had to be "Cleopatra to his Marc Antony."—It was so corny.** I thought he was pushy actually. I just gave in.

No good single guy close to my age was on the horizon. Kyle poured on all the gooey charm he could. He kept grabbing my hand and reciting lines from "The Princess Bride" movie at me when we were out in public.

Early in our relationship, I told Kyle that I had been Marilyn Monroe during my last past life. So he began to call me Marilyn as well as Michele. Unfortunately I also soon found out he had some kind of "momma-complex" and he then began calling me "Momma" a lot.— I was shocked the first time and asked him to stop... which he didn't. So I was then called Michele, Marilyn...and Momma. He also made up words and acted like a little boy when he wanted his own way. That did not turn me on. I told myself, "Kyle's just creative"...it helped... temporarily.

Kyle also gave me a framed high school photo of his real Mom to hang in my bedroom. Her name is Bonnie. Pretty. At first he seemed to cherish it. But later I got the impression he had a love-hate relationship with her.

Sex, sex, sex....

Kyle was pretty good looking...with radiant blue eyes... but our sex life was just so-so and got worse over time. (Don't call me "Momma" if you want to screw me!) **However, on that note...he is the only guy I have ever had sex with in my childhood home.** During one visit, Kyle followed me to the back of the basement where I was checking on the laundry and he grabbed me and bent me over in front of the dryer and pulled down my jeans. I would never have thought to do that there because I love my parents who are very religious and won't allow premarital sex under their roof no matter how long I know the guy. But so many years have passed since then. I still feel a bit guilty.... but also think, "Wow!"

<u>So let me broach this distasteful subject now.</u>

I recently read some article about a guy who claimed that he had been Marilyn's lover and had the inside scoop on all her sexual preferences. Supposedly he wrote a book that was even going to reveal whether she liked anal sex.—Who cares! I don't know one way or another what she thought of it, as that is simply not part of the memories about that lifetime which have resurfaced. But...who cares?!? That's another Marilyn book I will never pick up! (There were more important things in that lifetime.)

During our first year together Kyle was working at a computer lab and doing a lot of "guy talking". He came home one day convinced that he was missing out on something because he had never "gone up the butt" and he claimed his friends were raving about it. After saying "no" many times, I caved in. Yep, it was still as painful at age 37 as it was at age 24. I had tried it twice with Trevor too. Thankfully both guys dropped the subject after a couple times. But the first time Kyle taped it. Again, something to be thankful for, the computer it was saved on went haywire and kaput!

I figured I would just explain my take on this act, lest the idea come up in anyone's imagination as I am talking about all of my crazy experiences.—End of that! No thank you! I may be crazy but I'm not THAT CRAZY!

Marilyn...Michele...Momma...

Over time, I felt more and more conflicted as I actually felt like Kyle wanted me to "be like a Mom to him". I suppose I hung on because of the times he called me "Marilyn" which I liked. And I appreciated that he liked to dress up in suits, wore really nice colognes, and was somewhat musical. He dabbled on the piano and guitar...and he "thought" he could sing. Yes, I am a girl who is a sucker for someone who performs or gives it a good shot.

Kyle introduced me to what became one of my biggest addictions of all time...chai tea! We went to a lot of movies our first year together. Kyle loved to roam around big stores and he especially liked the jewelry and electronics. He kept claiming we should marry. At his insistence, we (I) purchased some man-woman engagement rings. Kyle kept saying he wanted to have kids with me. I told him my tubes were already tied and we shouldn't rush into marriage because of our age difference. He said he would change my mind...he seemed sure if it.

Kyle would constantly use phrases that at first seemed respectful and endearing, but as time went on I thought they were more manipulative. He liked to say things like, "I honor you" or "I did it to honor them." I am not sure where that came from but after a while I realized he honored very few people and in fact turned on them. For instance he had a young friend he met at a computer lab. He and the guy began palling around more and more. They began going out to eat together and going to the gym. I was glad he had a friend. But then Kyle began saying he thought he was the younger mans "mentor". Down-the-line, the friend told me that Kyle was bossy and trying to make him into "a clone of himself". —Ego! I guess he didn't really like people unless they "listened to his wisdom".

That was actually another phrase he used. Kyle would say, "Thank you for your wisdom." But I soon caught on that he didn't really listen to what others told him. He just thought that made him sound good. For a while he even tried to dictate to me what color of hair I should have.— Uh...no!

One time I asked Kyle, "Why are you even with me?" He said, "Because people like you everywhere we go."—I was shocked. OK, so they liked me, but I'm not really sure he did. Kyle continued to say, "I honor you."

So....what were Kyle's good points again??? Here's a winning point.

It should be noted that Kyle met my Nunny the year she was living with my parents and slowing down.—She was in her mid 80's. She seemed to really light up when he came into the room. I think she recognized that he was "cute boy" even if other things didn't make sense to her anymore. Kyle would talk to her and one time he kind of ballroom danced with her in the livingroom.

On another occasion Kyle and I took Nunny on a drive around town and she sat in the back seat eating candy and seemed very happy. It meant a lot to me that Kyle was kind to her. He told me, "Even though she is having problems, I can still tell who she really is." Of course this was very endearing and hard to overlook. It melted my heart that Kyle and Nunny got along well. He went with me to visit her when she eventually went into a home.

The big exam...

At first I thought Kyle was ambitious about having a career in real estate. He talked about it all the time. He talked fast and dreamed and schemed about getting rich quick. I soon realized he was very unrealistic. I asked a woman in the biz to chat with him about the practical realities of it. She tried but said he wouldn't listen. He was so sure he was going to succeed quickly and *in his mind* talking to someone who actually worked their way up the ladder in real estate was a waste of his time. I have no idea who or what gave him that much arrogant confidence. He hated to hear about "paying dues and working his way up". I tried to explain it, and he always protested.

Eventually Kyle took a real estate class, but he did terrible on the test because he was a know-it-all who didn't think he needed to study. He took the real estate exam a second time. Failed again. At first, he blamed it on his study partner. He said he had to spend so much time explaining things to her that he didn't do well.—That made no sense. The truth is, he told me himself that he didn't have to read the book to ace the test. Failing twice seemed to push him over the deep end. He was beside himself! He blamed it on the State of Pennsylvania then. He decided it would be easier to pass the test in California.

California called....

About 10 months after we met, Kyle took off for SanDiego while I was at work. —He left a note on my computer keyboard. It said he was going to Boston, but then he contacted me and said he really went to California. I was in shock... confused and heartbroken. I should have just let it go and gotten on with my life. I probably should have stayed in Pennsylvania. Various people bombarded me with reasons why I should stay.

(The only thing I can say to defend my decision is that I doubt I would have met my current boyfriend Jay down-the-line if I hadn't switched jobs.)

I was very attracted to a curly haired co-worker named Chris who had big blue eyes.—We got together. A cute drummer named Steve also came into the picture and tried to convince me to stay.—I spent a month dating him. Steve had the most wonderful dog named Charlie. He was a greyhound-collie mix, and he used to crawl in bed with us in the morning. I loved that dog, he was so cute! Even people at work tried to convince me not to go but somehow nothing pierced my logic. Maybe it was all about "feeling rejected" because Kyle left me... so maybe I thought I had to try to "undo the rejection" by hanging on. It's hard to say for sure.

While apart, Kyle was still always emailing and calling me, even though I got the impression he was involved with some Spanish girl in California. I didn't think Kyle and I were necessarily a good match... yet I seemed unable to throw in the towel and tell him to stop calling. What was it that I was addicted to? Was it that mysterious ball of energy that attached itself to me after he was in my bed? Did it keep me bound to him for a time?

Kyle bought me an airline ticket and I gave up my good job, fabulous apartment and life in my hometown. I moved to SanDiego, CA... to be with this man who called me both "Marilyn" and "Momma". I love Pennsylvania but had lived there all my life. For years I had had friends who moved away and urged me "to get out in the world and see new things." So, I finally made plans to go! And afterall, I would be closer to Hollywood. I gave my sister my beloved goldfish. I gave her kids a bunch of toys and dolls. I gave my neighbor friend my furniture. I was off!

Kyle moved to California in May 2002, driving across the country in is gold Camry. I retired from The University the same summer my Dad did. But thankfully I was still around to attend his office retirement lunch before I left the state. **I took a plane to San Diego in August 2002.**

Kyle met me at the airport. As he drove me to our new apartment he rattled off, "This freeway is here and this freeway there."— And this is what makes the "Saturday Night Live" sketch about "The Californians" so accurate and funny to me. In California we were always going down the highways...and they were all very confusing to me.

Our first apartment was small but clean. The location wasn't great but I urged Kyle to get an inexpensive place, and therefore we were a good distance from any really ritzy stores or fancy office buildings. Our landlady was a very friendly, talkative woman named Judy. She was delightful. I didn't know anyone in the whole state accept for Kyle... and there she was, smiling and welcoming towards me every time I saw her. Her office was across from the apartment postal boxes and the community laundry area. She would ask me to sit down across from her desk and visit. Thank God Judy's friendly face made my transition from Pennsylvania much easier.

At first things were new and fun, but Kyle and I only had one car. Kyle went to work during the day and I did laundry and spent hours on the internet and watching TV. It was the first year the Dr. Phil show was on and I watched five days a week. Finally after a couple months, I bought a used red BMW with some state retirement money when I finally received the check.

Then I found employment through a couple different temp agencies that took turns finding me assignments. I really liked some of the women who found me jobs and I'll never forget their kindness...Tammy and Sabrina. My jobs ranged anywhere from one day to 2 months. People always seemed so grateful I showed up for assignments. I guess they didn't want to be stuck answering the phone.

As time went by, Kyle seemed to be increasingly imagining that I was with this guy or that guy. For instance, he would arrange for a water delivery guy to come by when he knew only I would be home...and then he would accuse me of having sex with him.—I didn't. I told him to change the delivery times so that he could be home too then. But I distinctly recall a time that he answered the door and then called me out into the kitchen when there was no reason at all for me to be there and he knew I still had a nightgown on. He accused me of being with some package delivery guy too.

During the 10 months I was in California, we moved from Lakeside to Poway to Rancho Bernardo....but all my jobs were in SanDiego. Kyle was always trying to get us a fancier apartment so we kept changing our address. At the first place we had, we furnished the bathroom with two round, bright red fluffy rugs. Kyle called them "The Marilyn Monroe Rugs". They seemed quite special...for a day or two. Then they began to shed like a collie dog! There were red fuzzies all over the room... and then the fuzz traveled into the hall. They shed and shed and the whisps still kept coming. It seemed like an endless supply, yet the rugs still looked thick! Needless to say, we did not take them to our next abode. Like Marilyn herself, those rugs are long gone but made a lasting impression! (Is that egotistical to say?)

At first he worked as a "talent scout" in a modeling agency, but then he became disenchanted because the commissions would almost always fall through. Kyle claimed he was tired of swindling young girls and their families into buying expensive modeling classes and make-up packages which he knew most couldn't really afford. He said some parents would go into debt because they didn't want to crush their young daughter's dreams after they had been "discovered" in a crowd and told that they were beautiful and modeling material. Kyle said he felt like he was selling a false dream. He also said a lot of people would agree to buy a package deal and then not do so. Therefore he constantly got his hopes up that his commission was going to be much better than it ever turned out to be. It was during this period that a lot of my good jewelry went to the pawn shop and was never seen again...gone. But at least at this time, I thought Kyle seemed empathetic toward other people...he didn't want to dupe people on his job.

Kyle got a new job in the financial field. But as good as that seemed at first, things began to disintegrate. Kyle was very envious of some manager who was five years younger. He was often perturbed that the guy was higher up in the company and jealous that the guy had gotten a lady pregnant and therefore he had a son. Kyle was already 31 and he said one of his life goals was to have a child by the time he was 30. He felt he had fallen behind. He often told me we should have a child together.

The manager he was so envious of had visitations with his child, but could also live the single life. He pulled Kyle into the strip club scene. Kyle began going out with the boys after work on a regular basis and he'd come home later and later...sometimes not til 5:00am. He went from being a seemingly doting boyfriend to being absent until the wee hours of the morning several nights a week. I never knew what to expect, he never told me beforehand. I felt pretty alone and devastated.

But eventually I also realized this was not the beginning of his lies. I found a photo of one of his "models" hidden at the back of a closet. Kyle said they went to Disneyland together. I got the impression there was more to the story than that. He often called the models "Princess" but told me it meant nothing. He said he was simply "trying to flatter dumb silly girls who everyone has pampered because they are pretty." But I suspected more to it.

By May 2003, things had eventually become so weird between us and I became extremely depressed. It also didn't help that temp jobs were interesting but also inconsistent. I was off-and-on employed. At one point Kyle backed me up against a wall and was just about to slap me across the face but stopped short of doing that. I don't even know what set him off. I think it was something small. He never did that again.

Now, here is something that drifted throughout our relationship. Just like with my ex-husband, Kyle had a long sob story about all the people who had done him wrong in the past. And somehow he felt that that gave him permission to be odd with me.

His sob stories ranged anywhere from multiple bad relationships within his family, to an ex-wife he called bitchy, to step kids he said broke them up, to a time he was molested as a teen. I felt badly... and I stayed...

Why isn't this lifetime working out?

Then...one night I took blue over-the-counter sleeping pills and didn't give a damn about waking up. Afterall, I was 38...I had already outlived Marilyn by two years. I threw the boxes out in the dumpster across the apartment complex, so no one would know what I took.

I passed out after about 30 seconds of experiencing my heart rate rapidly decrease to barely existent. I was ready to move on. I was in despair then peace. But oddly enough, Kyle came home much earlier than usual that evening and found me out-of-it. He called an ambulance. I have no recollection of anything between the time I passed out and the time I was awake again. It's still odd to me that I don't remember an inbetween life state. Maybe I just thought I was close to dying but wasn't.

I woke up in a hospital bed the next day. Kyle was at my side and said they pumped my stomach. He said they also wanted to do a spinal tap but he convinced them not to. I pulled the catheter out of me.... It actually took quite a bit to work it out. I was still in a paper gown.

Then, a handsome dark haired doctor named Brad-something came into the room. He paced in front of me and said he didn't know if he should discharge me because "taking 16 pills is quite serious." I just smiled and kept my mouth shut. Kyle convinced the doctor that he would take good care of me. I got dressed and we left.

As we got to the parking lot, I asked Kyle why the doctor thought I took 16 pills. Kyle said I mumbled something about 16. I said, "Oh. Well, I took 6 packs of 16 pills...so I took 96."

I honestly couldn't believe that I was still alive. I didn't feel either good or bad about it. I just kept breathing and immediately wondered where I would get my next job. I also noticed that Kyle had begun wearing some new cologne and it was really awful. His old ones were much nicer. It all seemed so symbolic.

During this time we were constantly switching back-and-forth which vehicle each of us was driving. It all depended on which one he deemed most prestigious at the moment. One day I found a bag of fancy chocolates and several pairs of cute new underpants in the trunk of one of the cars. He said that they were for me. I really didn't believe him. But since he had given me a couple nice rings for holidays, I told myself it could be true.

Life after the blue pill...

Anyway, after I came home from the hospital, I immediately got a bunch of temp jobs and met more nice people around San Diego. Things were better for a couple weeks and then they went back to bad.

Kyle had an affair with a pretty young woman who was his client. He had to drive to her house to get her to sign some financial paperwork. Her name was Lisa-something and she had two small boys and lived in a ritzy neighborhood. Kyle seized the opportunity to screw her and spoil the children so he could play Daddy and fulfill his dream of being a father by age 30....by then he was 31. I saw a photo of Lisa and she was small, tattooed, blond and pretty. But Kyle always said he hated tattoos and she had more than I did. I think he was also in love with her house. He told me several times that "some actors live in the area".

At one point Kyle got into an auto accident with Lisa. She was driving her van and turned off the highway at a high rate of speed and rolled over. She hurt her leg but would recover. He called me and asked me to pick him up at some hospital in the middle of the night. I had no idea where I was going but mapquested directions and found him. Kyle had some bruises on his face and a sore arm, but was getting around. I drove him to a doctor's appointment the next day. But a few days later he went back to her. I guess I was just his "Momma" and she was the "sexpot".—How ironic really. **There I was....living in California...and losing my man to a blond! Karma.**

Lisa called me up and griped about all the things she thought Kyle was doing wrong with her kids.—There was a long list. She seemed to want empathy. But yet, she was mad at me when he would call me. She would scream so loudly I could hear her through the phone. Nevertheless, he chose her. At the time I didn't realize what a blessing this was. I was sad...and had become very thin. I briefly looked for my own apartment but then gave up. I could really only afford a room in a house.

Meanwhile, I made arrangements to fly back to Pennsylvania. I began shipping back my bigger items and my parents arranged to have my car hauled across country. Our apartment phone got disconnected and I didn't own a cell phone. I remember calling my Mom from a pay phone and constantly feeding it quarters.

When Kyle realized I was really going he suddenly decided to stay at our apartment with me. When I intended to sleep on the couch, he insisted I sleep in the bed with him. He kept saying I should stay in California but just move to a different apartment. He even introduced me to a girl named Teri and said that we should be roommates. But she had a young child and really not much room. Teri was nice and we ended up keeping in touch even after I left the state. Kyle seemed to want to keep me waiting in the wings just in case he needed me. But I wanted to be *wanted*...not just needed.

I had moved to California to be his girlfriend. Thank God I had never done anything rash during all those months he kept saying we should get married and adopt a child... or I should get my tubes untied! He really tried to manipulate me to do so.

I returned Kyle's Mother's high school picture to him. He had left it behind when he moved from Pennsylvania to California. It was with him again.

Kyle gave up trying to convince me to stay as he drove me to the airport. We barely got there in time for me to check-in and catch the flight. We ran to the proper area and were out of breath. The security made a big deal about scanning my luggage and seemed especially suspicious of some troll dolls and went over them with a wand. I also had a bottle of vitamins that caught their glare. Thankfully the trolls and I were all allowed to board.

I sat next to a couple really nice guys on the plane and we opted to spend our layover together, although we were all going in different directions. The guys had beers and I had something else. We three chatted. Then the dark haired man told me I was pretty and got on his plane. The blond guy stayed so long to hang out with me that he missed his flight. I had reminded him it was time to go but he just kept talking. He was in the Navy and going off to some base. He got assigned an alternative flight.

So, I had companions for what could have been a boring or depressing time at the airport. We emailed each other the next day just to say we had arrived safely at our destinations. I was back in PA. It was time to pick up the pieces of my life...again. **My Mom told me I didn't have to be in a hurry to find my own place.**

The California experience...

My 10 months in California were over, and I only spent half a day in LosAngeles...and I didn't even see Marilyn and Jane Russell's stars on the sidewalk or visit the Hollywood sign. I did, however, purchase a replica of the Oscar Award at an LA gift shop. It's in our bedroom in Indiana now. It says "Hollywood Best Couple" on it. And I think that applies quite nicely to the love of my life Jay and me.

One good thing, Kyle and I did hang out at the pool at the Hotel DelCoronado a handful of times. We never stayed the night but we ate some good meals there. I bought a book about the lady ghost who supposedly haunts the place. And I found out that this particular hotel was the backdrop in one of Marilyn's movies... "Some Like It Hot". I don't think visiting there stirred any new memories though. As a matter of fact, I don't think I thought about past life stuff while in California... not deeply anyway.

The day before I left California, Kyle gave me a CD with a bunch of Marilyn's show tunes. He bought it at the hotel. I didn't really think I'd enjoy the music, but truthfully I was surprised to discover Marilyn could sing for real! (I remember as Marilyn being insecure about my voice.) I played the CD in my car every morning the first month I was back to work in Pennsylvania. It was somehow comforting...uplifting. I began a new job, but I didn't go back to the college. It was at a broadband management company not far from the campus, and across from a McDonald's and a shopping mall. This seemed like the perfect location!

California calling...again....

Now, one would expect this to be the end of the Kyle-saga...but it wasn't. Before I left California, I had gone to see a psychic. She told me Kyle would want me back in about 6 months.

So when I first returned to Pennsylvania, I carried his photo around and told people he was going to want me back. In fact, it was a photo of him, dressed in black, standing in the modeling agency he had worked for and holding a fake pink rose. I thought he looked cute. The lady at my new job smirked but was kind.

Not only that, but one day my parents, some of their religious friends and an Aunt and Uncle of mine traveled to a church in Johnstown because there was someone there who could supposedly perform miracles. You were supposed to think of what miracle you wanted when you walked up the isle to receive your blessing. I of course was still somewhat broken inside and prayed for Kyle to beg me back. That was really all I kept thinking about at the time.

Well, I'll be darned. Six months after my return from California, Kyle got ahold of my work number and began calling me. I have no idea how he knew where to find me. I told him I had already met someone else and was happy. He did his best to convince me to move back. His relationship with Lisa had fallen apart. Things didn't work out well with her or her boys. As a matter of fact, he seemed to despise them all at that point. He told me a very sordid tale about how things supposedly fell apart. The story he told was a bit depraved. I wasn't happy about all this...but I also wasn't overly sad.

By the time Kyle began calling me, he had already moved onto a new relationship with a lady he met on a beach, but things were already getting shaky. He truly didn't want ME back, it was obvious he just wanted me to rescue him until he found someone else he thought was better. Then he would be off again! I said "No, no, no, NO!"

Kyle made one last ditch effort to win me over. He sent me a cute charm bracelet he remembered I liked at in the Hotel DelCoronado giftshop. And he sent me a note on a Marilyn Monroe postcard. I still have both.

Phoney-Baloney!

But then the story takes an even crazier turn. Kyle emailed me a few times after we were over for good. He told me he had finally found a wife and they were having a child. He said he was working for a real estate company along with some woman, and that his work was very stressful because he had to manage three buildings. I thought he seemed slightly unhappy, while also accomplished. I assumed he had finally passed a real estate test and reached his dream. I didn't know what to think. I sent him back some encouraging response to keep going for his goals...something like that. We had been apart for several years at that point.

One night (around 2009) I was watching "Ghost Whisperer" on TV, and out-of-the blue I decided to google Kyle's name. I just wanted to see what real estate place he was working for. Up popped the words "scam" and "manhunt". There was no mistaking the news was talking about him because of the photo I was staring at! It turned out that he was wanted in a couple states. Kyle had become a major scammer and swindled multiple people and institutions. He was on the run!

I emailed my Mom and said, "Turns out Kyle is a criminal and on the run. If for any reason he calls you, don't talk to him. The Police want him." I guess I was paranoid.

Apparently Kyle was finally caught and detectives discovered he had quite a bit of incriminating material at his home and appeared to be ready to pull off future scams.

I know that while we were still together Kyle had used some personal information of mine one time to get a laptop I knew nothing about prior to its purchase. However, the thought of him being a big time con was still shocking. I knew he was shifty with me personally, but I thought that was just something he was doing to be mean to me "as his girlfriend". I never saw fake ID's or checks when I lived with him for two years...never. What pushed him over the edge?

His legal battle dragged on and on for several years and I kept watching it unfold through articles online. Half the time he had a public defender...half the time he was his own representation. Kyle once told me, "I could be a lawyer if I wanted." I guess this was his chance to try it! Eventually he admitted to many felonies and was sentenced, I believe, by courts in both states. He did this to himself.

Looking back, I remember years earlier when Kyle wanted to go see the movie "Catch Me If You Can" and he said "that is about me." I should have caught on! I thought maybe Kyle was relating to being a cute guy like Leonardo DiCaprio. But apparently he was relating to being a swindler like the character in the film.

Then, one day I received an email from someone anonymous. They sent me Kyle's address in jail. I replied that I would not be writing.

I sometimes wonder how Kyle is doing, and also what his life will be like one day when he is free. If he wasn't satisfied before lock-up, how on earth is he going to fare when he is an older man, with a record, and hasn't had the chance to raise a child, which he at least claimed was important to him. What kind of job will he get? He often spoke as if he had ideas of grandeur. I do feel deep concern for him now and then. But there is nothing I can do.

I don't know why he ever picked me out of the crowd. I don't think he loved me. But if half of what he told me about his childhood dramas was true, then I guess he really had emotional scars. Unfortunately he hurt others instead of getting counseling and finding a productive way to work things out. **A man who can put so much energy into a con racket, could channel all that know-how into doing something good.** He wasn't stupid.

Part of me will always love him if for nothing else, then because Nunny liked him. He also called me "Marilyn".

Enough with the "sex and tears" already!

During my early thirties I made a good friend in my apartment complex...it was really a condo building, but unlike most of the other tenants, I didn't own my unit, I just rented long-term.

When I was in between boyfriends, I began seeing various guys and a couple ladies in the building became very, very curious...nosey! They sat in the lobby, observed, stopped me and asked questions. And then the next day and the next. They were a mother and daughter who each lived in the same building but on different floors and then rented out a third unit for income.

The Mom was very tiny and fragile looking. And the daughter was 12 years older than I and had just had weight reduction surgery and was working on her fitness. I'll call the daughter "Frenchie" because one time she had me take her picture in a brown wig and we thought she looked like a mysterious cute French woman. She used that in her personals ads for a while.

Anyway, Frenchie and her Mom were suddenly very much in my life. I was constantly talking to them in the lobby or in the laundry room in the basement. Frenchie would just show up on my doorstep and sometimes bring a guy friend from another floor in to watch TV. She didn't have a job for a few years and I'm not sure what he did, but they said they were both hoarders and couldn't sit down in their own units so they would come to hang-out on my couch. Eventually I saw their places and found out their stories were true. But the issue I had was this...I worked all day at a very stressful job....so them showing up at 5:30 PM all spunky and ready to hang was a bit trying. I just wanted to hide.

Eventually the guy cleaned up his apartment because he wanted to impress a girl, and then he moved out of town. But Frenchie and I continued to hang out. Most of the time we shopped and laughed and talked about guys.

Frenchie knew me during the time right after I broke up with Demetri and was going out with lots of young ones. She knew me during the time I was involved with Kyle. And she welcomed me back when I returned from California. By then she had gotten a part-time job and was busier than before. She also met a couple girls who said they were Jehovah Witnesses and they wanted to do good things for people. So Frenchie put them up to clearing out some of her hoard.

But here is something Frenchie would do continually over time, and it really irritated me. She would tell guys I barely knew that I liked them. I would be confounded! Frenchie explained that she figured these men would never give her the time-of-day, so she set me up to see how they treated me and in effect she lived vicariously through my experience. I didn't appreciate this.

When I first left California and moved back to Pennsylvania, I was hoping against all hope that things could work out with Kyle. I began a job a few weeks later. Then there was some guy Frenchie met down-town and she introduced me to him. He wasn't bad looking and was close to my age. As he was about to leave, she ran over to his car door and whispered something, and then I saw him staring back at me. I knew something was up.

Frenchie told him I was attracted to him and then he wanted to meet for coffee. I was not happy, but ended up alone with him at a diner. Turns out the man was very pleasant, and the conversation was jovial, and he was the cousin of someone who worked in the same building where I had just become employed. The more we talked, the more he grew on me.

But here is the thing that made the biggest impression. Somehow in the middle of all of that talk, I confessed that Frenchie had just set us up and I still liked some other guy. He was a good sport, although I think he was trying to break me down. **This man began to tell me that he read some article and it taught him how to give women multiple orgasms. He said it was so effective that often women ended up in tears.** I had never had an orgasm at that point despite all of my dalliances, so my ears perked up.

I wasn't sure I quite believed him and asked him why the women would be crying. He said that continuous orgasms were just so intensely physically demanding and powerful. I think he thought I was sold…I wasn't. I took one look at him…and thought for a long hard moment…… but for the life of me, I didn't actually think that sounded fun at all. I could picture this guy on top of me, and that didn't seem so bad. But why would I want to do something that made me CRY? It just plain sounded draining.

He told me to think about it.—I did. I was fine waiting. I didn't want to have an orgasm with someone who was just proving a point and treating it like an Olympic event. I guess I'll never know if I passed up a complete disaster or the time of my life. But a few weeks later, I met the love of my life. And he managed to "fix my problem" and I've never cried during sex.

I finally met the love of my life!

When I was 39: **This brings me to my next man…the best one…. my boyfriend of 16 years named Jay.** Jay is 4 years older than I am. He is tall, has wavy hair, and freckles on his arms. Jay is a computer programmer who plays in a band on weekends.

I met him a few months before Kyle tried to convince me to move back to California. So when I told Kyle I had someone else, I wasn't lying. Jay's presence truly saved me from even considering the insanity of reuniting with Kyle. I was so happy with Jay within a very short period of time. I was truly bedazzled by his blue eyes, quick wit ...and physical prowess.

So...here is how my story with Jay began.....

Summer 2003:

I got a 40-hour a week job through a temp agency. I listened to my Marilyn CD on the way to work each day and drove my used BMW... which ended up in the garage quite a lot. I began to love country music that year. I thought for sure Kyle would come back to me because of what the psychic in California told me. I still cried as I drove to work most days.

I really didn't talk to many people in the building where I worked since my job was right inside the front door and I had no reason to walk down any of the hallways, accept to go to the restroom nearby.

I also would go to the sink to get water for the plant in the front lobby. When I told my manager that I was Marilyn during my past life, she named the plant "Marilyn" and said I was in charge of taking care of her.

I talked a lot to three very nice ladies, Jane, JoLu and Pam. Eventually another temp worker named Jeff talked to me. But that was about it. I was living in my own little world, trying to mend my heart. Shopping at the mall during lunch hour and eating dinner with my parents in the evenings. One time my Mom and I walked around the neighborhood I grew up in and marveled at all the bigger fancier homes built at the end of the original streets. I was struggling to move on, and every day was still a little painful.

On the job, I sat at the front desk and I had to screen people who came through the door without a badge. It's pretty funny to me that I was considered some form of security. But I had a list of all the employees at my desk, although I barely knew what any of them actually looked like.

I remember that year a lot of crazy calls came in on the always-busy phone lines, because some guy at the back of the building was caught up in some love triangle. Nevertheless, it was a good job which I was lucky to get.

About a month into my job, in strolled Jay. He was energetic, nervous, and gave me a chilly handshake. (For some reason my hands are usually warmer than his.) He proclaimed he had lost his security door badge so he was coming in the front entrance instead of the usual back of the building. I thought he was cute and I didn't notice a ring on his finger.

The next day Jay came back again and apologetically said that HR was working on getting him a replacement badge. I figured I better flirt with him, or else I would never see him again. I thought as quickly as I could ...afterall, I had been Cleopatra and Marilyn during my past lives. Surely I could come up with *something* clever to say.

Michele:	**"May I ask you a personal question?"**
Jay:	**"Yes."**
Michele:	**"Are your eyes really <u>that blue</u> or are you wearing colored contacts?"**
Jay:	**"Are they <u>really</u> blue?"**
Michele:	**"Yes. But I hope you don't think I'm sexually harassing you."** (I had to put the idea in his head...SEX.)
Jay:	**"No."**

*****I felt pretty confident he had gotten "the message". He did.

Ten minutes later Jay called to see if I wanted to go to the mall across the street and get a sandwich for lunch. We went. We talked easily and had a nice first date. This is when I found out Jay was a father and that he and his ex-wife had gone their separate ways almost two years earlier. His ex had taken their small child back to Indiana, which is where they both were originally from. Jay stayed in Pennsylvania because of his good job...and all of the child and spousal support payments he had to make.

Ten minutes after our first lunch date, Jay called to see if I wanted to take a walk in the park with him after work. We walked around the park... we went back to his place and he played music... we took another walk in the wooded area behind his house... we went to his room....we stayed in his room. The rest is history. We were pretty inseparable.

As the days went by, we both found it quite convenient that we worked in the same place. We were on opposite ends of a very long hall, but we continued to get together during lunch hour 2-3 times a week.

I told Jay I like McDonald's a lot. I was happy with a $5 meal and we ate there often...and still do. We were in the restaurant when Jay asked if he could wear one of my big silver rings. I took a band off of my middle finger and Jay wore it for about a month. He doesn't like wearing jewelry but it was a cute gesture that he wore it for a while. The band is still in his top dresser drawer.

Shortly after Jay and I began dating, we did the usual "lover thing" ...which may sometimes be a no-no and trouble-maker. **We decided we were going to tally up how many partners we had "gone all the way with" including each other. I said 31...he said 41.** Jay was amazed and said that for years his family's home phone number ended in "3141". His parents still had that number. We chuckled and said that seemed like a sign.

Our first year of dating was so exciting. We couldn't get enough of each other. Jay is a great lover and I experienced things with him I never had before. Despite doing many things prior, I still had a few sex-glitches to overcome. But....Jay had the cure!

I think I had some residual emotional issues because of the way Marilyn was killed as blue-eyed Bobby stood by. And I wasn't particularly physically sensitive despite all of my enthusiasm for mingling with men. I attribute this to perhaps being the result of several of my past life deaths over the last 200 years... Marilyn's, Lizette's, Charlotte's.

Somewhere along the line, I also realized that Jay reminded me an awful lot of James Dougherty, Marilyn's first husband, who was truly a nice guy. So often during this Michele-life I had thought I had met "a nice guy"...but the guy turned out to be "a bad boy". I really do prefer a nice good man. I don't thrive on lies and being part of a harem.

I know some girls think nice guys are boring and "just friend" mate-rial...but in my experience, they are actually the best lovers. Just because a guy is polite, doesn't mean he won't fuck you really really good. And he will even do it while he's sober, he'll remember your name afterward, and be around next month because he isn't locked up in jail. I feel very very lucky I finally found "a good guy"...one with freckles too.

Swing on by...

Something amazing happened with Jay during our first year together, when we were still living in Pennsylvania.

Jay and I would sometimes discuss our past relationships. I told him about all the sordid stuff I did with my ex-husband who wanted to dabble in the swinging lifestyle. I told him about my mid-life crises during a few years of my 30's. And I asked him if he ever wanted to swing. I don't quite know why I asked him...it wasn't a test.

I think it was mostly because he told me he was still broken up about his marriage falling apart and he said that he had had a hard time going back to the single life initially. When he finally began dating again he found himself in the middle of various strange situations... and then he met me. I kept saying that the only reason he liked me was because the other experiences were so bad.—We would both laugh. The truth is, Jay is actually still long-distance friends with one of the ladies he dated right after his split, but the others were quite entertaining nightmares.

Then Jay and I ended up meeting another couple...although I can't recall how we made initial contact. We talked about swinging and the couple claimed that that is what they were looking for too. The pair was just a little younger than us and fairly attractive. Britt had pretty eyes and a large chest. And Derek was very upbeat and ruggedly appealing. They came to one of Jay's music gigs at a coffee shop and then we also went out to dinner.

But we never had a tryst because it seemed that each time we talked either Britt or I were not feeling well. Derek did talk to us on the phone one night and assured us he was up for pretty much anything and ready to go.

Finally I just happened to run into Derek by chance one morning when I stopped somewhere on my way to work. Derek looked cute with a big bright smile and he told me he thought I was nice and slender. He said they were still interested in getting together and I told him I would talk to Jay. By this point I was pretty in love with Jay so I had mixed feelings about the whole swinging notion. However, since I was the one who had started it I wasn't about to back out.

But I will never forget this...the sweetest thing happened. Jay was sitting at the dinner table and I was standing there telling him about Derek and Britt. He said he thought Britt was attractive and he would definitely have fun....but then he said something else.

He said, "I don't know if I want to do this. I'm really torn. I do, but I don't. You are my <u>special-Michele</u>, and I don't know if I ever want to change that. You are my <u>special-Michele</u>. I want to keep our love sweet." I was completely amazed. If you are with the right person, monogamy is hot!

Here was this man who certainly likes sex and is very good at it... and he was thinking about me...and our relationship...not just "playing stud". This was such a touching thing to me. Afterall, I had experienced men who were aggressive with me, manipulated me, seemed indifferent to me, and seemed to want to sleep around with everybody-and-any-body. This is a real relationship...with a real man...the man who I had been waiting for. It was actually hard to believe I heard those words.

At age 39 I met the man of my dreams. If I had died at age 36 like Marilyn did, I never would have met Jay. If I had died at age 38 when I tried to kill myself in California, I never would have met Jay. I honestly began having the best sex of my life...AFTER that point in time which people like to label "a woman's prime" as far as outward appearance goes.

People who want to judge when our prime is are only out for them-selves. Don't ever let anyone tell you when your prime is! Maybe when I was younger I was prettier...but then again I think a smile on a happy person is very pretty too. And I am very happy with Jay...in a lot of different ways.

Jay and I had so much fun together...

Jay is a musician and at the time we began dating, he would get small one-man gigs at parties, fairs and coffee shops.—I was his biggest fan. We worked out together at the YMCA, and went dancing at a favorite piano bar. We always requested "Lady in Red" ...it was "our song". One particularly fun time we went on a gorgeous scenic hike with a couple of Jay's co-workers. And sometimes we grocery shopped as a couple and then made meals together at his home. Everything seemed effortless. **During this era, *everything* also seemed like foreplay to us.**

We took many long weekend road trips to Indiana to see his parents and get his daughter for a day. I was lucky enough to hang out with his Dad a handful of times before he passed away. We lost him right before I moved to Indiana. The man was a consummate musician and specialized on the banjo. It was amazing how many songs he knew. Jay's Father seemed very proud that his son followed in his footsteps. Jay has one of his banjos.

Eventually the decision had to be made...Jay decided he had to move. His daughter had turned 5 shortly after we met and he felt he was missing too much of her childhood. I wasn't about to say good-bye if I didn't have to. I was way too in love. I often wore the heart lockets he had given me our first Christmas and first Valentine's. Jay and I started making plans.

Racing off to Indiana...

Jay moved to Indiana June 2004, two months before I did. He got a nice rental home and broke the news to his daughter that he was in the state to stay and spend a lot more time with her. I finished up some things at my workplace and had major crucial repairs done on my car. Jay and I were in constant touch and he came to visit me once in the middle of that time. Actually, months earlier he had already agreed to perform a music gig in a park and he returned to Pennsylvania for a couple days to honor his commitment, but I benefited. We made our hotel pitstop afterwards. We couldn't stay at my parents' house because "we were living in sin".

I turned 40 right before the August I moved. By our second year together, Jay and I had both relocated to Indiana. This was when we began living together. We had spent a lot of time with one another in Pennsylvania, but had different addresses there.

I gravely wished it had not been necessary to move because this put me in the position of being very far away from my own family and friends. At the time I had returned from California, my parents were so nice to me that I really just wanted to stay in my home state. But I was too smitten with Jay to just say good-bye. From there-on-in we were together every night and morning. And...Jay had to train me to cuddle. Yep!

People joke on TV about "cuddling". Shows make it sound like every girl requires it and every boy denies it.—That's not true. Jay has to practically pin me down to the bed to get me to lie still enough to cuddle sometimes. Well...not really "pin me down". But he has to give me the cute-face or sound sad and lonely to get me to do it more than a minute. Is this because I spent so much time "not dating" during high school and college? Is this because I expect someone to beg me to stay? Or is it because sex just wakes me up instead of putting me to sleep? I really don't know. Maybe all.

My Nunny-Bunny...

Sadly, we lost Nunny a couple months after I moved. Jay had never met her because by the time we began dating she wasn't doing well and was in a Christian run nursing home in her hometown. Although my family visited her often, I never introduced Jay to her, because I wanted him to know her through me and the stories I told him about her. **Nunny was a very cute, caring and dynamic little lady. And that is the Nunny I wanted him to know.** (Papa had died 11 years earlier).

I tell people all the time, "Nunny was my favorite person in the world." One time I had a boyfriend be jealous of that!—Sorry, it's just the way it is. All my Grandparents were wonderful, and I was blessed to have them all in my life. Nunny was my last.

The stressful years...

After the move to Indiana, I dealt with a lot of frustration for many years. It's hard to re-arrange your life around someone else's family needs and whatever dynamics come along with that...especially with a hostile ex in the mix. I tried keeping track of my feelings in a diary, but I ended up ripping it up. My coping mechanisms kicked-in. I did a lot of shopping and fed a lot of birds, ducks, squirrels, chipmunks, bunnies....etc. The wildlife critters who came into our yard gave me a purpose. I adopted pets. I collected artwork and trolls. I worked lots of overtime.

I worked to make things run smoothly, and Jay and I tried to set up a nice living space for his young daughter to stay in when she came for weekend sleepovers. But I'm far from the ideal partner. For some reason, I rebel against doing too much cooking. I like to eat out, even if it is inexpensive and fast. I'll do grocery shopping, laundry, dishes, and even take out the trash, but I leave most fancy cooking to the chefs. Maybe I have a fear of being "too traditionally the girl"...? I tend to be with men who don't like yard work much, and don't know how to fix things a lot, and care very little about watching sports. Works for me! If my guy doesn't have to revel in sweating and getting greasy, why should I have to wear an apron and baste turkey?

Maybe that is just an excuse. I'm not sure. I remember when I was teen Norma Jeane, and I married James, I tried really hard to be a house-wife. —I tried. He was a good man and deserved better than I was. But I really didn't feel cut out to be a homemaker. I was trying to convince myself to do it. It is an art. It takes hard work. To some it is very satis-fying. To some it is boring. The result is always a wonderful thing...a cozy home. But I still think part of me rebels against it. Becoming a good cook would possibly symbolize never leaving home. I guess as long as I don't commit to cooking I feel like I have one foot out the door...and perhaps pointed towards something else exciting...I'm not quite sure what. But unlike during Marilyn's lifetime, I would not want to leave my man behind. Afterall, if I moved on without him, who would force me to cuddle...?

Chemistry still bubblin'...

One good thing, Jay and I went into the second year of our relationship with all the physical passion we had the year prior. Our chemistry was/is amazing and it seemed we couldn't get close enough to each other... we tried. Our relationship is deeper than any other I have ever had with a man before and he pretty much demands we laugh through nearly everything.

Jay has named my breasts "A" and "B"...one has tattoos and the other doesn't. We laugh as he pretends he is trying to figure out which he likes more..."A" or "B"... "A" or "B"? He still can't decide...16 years later. (Which one is "A" and which one is "B"? Only WE know.)

Anyway, we coped with our new life together in Indiana as best we could. We dealt with finding permanent jobs, fluctuating visitation schedules, city traffic, quite a few car problems and his hostile ex. We had each other. And a very big plus is that we are from the same generation, so when we talk about this and that from way back when we often both can relate!

Chaos continued as Jay's ex-wife was constantly screaming at us, and leaving rude phone messages, and jerking him around on visitation. This meant lots of arguing and stress while they haggled out details over and over again.—This went on for years...years. Jay missed having daily contact with his child who was quickly growing up. And his daughter often expressed a desire to come live with us. Eventually a day in court turned things around. She came to live with us just before her sophomore year of high school. She is an excellent singer who thrived in a school that has a top notch music and theatre program. Then she got scholarships to college.

Life goes on, and Jay and I continue to work, love, and pursue our hobbies.

There ya have-it....

So...as you can see, I have had some things going on in my current "Michele Life" and ultimately I didn't pursue show biz this lifetime.

I have worked at a store, a restaurant. a library, an engineering office, a science office, a housing office, a research and assessment office, a computer company, and in several legal offices...not to mention short-term temp jobs and lots of babysitting. I've actually worked in the legal area in two different states and in three different offices throughout all of my career endeavors. But I have been in the same job from 2004-2019. The first two jobs I had in the legal field didn't teach me much. The last one has.

I find it somewhat interesting that I never intended to end up in the legal field...yet so far I have. Afterall, Marilyn was murdered. And murder is against the law! But somehow the legal field has seemed to absorb me. It has kept resurfacing.

Years ago in Pennsylvania, I had a job in two other units and the director of that area suddenly decided to throw in a third unit....legal. I didn't actually have to do more than schedule appointments for the attorney, but still there it was...The Law! And funny enough, I initially got my current job through a temp agency...which had placed another candidate in the position first. The candidate didn't show up! So, I got the call to report to duty the following day. Seems like fate. Legal! I'm a Legal Assistant!

Some doubters may think it is odd that I claim I was Marilyn Monroe and reincarnated rather quickly, but yet I have ended up working outside of show biz. But is it really? Towards the end of Marilyn's life, she seemed to gravitate towards powerful men wearing suits. And...well...haven't I kind of too? –I mean, professionally. It's really kind of sexy when the men I work around come back from the court house and they are all dressed up and talking about how they won a case using their evidence and wits to outsmart the opponent.

211

Is it mandatory to stay in show business in order to prove where I've come from…who I am? I have posed for very few photos during this current lifetime. I'm not particularly photogenic. However, before photography was invented people didn't have pictures taken, and very few could afford portraits. Do we doubt those people existed?

We may be born with different talents during each lifetime, but maybe our similarity from one life to the next is in how hard we work and how kind we are. Maybe our similarity is in our inner dialogue. The things we tell ourselves that no one else can hear. How we admit things, or excuse things, or grieve things, or love/respect things, or try to understand things…or in how we talk to whatever higher power we believe in.

Maybe we can change professions …maybe Marilyn's soul didn't have to return to the stage in the next consecutive lifetime…? Maybe it wasn't even allowed to. Since I can only remember a very tiny part of the in-between life, I am not sure what my soul agreed to. I only remember a few things during the in-between state:

—I recall being Marilyn and approaching another woman who looked like me. When I spoke to her, she would repeat back to me the same words, but in a different…more stoic…way. I felt like she was sucking some of my emotional energy out of me.

—I also remember seeing Cleopatra and being shocked she was so tiny.

—And I remember seeing what appeared to be a council of men in dark suits making some decision about me. But I don't know what they were discussing or how it all came out. I felt they were from two lifetimes ago.

Chapter Ten:

MICHELE: MY SKIN
CANCER ORDEAL:
TRAUMA...KARMA...BOOK!

So...why did I write this book at all and why write it now? Well........

*U*p until 2009, one of the people who killed me/Marilyn was still alive...and I thought he wouldn't hesitate to kill me again. Even though I look completely different than Marilyn, in my mind I thought that if I were ever on TV, he would surely recognize me...somehow. Maybe that is paranoia, but it crossed my mind sometimes. So, for that reason alone, it was easy to put off going public with any information.

I never intended to write a book. I never thought I'd have anything to say, or would know how to say it. I certainly never imagined I'd have more than ten pages to write...100 at most. For years I have told people verbally how Marilyn actually died. My friends would humor me, since most of them don't really believe in reincarnation and were probably afraid to tell me they think I'm nuts. Murder isn't a pleasant subject... and I'm surely not happy things happened as they did. But I have felt the need to inform people of the truth. There seems to be a lot of ideas written about the subject.

HOW DID MARILYN DIE...WAS IT MURDER OR SUICIDE? Well, I want people to stop the speculating and understand ...I know what happened...I was there...and I remember. But I realize that unless you know who I am first, you won't know whether or not you can trust and believe me. I want to solve this cold case for everybody. There won't be any arrests like there should have been, but at least you will know the truth through this book.

<u>**Very simply......there are a few reasons I wrote this book:**</u>

I was severely depressed after skin cancer...thought about my karma ....and...

1) For years, I've wanted people to know how I died during my last past life, as Marilyn Monroe. So many scenarios being tossed about. Marilyn died in 1962, before DNA testing...and I also read that her case file was pilfered so a lot of evidence is missing.

2) Fall 2018, I wrote to a popular and respected talk show and a booking agent called me about a month later. There was some interest in my subject matter. However, after several weeks of talks and emails, they wouldn't go ahead with my story because I couldn't get anyone from my family or my boyfriend to come on the show with me. And the other "Marilyn Claimer" who they tried to get on too wasn't returning their phone calls. Simply presenting me isn't enough! I decided I had to do something else....so....

3) I hoped to drum up someone else to go on the talk show with me. I wrote to three popular TV psychics...two past life regression hypnotherapists...a couple of the other "Marilyn Claimers" who have their own books...and to the website run by Marilyn Monroe's beloved niece Mona Rae. In some cases I felt like I was actually writing to entertainment corporations where they

were probably going to dismiss anything I said and be dead-ends. But I tried. I tried!

4) After receiving no response from any of these people yet, I decided I had to write a book. One of the "Marilyn Claimers" inspired me to self-publish as she did. I took out my laptop and began assembling my words. I had to find a way to tell people Marilyn's truth.

The talk show I wrote to doesn't necessarily need me to produce a relative who believes I was Marilyn or even believes in reincarnation. They just need someone to vouch in-person that I have held my beliefs long term and this isn't a passing phase for 15 minutes of fame. Despite the fact my boyfriend is a good musician and plays out in public on a regular basis, he is somewhat timid about going on TV. I suppose with all of his usual hilarious quips, he might redirect the show anyway. It might become the "Jay Comedy Hour".

As far as my family goes, at the time the agent was talking to me, I didn't even mention the show to them for various reasons. They don't believe in reincarnation at all. There are health matters as well, and traveling across country just doesn't seem in-the-cards. But I was Marilyn before I was Michele, and that is just the way it is. I'll do what I have to do! I was murdered. I finally told my parents about the talk show situation months later when I eventually told them I was in the middle of writing the book.

Now, I need to tell my skin cancer surgery story, so people understand what drove me to a very low point, therefore leading to the soul searching which lead to writing this book...and telling Marilyn's story.

I began writing this book Winter 2018
This is my real life cancer story from MY point of view.
I have <u>NO medical</u> background/education/expertise...none!

Over the past year I have read many online Question/Answer blog type sites, and I know that when skin cancer patients are upset

about the outcome of their surgeries, doctors tend to respond as such: "First you must understand that skin cancer surgery is for the purpose of removing all the cancer. It is not a cosmetic procedure."

To that I say, "Thank God for the medical professionals. But... doctors should still feel a reasonable obligation to inform patients upfront if they are planning to perform an operation on them that may have dire side-effects. Face-to-face, doctor-to-patient explained information."

There are several reasons for telling you about the following SKIN CANCER ORDEAL I went through:

1) So you understand more about where I am in life right now.
2) So you get suspicious blemishes checked out sooner, not later.
3) So if you do require skin cancer treatment you are smarter than I was, make no assumptions, ask a lot more <u>specific questions</u>, and aren't taken advantage of. (Some doctors are wonderful, some are not.)
4) So if you have skin cancer and feel alone, you know you are NOT alone, and in fact there are some support groups online.

The summer I was 19 going on 20, I had a bad case of mono. This was the summer a year after I began to remember I was Marilyn. And also the summer right after my semester with "Mr. Cruise Control".

Being vain and insecure, I was styling my hair to go to the doctor. I was pretty out-of-it, both mentally and physically exhausted. I accidentally burned myself with a curling iron and it left a large mark because I was slow to realize where the pain was coming from and pull the hot metal off of my skin. The mark was on my right temple and never went away. For several decades it looked red, oval and a bit shiny.

I got used to covering up my injury with make-up each morning, but finally in my late 40's to 50's it began to look different. I told myself I was probably just allergic to some of the hair dyes I was using, because I tended to change colors a couple times a year and also use different brands. I thought maybe that was the reason the mark was looking odd...chemicals.

I drove 10 hours from Indiana to Pennsylvania to spend Thanksgiving 2017 week with my parents. By the end of the day, my eyeliner was running and the cover-up on my burn-mark was smudging off. I sat at the dining room table talking with my Mom going on midnight. She noticed my mark and thought I had ring worm. I reminded her I had burned myself badly when I was 19...and it was at *her* house. She insisted I had ring worm.

When I returned to Indiana, I didn't believe I had it but I figured I would humor my Mom's idea and I went to the drug store and got the ring worm ointment. For a few days I didn't cover up the red mark with make-up, and I applied the medicine. It looked really bright red and worse!

I made an appointment with my dermatologist's office. I laughed to myself about "ring worm" all the way there and figured she would just say I needed Vitamin E. Instead, I was immediately diagnosed as having basal cell skin cancer. I didn't believe it and told the doctor about my burn. So the young doctor called in the older doctor for a second opinion. He immediately called it cancer too and gruffly snapped at me to go see his specialist. They scraped off a piece of my skin to send to the lab just to be sure.

The girl assisting the doctors told me that basal cell was "the best cancer to have because it is slow growing and not life threatening." She handed me a little pamphlet and the specialist's name and number. I asked her if insurance covers cancer surgery and she said it did.

She told me, "Just go to the specialist and he'll fix you right up!" She said it in a perky way as if I would be purchasing a burger and fries and it would be fun.

After that appointment I had to go to work. I immediately went to my desk and googled skin cancer surgery. An array of very graphic medical photos popped up on my computer screen! I immediately went to my co-worker's cubicle and she could see the horror on my face. She calmed me down by insisting that the internet isn't the best place for information and most of what I saw probably wasn't going to apply to me, so I shouldn't read it. I liked that idea.

How much surgery could my little 'ol burn mark require anyway? Denial continued. I believed her mainly because she has had many surgeries herself, although none for skin cancer. I felt my friend was "an operation guru". I didn't want to think about anything unpleasant.

Two weeks later the test results came back from the lab confirming it...my burn was now CANCER. I still wasn't overly worried despite a couple friends reacting as if it was <u>really bad</u> news. I kind of felt like I had to be strong for *them*. I really didn't want people fussing over me and I suppressed whatever inklings of dread that began to creep in.

Denial...

The truth is I was in denial a couple years and should have gotten the mark on my face checked out significantly earlier. I actually had a friend who asked me repeatedly, "What is that mark from again?" I would tell him about my curling iron fiasco. But he never once told me he thought it might be skin cancer, even though he had had some himself. (His healed by <u>secondary intention</u>...allowing new skin to grow over the area after the cancer is cut off.) I continued to blame my hair color for the strange way my burn mark was looking. Suspicious marks should be checked out!

My doctor and nurse:
For the sake of my book, I will call my skin cancer doctor, "Dr. Nixby" because he gets rid of the cancer... "he nixed basal cell on me." I will also call my main nurse who I had for 5 different appointments, and more specifically the day of my big operation, "Gwen". These are not their real names, just fictitious names for my book, and NOT relative to anyone or anything else that might be the same or similar.

I in no way wish to imply all doctors...or even all skin cancer doctors...operate in the same manner as mine did. Even doctors with similar training are individuals who make their own decisions while treating. I can only tell you that I was unprepared for the extent of my surgery and the upsetting manner in which it was handled.

I think I need to mention this: Some people have told me they don't believe you can get skin cancer from a burn. All I know is that from the day I got burned, I had a continuous red mark in the same place on my temple up until I was diagnosed with cancer and got my operation.

I wish I had realized the seriousness of skin cancer before I had my surgery. Some people join support groups right after making their appointment for surgery, so they have some idea what could happen and what they should ask. While other patients don't necessarily have medical background, they can still be a great source of information and inspiration while going through treatment.—Proceed with caution. The doctor is the trained expert.

I called the certified skin cancer specialist's office and scheduled my surgery. January 23, 2018 was the treatment date...a month away.

I asked a few questions and was told, "Well, the doctor will test layers of your skin and you will have to do a lot of waiting around. You won't be put under, just numbed, so you can drive yourself home if you want, but you may not feel like it." That *sounded* pretty simple... not complicated.

I asked how much time I should take off work and I was told, "A day to be safe but you may be out in half a day." I had no idea that some people take off multiple days...a whole week...or even a month after skin cancer surgery. I had no idea the healing period could be quite gruesome and uncomfortable. I expected a scar on my temple and a couple weeks of pain, but that's all. Afterall, I only knew one other person who said they had it and even though he was a repeat patient none of his cases seemed bad.

I had my last alcoholic drink two days prior to surgery. I didn't drink alcohol at all for <u>over a year</u> beyond. I heard it slows down the healing process and I was not going to be the cause of things not getting better as fast as possible.

I remember happily putting on my usual make-up the morning of my appointment...mascara, eyeliner, blue eye-shadow. I had plans to go shopping later that same day. I wanted to clean my big fish tank. I was actually cheerful. I had an iced-coffee on the way there. I was just happy I could afford my deductable. In the parking lot I sprayed myself with banana crème scented perfume, because I love aromatherapy, it brightens my mood.

Again denial...

Honestly, at that point, the word "cancer" wasn't even in my vocabulary although I was told I had it. <u>I never even liked admitting that it was my astrological sign because it sounds so bad</u>. I couldn't admit what I had was cancer until several months after my surgery. **Up until that point, I just kept thinking of it as "my curling iron burn gone bad"... but NOT CANCER.** Thinking of it as cancer just made me feel more stupid for not getting it checked out sooner. It also just sounded so icky and embarrassing. <u>It hurt my pride to think I had it</u>. I truly couldn't wrap my mind around that word, I just couldn't. This sounds so cliché, but I could barely say the word. Inward I cringed.

Surgery...the day my face changed forever...

I arrived at Dr. Nixby's office and I was ready to get it done and enjoy the second half of my day off. The lady at the front desk kind of smirked and called me over, asking me to sign several documents. I should have read them more closely than I did. I found out a month later that the nurse believed I had gotten those materials in the mail prior to that day.—But I didn't. If I had received them ahead of time, I would have read them more carefully instead of hastily signing them at the desk before the 8:30AM appointment began.

The truth is, I googled my surgeon before I ever met him. I wanted to see who he was. Dr. Nixby is very cute in photos and even better looking in person. The first moment I saw him was when the nurse was taking me down the hall to Room 4. The doctor was laughing about something and looked really sexy. He has very blue eyes. I even emailed a photo of him to my friend while I was in the waiting room. Handsome doctor. Firm handshake. Good eye contact. He made a very good first impression. Initially I really liked the doctor and trusted him.

I was at the office a little over half a day. I was shuttled from room to room by the pretty blond nurse named Gwen. I was shot in the face multiple times to numb my skin. The shots were quite painful. Gwen chatted with me about how she ended up in her profession and about all her kids. We laughed about getting tattoos and our parents' disapproval. She was pleasant and I really liked her. Something about her was very calming. I felt like she was "my friend". Gwen and Dr. Nixby looked like they stepped out of some TV medical drama where central casting obviously sent "pretty people".

When Dr. Nixby first began to work on me, he said that in the temple area, if you go too deep, you could hit the nerve that controls the eyebrow movement. I thought for a moment about how it would be if I couldn't use my eyebrow, but I really didn't understand the full extent of things...and it was not at all explained. Thankfully that is not an issue, because I can still move them both. However, during the month after my surgery I read that hitting such a nerve can also make your eye droop etc. It seems the doctor could have explained that part. If he had, I would have known to ask specific questions every step of the way. I feel that he told me about things in passing like a disclaimer but not to give me real information to make actual decisions.

First the doctor has to remove a layer of skin, and test it for cancer. Then he determines if he has to go back in and remove more. There is about 50 minutes between each round of testing. Whether or not an actual reconstruction procedure is necessary or what kind is determined after all the cancer has been taken off. You cannot predict how much it will be necessary to remove just by looking. Cancer can grow and spread out further or deeper than what a mere mark on the skin may indicate. I didn't realize this tidbit prior to my appointment.

A lot of the morning was spent in the waiting room and I found a really nice woman to talk with for a while. She was with her 91 year old father who was a patient. Fear wasn't at all in my mind and I was grateful the office provided some snacks... I had some hazelnut coffee. Thankfully I brought my laptop. My friend Meredith and I emailed to pass the time.

But really, I tried to convince myself I wasn't bored out of my mind. Waiting around between various treatment phases was tedious and I was on auto pilot. I let my guard down. I trusted blindly. I continued under the assumption that my doctor and my nurse would never do anything to hurt me, and that if something extensive might be done to me, I would get a detailed explanation, a "warning" if you will, and have a choice in my treatment. I naively proceeded through the morning, towards afternoon.

At some point in the day, nurse Gwen commented, "You have light skin and red hair so you are more likely to get cancer."
I told her my hair is really dark brown. While fair people may be more likely to get skin cancer, others get it too. It's a misconception that you are safe if you are darker. I'm so glad I stopped sunbathing many, many years ago.

I found out that the area that is operated on is referred to as a "wound". In between the rounds of testing my skin samples, I recall a second nurse with pretty long eye-lashes apologetically commenting on the smell of the cauterizing of skin while closing the wound. I told her I hadn't noticed because of my perfume. She said I was "refreshing," so I figured many patients must complain.

When I eventually joined a skin cancer support group, a few people remarked that that was something that really unnerved them during treatment...the burning smell.

I was burned at the stake during my past life as Charlotte during the 1800's. I'm surprised the cauterizing didn't disturb me more. Then again, I was trying to be brave, be strong....and basically suppress all feelings of fear to get through my appointment. Suppress!

After two rounds of the doctor shaving off my skin cancer and testing it, I was ready for reconstruction. I was told I was lucky he didn't have to go deep and hit a nerve. At that moment I thought I was "lucky".

Gwen put a mirror in front of me for a few seconds and showed me the hole in my skin at my temple. I thought it was about the size of a silver dollar. I saw it very quickly. I saw it from the front, not from the side like in my medical record photos. I could have sworn it looked gray and not red. Did they do something to it between the time they took the photo and the time they showed it to me? Or...was I in shock? **When I saw the hole I remember thinking, "This is real." But I just figured I could hide a scar on my temple with bangs.**

Lying by Omission...

Gwen and the nurse with long eyelashes both came into the room and Gwen informed me: "The doctor's going to stitch you up to get rid of that big hole in your head."

That didn't sound too ominous or detrimental... "being stitched up". As I was being prepped for reconstruction surgery, I was given many numbing shots which were quite painful for several seconds each.

And there was a point where I heard Gwen, to my left, whispering to the other nurse, "Just a little more." Then I looked to the right and realized they were shaving my head, but I couldn't tell how much because I was numb and the raiser was quiet.

I asked why they were shaving me and all I was told was: "So the doctor doesn't get hair in the stitches."

I just assumed they were shaving me a little bit around the temple area only. Gwen must have held her breath and hoped to God I was too stupid to ask any more questions, and I was. Two weeks later, the memory of this conversation made me feel so betrayed. I would play it over and over in my mind, and wonder what I missed. I feel that I was deliberately spoken to in a manner so as to lull me into thinking that the surgery I was about to get was going to be much more simple than it really turned out to be.

The reconstruction surgery began, and it was done while I was fully awake and not on any sedation. I went into it feeling pretty calm and just going along with whatever I was told to do. **The truth is I had no**

idea how much my face was going to be moved around until I was in the chair, already cut and my cheek was being pulled up towards my forehead.

What I still don't understand is how I didn't see what was happening out of my peripheral vision. Was it because of the angle the reclining chair was on? Was it because the shots in my head blurred my vision for a while? I just don't know. I really didn't know how to react, but I knew crying wouldn't halt it. And I was oddly surprised I didn't start crying. **It was a very perplexing and awful moment.** I made a little joking comment about how I had extra fat on my stomach they could use to fill in the hole, but it was too late of course to do anything but what was already in progress. **I had already been extensively cut up the side of my face, way beyond the area surrounding my old skin cancer burn...but I didn't know it.**

Dr. Nixby and I had a little conversation about football teams while he was still stitching me up. I'm not into football but I do like a blue-and-white college team. That only disguised what was really happening. It delayed my thinking about how Gwen had sugar-coated the explanation about the procedure while she was prepping me, and the doctor had told me nothing at all. I'm sure even the nurse who was shaving me knew I was going to walk out the door looking mangled up.

After I felt my skin being rearranged, it did feel noticeably tighter on the right side of my face. Things were definitely "different". The idea of having my face cut and stretched felt simply <u>degrading.</u> I feel that if a doctor won't even explain it to you, he shouldn't be allowed to do it to you.

I believe I remember being out-of-body Marilyn and seeing myself in an autopsy room. Maybe this current day operation experience felt eerily similar to that memory..."things just happening to me".

Dr. Nixby made some comment about how it was like I got a bit of a facelift on the right side. He said some people want the other side done too, even though they can't just do that. He seemed to think that was amusing. OK, seriously...I don't need a lopsided face. Getting a facelift on just ONE side is NOT a plus...don't even joke about it. What if I would have rather left the office with a hole in my head than had them do that to me? What if I wanted another option? Anything but what I got!

While the waiting room was packed that day, I actually looked like one of the younger patients there. I saw only one (maybe two) other patients who were definitely younger. So perhaps if I was 80 I would have found it funny that I got an unexpected facelift on one side of my face, but not at 53. (On the skin cancer sites I have been on, there are both young and old. At any age it is important to get things checked out as early as possible.)

Mid-operation, I told the doctor I was going to visit my parents in 4 months and I asked if I would be *relatively normal* by then.

Dr. Nixby:	**"Well, <u>that's</u> a loaded question."** (laughingly said)
Michele	**"I said <u>relatively normal</u> not totally normal."**
Dr. Nixby:	**"Have you ever had surgery before? Do you know how well you heal from any previous operations?"**
Michele	**"No."**
Dr. Nixby:	**"Let's just say, <u>some day</u> you will almost forget this ever happened."**

I really doubt that...maybe I'll forget when I'm in the next life. But the whole situation was way too traumatizing. And the outcome horrified me.

In the moment after my face was shifted around, nurse Gwen asked me if I was alright. I said I had to pee. I am sure the doctor didn't want to hear that because he was not done "stitching me up". But about ten minutes later he bandaged up my head and the nurse shuttled me to the restroom the staff use in their suite. Maybe they were afraid I'd take a peek if they let me go down the hall and out of their sight more than a minute.

I did look in the mirror after I used the facilities but I didn't see anything unusual… at that point swelling and distortion hadn't set in. Nor did I look very closely. The big white material bandage was quite well wrapped around my head and I left it like that. I wanted to be "a good patient" and get back to the operating room. I still trusted them and felt badly for the interruption. I thought it was very considerate of the doctor to allow me to go. In that respect he was more understanding than the rude urology specialist I had had years earlier. Dr. Nixby then put more stitches in.

Finally the full operation was done, and I really have no idea how long it took. It might have been 45 minutes, I'm not sure. Being at the doctor's office felt like being in a vacuum, a void, a time-warp. Gwen quickly took a photo of me.—That is the picture in this book. A short time later she took another one and in it my face is bruised and massively swollen-over in embarrassingly grotesque distortion.

Before they actually said I could leave, Gwen took my blood pressure. She said repeatedly that it was very, very high and her face looked quite concerned. Normally it is good and she said it was good before the operation. She then reasoned that maybe it was high because of all the shots they had given me.

She also asked if I was wearing contacts, and she said I should take it out of my right eye before it completely swells shut.—That was actually the first moment I realized my eye was even closing, and it was a bit startling because I was driving myself home. Funny she said that to me then instead of before the operation, but I guess she didn't want to tip me off that I was getting a more drastic procedure than she or the doctor let on.

I was told to try to leave the head wrap bandage on until the next day. I also had a couple smaller gauze type bandages taped over my stitches. And I was told not to bend over or pick up anything more than 10 pounds…not even my cat. I was not allowed to clean my fish tank like I had planned. I was not allowed to do that for at least a week. I had to keep my head elevated. I had to keep my stitches dry. And I had to put something on them to keep the area moist. I was given an instructions sheet.

By the time I got to my car, my eye was half swollen shut and the skin all around it was turning bright purple. I drove home with my eye rapidly closing and my peripheral vision on the right-side quite diminished. Thankfully my drive was only about 25 minutes long.

I quickly took my contact out. Typically I can even sleep in them, but I realized I wouldn't be able to apply eye drops if it was tightly shut for a long time. I then drove to the drug store down the street to fill my prescription. I got the antibiotic but not the pain killer. I didn't need it.

For the first time I realized how truly awkward and SAD it is to be seen by strangers as "very different" and deformed. I still had the big bandage wrapped around my head. And my face, which was very swollen and bruised, was only partially hidden by my sun glasses. I noticed someone enter the isle I was in and then look startled to see me. They abruptly turned around and walked in the other direction and down another isle, as if what I had was contagious. I told myself, "Just be brave."

At home...and at work...facing MY FACE...

My boyfriend got home from work that evening. I wore sunglasses and hid my severe condition from him as much as possible. I told him the doctor and nurse never informed me about the extent of the treatment before it was performed. Thankfully he was understanding. I am sure that every one of my previous boyfriends would have run out the door immediately.

I took over-the-counter pain relievers and antibiotics later that evening. Now, I never really sleep all-night-long uninterrupted. Between my bad back, small bladder, and two jumpy cats, I am often awakened several times. But that first night after the operation was worse than ever. The big bandage was really snug and painful. I kept trying to rearrange it over the top of my ear but it would slide back down and then hurt again. I finally tossed it off around 2AM. I figured that was technically "the next day".

Once I ditched the bandage, our big orange cat wouldn't stop sniffing the top of my head. Maybe I smelled like blood, I really don't know. Our little kitty has always liked to lick that side of my face when I'm lying down. My boyfriend thought maybe she sensed the cancer was there before we knew.

My right eye was very twisted up on the end. I began looking at people's eyelids when I watched TV. I was so envious of people who looked normal and had two matching eyes...like mine pre-operation.

Even over a year later, I catch myself looking at eyelids on actors.

Online I would see photos of other skin cancer patients who also had swelling: I would feel jealous of others who had "normal swelling" in their eyes as opposed to twisted up like mine. I felt so deformed. It also didn't help that even when I saw other people with cancer in the exact same part of their head, their surgical procedure was a different one. I really felt like my life flashed before me and every insecurity I had ever had about how I looked loomed in the forefront of my mind.

I took the following day off work. I had not planned that, but since I only had one good eye and there was an icy snowstorm I had no choice. I went back to the doctor's office two days post-op and nurse Gwen changed the gauze bandages that were taped directly over my stitches. She gave me some sample tubes of stuff to keep putting on my scar to keep it moist.

Gwen said she was surprised I looked as good as I did. I had used an icepack quite a bit and my eye opened up a day and a half after it closed. I was determined not to call in sick again. At that point I was still trying to "be strong". I had no clue what slow recovery lay ahead.

When I went to work people were horrified despite the fact I emailed a warning to them about my appearance and tried to explain the procedure as best I could, without completely understanding it myself. I admit that when I sat down at my desk, it suddenly hit me that I may have gone back too soon. But working in a high pressure office makes the pile-up of work very stressful if you are absent more than one day. When my supervisor saw me and looked shocked at my appearance, I had to fight back the tears because I knew by her reaction that I did indeed look as horrific as I thought I did.

Three days after my surgery I was taking the minutes in a big work meeting a couple visitors were attending. They wondered why I was wearing sunglasses indoors. I quickly showed them what I was hiding...and they were a bit stunned. The sunglasses went back on.

One of the men at work does community theatre and I jokingly said to him, "How do you know this isn't just stage make-up?" He said, "Oh, <u>that</u> I can tell is <u>not</u> make-up."

I returned to Dr. Nixby's office a week after surgery and the stitches I could see on my face were removed. **I asked the doctor about my eye because I was becoming very concerned. My eye was twisted up on the end, extremely swollen, crunched down and I looked like a monster.** The doctor simply said he thought I would be alright and "there are things that can be done down the line if needed." He said it is important not to revise anything too soon because it can create bigger problems if proper healing time isn't allowed. He said, "It is better to leave too much than not enough."—Later in the day that phrase perplexed me.

I remember him making the comment, "I did pretty good. Did you see I hid most of the scar in your hairline?"

All I cared about was my mangled eye. He told me to come back in three months. I made an appointment and went off to work. I was in a low energy survival mode. I still looked like a piece of meat that took a pounding.

I wore sunglasses as often as possible in public and at home because I didn't want people to see me. I was no longer wearing my contacts and began wearing reading glasses to see. Unfortunately I had a hard time seeing my computer screen at work with tinted glasses, so I was constantly rotating the spectacles on my face...sometimes for vision and sometimes to hide my warped eye. **Some office visitors asked if I had been in a car accident.**

A big misconception I had was in thinking that when all the bruising was gone, most of the swelling would disappear too. That was not the case. By two weeks after surgery, the last bit of purple disappeared on my eyelid and my eye was still quite distorted and uncomfortable. This was when sheer panic began to set in...and so did my obsessive computer searches for information. I desperately needed to see that someone else had had the exact same procedure I did, for the same area of the face, and survived and looked normal again. I couldn't find confirmation.

At that point, I would have gladly sown the cancer back onto my head myself if that is what it took to get my normal eye back. I deeply regretted my operation. My friends kept telling me it wasn't so bad... but of course it was MY FACE not theirs that looked twisted.

Disheartened...

Three weeks after my surgery was Valentine's Day. I normally love that holiday, but not this time. I felt the complete opposite of pretty or sexy or even loveable. I looked like a mutant. I was so embarrassed. I thought all the time about killing myself as the day approached.

A couple days prior, my boyfriend went on a business trip to Kansas City and I had two days to myself to end everything. I was definitely "in the zone". (I had been there before, I wasn't afraid to do it.) In my mind, the impending holiday just magnified the torment I had been feeling after my surgery. However, I realized Jay would never get over it if he came home from a business trip and he found me dead on our bed. I began to consider killing myself in the upstairs bathroom...or even the fishtank room.

The morning of February 14th I got up for work as usual. I decided to try to put eye-liner on because I look very pale without it. My right eye was so squished up on the outer side that the liner immediately began to make my eye water and inky black run down my face. **I locked the door to our little pink bathroom, and melted down into the fuzzy pink rug...bawling as quietly as I could, and feeling completely destroyed.** I finally pulled myself together about 10 minutes later and aborted "mission eyeliner". I had to accept that I was going to look pale and gross even on Valentine's Day. I put on sunglasses and emailed my work that I would be an hour late.

I went to the office and moments after I sat down one of the men came up to my desk and said something slightly sarcastic. I took my sunglasses off and looked him in the eye and asked how he was doing. He could immediately see that all was not well with me. He graciously offered to do some of my tasks. I told him I just needed a few minutes and then I would get them done myself. I have always appreciated his sensitivity in that moment and enjoy working with him. A picture is worth a thousand words. I am sure my face was a vision of devastation. He was kind.

Even better, the same gentlemen never patronized me and told me "I can hardly tell a difference" like so many people did. I would rather someone say nothing than lie. A lot of people made well intentioned comments that actually upset me more than helped me. I struggled daily.

The truth is, Marilyn is known for not being dependable on the movie sets, and irritating her co-workers. Even during my most depressed state, I missed very little work because of my operation. I was absent just a few times for follow-up appointments and maybe twice because I went in an hour late when I was too upset. **I never want to go back to that point of being someone people can't count on.**

Support...

As things continued, my boyfriend was loving and supportive. He knew I was disturbed but he had no idea how much. At first I tried to hide how upset I was. After about a month I couldn't. Me wearing sunglasses in the house was usually a tip-off I had been bawling. He focused on "other parts of me" so I guess that helped him deal with the situation. I felt unworthy. I really cared more about what I personally thought about me.

I didn't feel like I had my own face anymore...and I still don't. I feel like I have "the face my doctor gave me"...but it's not mine. If he had explained the surgery and side-effects to me, and I agreed to have his procedure after being fully informed, I would have also been responsible for my condition. But I didn't/don't feel that is the case since I was never given the opportunity to 1) understand the situation fully and 2) approve or deny the treatment. So, THIS IS NOT MY FACE.

I read online that the nerves in my face had to regenerate. And later at an appointment the doctor said the same thing. At first I had quick funny feelings in my face. Then I had a lot of pressure and often I felt like my eye was going to cave in. One day I felt like the whole right side of my face was going to explode. Many times I would suddenly feel as if someone was sticking a finger up under my eyelid and leaving it there for several hours. Sometimes I felt like something was poking my eyelid from the inside. There were a couple weeks it felt like sand was falling out of my eyelid and into my eye. My eye would water. One week I had severe pains in the top of my head. They were fleeting but I felt like I was being slashed by a knife. I just took over-the-counter pills and tried to get through things as often as possible without taking them. Around week 7, my eye started making squishing sounds when I blinked. I figured fluid was trapped where everything was puffy. The squishing sounds lasted past the year mark.

Just because a Release claims risks have been discussed, doesn't mean they necessarily have. Read before signing. If it says that a procedure could possibly create <u>"distortion/alteration of surrounding anatomic features"</u> it *might* apply to YOU. It is easy to gloss over wordy documents... hoping it won't. Some people do experience pain etc. too.

My boyfriend would tell me, "Just don't look in the mirror and you won't think about how your face looks." But HOW do you forget your face is a mess when it feels like it is attacking you from inside most of your waking hours? The discomfort was a constant reminder. The first 4 months, constant discomfort. Then significant drop-off occurred. The following 3 months discomfort 30-50% of the day. My eye continued to water often.

I really didn't want to be on planet earth anymore. And people trying to tell me the results of my operation "weren't that bad" was making things worse. I looked at medicines over the internet and I also began reading about suicide by taking lots of pills. And then I saw an article that claimed taking a large inappropriate does of over-the-counter pills is more likely just to ruin your liver. (I had never heard that before.)

I felt defeated for a moment but then realized I could take sleeping pills and aspirin and stab myself before I pass out. I remember that I had passed out pretty quickly when I had tried to kill myself with pills at age 38. Surely I could stab myself swiftly and get it over with. (I stabbed myself two lifetimes ago I reasoned.) But then I began thinking about how Jay would be affected if he found me dead some night when he came home. And I knew he didn't do well at the sight of blood. (I also knew I died more slowly and painfully than expected when I did kill myself 2 lifetimes ago. It may not seem so horrible in "Romeo and Juliet"...but it is in real life.)

I thought about killing myself in the car in some parking lot so Jay wouldn't be the one to find me. But I knew the Police would come to him first, or maybe even be suspicious of my death then. (We watch "Dateline" murder mysteries all the time.) I also didn't want to jinx the car because my Dad got it for me ...and also Jay likes it more than his.

I figured Jay's daughter would never sleep in the house again because she would probably think it was haunted if I died there. She was also right in the middle of her first year of college and I didn't know how financially strapped Jay would be if he suddenly had to pay all the rent and all the household supplies and food. I know college is expensive. And Jay's trauma would become his daughter's too. I felt so trapped. I fleetingly wished he would find another girlfriend so he could do without me.

I was constantly losing sleep, working a stressful job, doing all the normal activities but thought about dying every waking moment of every day. This continued for about four months. I especially felt so humiliated when I had to go to the grocery store...for some reason that just really affected me and I hid my eyes as much as possible, even though I normally like chatting with people. Every trip to purchase food felt like some "torturous test".

At work, one of the women left for another job and the higher-ups wouldn't let the boss replace her. Everyone was so surprised and over-worked. I thought about killing myself but that would make things worse for everyone at the office because they would have to take on even more work. I imagined them all mad at me for abandoning them. And I also didn't really want to hurt them either. Again, I felt so trapped.

Why did I bother getting surgery at all? It seems there are two reasons people do: To keep from becoming deformed and to keep from dying. Well, this surgery made me deformed at age 53 and I wished I was dead.

I remember reading a lady's entry on a medical blog. She was left with a scar on her cheek and said her husband was upset and she wanted to die. I knew someone else understood. It isn't just being vain and melodramatic. Was The Universe getting back at me for relying on my looks too much during my last lifetime? Was I paying for decisions Marilyn had made?

Up to the point of my operation, quite often people would tell me they thought I had been aging really well. They would say it. I wasn't asking for their opinion on my appearance. But after my operation, I knew that era was over. I knew that from then on, all people would ever notice is how hard I was working and if I was getting things done. I also noticed that all the stress and worry post surgery was aging me as well. But I simply couldn't relax any more. In my head, I continually heard "the lies" I was told in pre-op prep... the sound of omission.

I continued to wake up in the middle of each night and couldn't fall back to sleep. I was running on empty. I found a couple online sites where my doctor was advertised and reviewed, and one where you could ask a question. But it became apparent that no one must be monitoring the site.

Back to Room 4...

Five weeks after surgery I made an "extra appointment" to see Dr. Nixby because I couldn't wait for the three-month session in April. I went to the office and told nurse Gwen I felt totally blind-sided by the procedure I got. She made some comment about how I must have received some materials from them prior to the surgery because she said she sent them. I did NOT receive materials. She said they were with the documents I handed in at the front desk. I told her I didn't bring any documents with me, they were handed to me the first day I arrived at the office. I never received them to read at my leisure. To this day, I don't know where they ended up or what they said!

I told Gwen that I searched and searched and couldn't find my exact procedure anywhere online. She said the doctor does them all the time... "forward advancement flap". She got on her little hand-held computer and seemed to be searching for an example but couldn't find it.

I then took off my sunglasses and she said, "Oh, you <u>are</u> really swollen." That was her instant reaction and she sounded surprised. I told her I had been crying a lot and I felt deformed. She then quickly back-peddled and told me that my amount of swelling was normal.—I didn't believe her. She then went and got the doctor.

I could feel myself getting very warm as I waited for the doctor to enter the room. I was hopeful that whatever he would say would allay my fears. Dr. Nixby walked in...firmly shook my hand... and then I told him the same thing. The look on his face was "very serious" and remained so the whole conversation.

He said I couldn't find the procedure on the internet "because not a lot of people do that type of operation." He didn't offer any more explanation or before-and-after photos. I was so depressed and subdued that I didn't push for any examples. I could feel my face turning flushed.

I asked him "where did you cut me?" He looked at me as if I asked him where he had hidden a murder weapon. I told him that I was numb at the time and couldn't tell where he had cut my face for the operation. He timidly gestured to an area of my cheek around the lower part of my ear and said he started there. He had the weirdest look on his face as he did so.

I asked him a couple other questions and then he suddenly offered that he had loaded up my head with a lot of extra <u>internal stitches</u> which would be there for 10 weeks. I was happy for the information which explained some of the lingering swelling, but I was baffled that he had not told me that four weeks earlier when I had specifically expressed deep concern for my swollen twisted eye. It could have decreased a lot of my panic. He assured me that the swelling should go down significantly by the next time I was scheduled to come back. He said I should keep my 3-month appointment.

Again, I tried to impress upon the doctor my eye was my deepest concern:

Michele: **"I'm a girl. It matters."**
Dr. Nixby: **"I know it does."**

I was told to begin massaging my scar a couple times a day. **I left the 5-week appointment with Dr. Nixby saying, "You trusted us before, trust us now." And repeatedly telling me to "trust us...just trust us."**
It felt kind of passive aggressive. I felt like he was implying there was something wrong with me and my lack of faith, although HE is the one who didn't tell me he was going to cut up my face and rearrange it...and twist up my eye. I hadn't outright thought to myself "I don't trust the doctor"...*until* he brought the "trust" word up himself. After that day, I thought about it all the time, and just felt stupid for trusting him...or Gwen.

Throughout all of the initial healing months, there were things I would research or experiment with. Having no medical background, I was diligently looking for answers to things. I was constantly hoping for some good news in what I read.

1)   I suddenly was reading all the time about internal stitches. I would read about how certain stitches were expected to last a certain number of weeks. But a lot depends on a person's body chemistry and sometimes they stay in longer than expected (like mine did). Also I saw online where some people claimed

theirs would poke out of the skin's surface so they could go back to the doctor to get them cut out. I was kind of hoping mine would do that so I could get rid of them sooner....but no such luck.

2) Another big thing for me was what to put on my scar once I was allowed to massage it. I had friends swear by a certain name brand scar cream they had used, but when I tried it for 10 days, it felt tacky and made me itch and turn red...so cocoa butter won out. I used avocado cream for a while too, and then went back to cocoa butter.

3) I also began putting coconut oil on my eyebrow which seemed thinner than usual after the operation. I read that it helps hair grow. I think it did. Then again, maybe my hair just looked thinner for a while because of all the blubber around it from the swelling.

Because I couldn't sleep well at night, I would often be obsessively searching the internet for information about skin cancer treatments and recoveries. I found a medical blog page and then one girl pointed me toward a support group site on facebook. **Several weeks later a lady on facebook kept urging others to get a hold of their medical records and read them to understand what exactly happened to them.** I timidly did that. I contacted the doctor's office and was sent a release and I signed it, returned it, and got my medical records a couple days later.

Some of the medical photos were quite hard to look at. It was also shocking to see that among the paperwork was a signed Release which was obviously an electronic one. —I could tell by the way I signed my name incompletely spelled out. I barely recalled seeing that document, but realized I must have signed it in a hurry because the type was too small to read easily and it was pushed in front of me in the middle of a long morning where I was just going along with orders. I believe the Release was on some little hand held computer type thing...kind of like when you sign for a delivered package these days.

The Release made it sound like I agreed that things had been suffi-ciently explained to me. They were not at all! I felt betrayed by my own haste to sign and the nurse who had me sign it. **I guess small electronic forms take the place of discussions now?**

On one part of my medical records it eludes to possibly having a video made of your operation. Because I was so depressed all the time, I contacted the doctor's office again and asked if any videos had been made of my reconstruction. I figured it would be graphic, but I wanted anything at all that better helped me to understand why my eye still looked as it did.

I was used to watching medical procedures on TV.

A doctor call...

I remember going to work. It was a Tuesday, just like the day of my operation. I remember thinking to myself, **"This is 9 weeks post-op-eration. But it is only 8:30 in the morning and I wasn't disfig-ured until about noon time. Nine weeks ago *right now* I still had a normal eye. I still had my old face. I still looked like *me*."** I very clearly remember mourning my face that day. I never thought it was all that great before but now I suddenly wanted it back the way it was!

During late afternoon, the irritated doctor called me at work and he wasn't happy I was contacting his staff and inquiring about a pos-sible video of my procedure. He said that phrase is just on the Release but he doesn't make videos of his work. He also said it isn't good for a doctor if his patient doesn't trust him. He suggested maybe he should give me referrals to some of his colleagues to find another doctor and get a second opinion. I didn't really respond to that suggestion. I didn't want one of "his friends" since I imagined they would just agree to tell me whatever he wanted them to. Plus it seemed too late. Second opinion on what?

One of the reasons I wanted to stay with Dr. Nixby was because HE was the one doctor who knew exactly what he had actually done to me, firsthand. I figured another doctor would kinda-sorta know, but not 100%.

I admitted to Dr. Nixby that I may have been in denial about the seriousness of the skin cancer situation and I told him about how my friend at work had discouraged me from looking for medical information online beforehand. I told him I knew I didn't have a very high forehead or fleshy face to work with. I told him looking at the medical photos helped but I said I was confused because no one explained the procedure to me before I got it. I told him his staff was nice and I was pretty sure I remembered all our conversations, so I didn't think I forgot something I had been told.

Michele:	**"I feel like I was treated like a "science experiment."**
Dr. Nixby:	**"I would have given my sister the same operation."**
	"I went to school for a long time to learn how to do this."
	"It was a big cancer. It's going to take a long time to heal."

While still on the phone, I was also told that there was a chance I might need some form of revised blepharoplasty because the procedure he gave me "is not an exact math" and extra skin could have possibly been pushed up into my eye socket. I felt so defeated at the thought of yet another surgery...especially one I might not be able to afford anytime soon.

Before hanging up, Dr. Nixby also repeated what he had told me at the week-five appointment. He said, "By your April 30th appointment you should be significantly less swollen." I still had another month before then, so I hoped for the best. (If only that had been true!)

After the phone call I couldn't help but be very cynical. I guess Dr. Nixby thought I was stupid enough to believe that he would have given his sister an extensive disfiguring operation without explaining it to her first. I guess he thought I was stupid enough to believe he wouldn't have discussed the side-effects with his sister beforehand. I'll just bet he would have sent his nurse to say to his sister, "Your brother's going to stitch you up," when she knew full well his sister was about to get the operation I did. I think his sister would have been given an explanation…therefore a choice. **How can you truly consent to something you know nothing about!?**

I also don't understand what it meant when the doctor said he "went to school for a long time to learn how to do this". Did he take classes, but I'm the first person he ever gave the operation to for that specific site? Why would he not have told me how many times he has performed that same operation for the same problem in the past, and how things turned out? **I felt like he used cute phrases to skirt the issue and try to confuse me. Again I felt manipulated.**

I also don't understand what the doctor meant when he repeatedly said "it's going to take a long time to heal". Is that ten years? What does that mean?

I was at work in a cubicle, at the front of the office, with no real privacy. I didn't want to debate anything there. I just thanked him for calling. Dr. Nixby apologized for calling me at work. It was all very cordial.

I know people heal at different rates but I still think a doctor could give a patient some kind of idea about range of expectations… with a caveat.

Trying to hold-on…

The next day I cried when I got to the work parking lot. I felt emotionally overwhelmed again. Then during lunch hour I said to myself, **"If you aren't going to kill yourself, you have to TRY to pretend to be happy…and maybe someday you will be."**

I went and bought new eye make-up and tried to apply it in the drug store parking lot. My right eye was quite warped but at least my liner stayed on that time. I still couldn't wear eye-shadow because the lower, blinky-part of my eyelid was swollen over. But at least I could wear liner and mascara again. It felt like a small success. I went back to work and a friend noticed right away and said I looked more like the "old me".

I cancelled my April 30ᵗʰ, 3-month appointment because of various things. Among them, I simply couldn't stomach the thought of returning to Dr. Nixby's office any time soon... I figured I would wait and go back when my face looked significantly better and I didn't need to hide behind glasses anymore. (I'm still wearing glasses.)

Each morning I would wake up and my skin would feel squishy and my eyebrow would hang funny until my circulation got going. I'd put on what make-up I was able, through tears. It was repulsive and dehumanizing. I didn't want to go anywhere but had no choice. I felt like I was applying make-up to an alien or a rubber dummy. The first hour each morning I was emotionally ill. But I could never waste time because I had to get to work.

My "10-week" internal stitches didn't seem to want to leave my face. I could see their pleated shape up against my skin which had gotten very red and tight around week 12. Most seemed to disappear at week 13...all accept for one which I had until week 18. The spot where that stitch had been left a lump of scar tissue that never went away on its own.

Around this point, I had posed a question on an online "question and answer blog" and a doctor from Vermont said that my eye could still be swelling because of disrupted lymph channels between my cheek and temple. She said it could be the result of either the cancer removal or the reconstruction. She said it takes time to regenerate. I was so thankful for that explanation. I held onto that concept which gave me hope the swelling could improve in time.

I had kept counting down the weeks and marked every Tuesday on my calendar at work for the full year after surgery. I always knew where I was past January 23ʳᵈ. I found that most of the people on the support group site I corresponded with did the same thing. We all were hyper aware of "what week it was" since our life changing surgeries. A couple of us even laughed about it a bit. I went home to my parents' house in Pennsylvania the week before Memorial Day...@week 17. My eye watered a good bit of the way there and I had to pull over in a parking lot for a while. It watered even more on the way back to Indiana a week later.

The truth is I didn't even tell my parents about the whole skin cancer situation until 2 weeks prior to my visit with them. I also didn't tell my sister Chris because I knew she would tell my parents. My Mom typically gets seasonal depression after Christmas and I didn't need to add to that. I didn't want to worry them. I wanted to focus on worrying about me. I didn't want to worry about them worrying about me also. This made emailing my parents tricky because when my Mom would ask what I was up to, I would have to watch what I said. It was hard not to mention the cancer situation.

I had kept holding out hope that I would be further along in the healing process, but finally I had to say something to my folks because I knew I was hoping for something that wasn't. The whole 10 hour drive back to my childhood home, I prayed to God for a miracle so my eye would be normal when I got to my parents' house. That didn't happen.

When I go back to Pennsylvania I keep in contact with my boyfriend several times a day. I had my medical records photos on my laptop which I traveled with. My Dad said he wanted to see my pictures. I showed him the view of me after the cancerous skin was removed...and then the shot of me with all the stitches. The pictures are a bit shocking and he got quiet. **A few minutes later he said, "Well Michele, it looks like your doctor knows what he is doing."**

I knew my Dad was "being supportive" but his approval irritated me because I still felt my doctor hadn't been fair to me. I wanted someone to understand MY side of things and say the doctor was wrong. One day a visiting higher-up attorney at work told me she agreed with me. She said that a procedure should be clearly explained before surgery... especially for a woman. (I think it should be for a man as well.) Her opinion comforted me.

After four months of major depression, the physical discomforts began to finally subside. It was gradual, yet remarkably noticeable. And my swelling went down some. Daily suicidal thoughts lessoned significantly but resurfaced on my 54th birthday in July. Ten minutes from the office parking lot I began crying. The thought of having spent nearly 6 months with my messed up eye made getting older seem sadder. At my office, the clerical gals decorate each other's cubicles, bring in snacks and gifts, and make a big deal about birthdays. But, I couldn't leave my car until I could stop crying. I saw my manager and flagged her down. I told her I would be in a bit late. She insisted on trying to talk me out of my despair. With resignation I went to work... all dressed up with my "squidgy eye".

Then again I wanted to kill myself in early October when another girl announced she was leaving work and stress was worse than ever. But alas, I didn't because my Mother's 80th birthday was a month away and she had begun mentioning it in her emails. I didn't want to hurt her.

I kept telling myself, "The one thing worse than being ugly is being cruel." I stayed alive. I also had plans to go back to Pennsylvania for the holiday and my parents and my good friend Meredith were counting on it. I visit in May and November. Meredith and I love antiquing.

I had reasons to stay alive but I had to get over my vanity issues. And I had to be patient some more...I had no choice.

Back to Room 4......10 months after surgery...

I went back to Dr. Nixby's office just before Thanksgiving. I really only went back because I was afraid my parents would ask me when the last time I talked to him was.—I didn't want a lecture. Nurse Gwen acted happy to see me, and as if my healing was amazing.

By that point I had already decided I needed to tell the public about how Marilyn died. I told her I was trying to get on a talk show to discuss Marilyn Monroe, and about a booking agent calling me. She said I should keep her posted. I remembered why I liked her initially.

The doctor had not seen me in person for about 8 months. Again he gave me a nice firm hand shake as soon as he walked in the room. He also acted as if I looked fabulous (the operation site, not "me" personally). The scar healed quite well. But my eye was still messed up. I asked the doctor about getting it fixed and he said I should come back a few months later and he would fix the lumpy area <u>above</u> my eyebrow for free.

When I asked him why I had a big lump above and under my eyebrow, he said, **"I think you are expecting to be normal, but your eye will never be normal again. Too many channels were cut. There's always going to be a little difference."**

Further, he said if I couldn't live with "the little difference" that was left, I needed to hire another doctor to fix it. My eyelid was far from fine. I felt like things had stalled after the 6 month mark and my eye still looked odd at 10 months...November 2018.

It bothered me that Dr. Nixby called my impending deformity "a little difference." I wondered if he was trying to convince me or himself that it is little. Was he trying to make it seem small because he was afraid I might sue him since I work in a legal office? He doesn't know that I have no desire whatsoever to do that. I just imagined he might be thinking that, but I don't know. **I wonder if he would have called the difference "little" if it were on his wife's face...?**

I made an appointment to go back <u>the day after</u> Valentine's 2019. I didn't want to look like a monster on my favorite holiday a second year in a row. I literally said that in front of Dr. Nixby and he looked at me funny. But see, he got to be handsome on Valentine's, I was the one all mangled up. I know revision surgery means more temporary swelling. February 15th was a full year past my first surgery. He optimistically said, "Maybe by February everything will improve some more." And I began seeking consultations with plastic surgeons in the meantime. One bad one, one good.

Revision and Derision....

Three months later I went back on February 15, 2019 to get the little piece of lumpy scar tissue above my eyebrow taken out. I felt a bit of excitement about going and maybe improving my appearance.

Writing of my book was already in full-swing and I had already written much of this chapter about my surgery. I figured I could keep it as it was "in progress" or soften the harsh account I had of my surgery, depending on how my doctor's attitude was at this appointment.

But unfortunately, he gave me no reason to feel differently than I had for a year. I still felt betrayed...and had to work at feeling differently.

First, I had a different nurse, and I admit I was very disappointed. The new girl was bubbly but talked a mile-a-minute like she was selling a used car. I noticed she had really perfect dark well-shaped eyebrows. My right eyebrow has been messed up since my cancer surgery. This new nurse was nice but not at all calming like Gwen.

I told her about the wonderful plastic surgeon I saw for a consultation on my eyelid, during early January. (My eye had not made any improvement on its own since November.) And I told her that that doctor thought highly of Dr. Nixby. She left the room and by the time the doctor entered, he had already heard that he was complimented. He mentioned the plastic surgeon's name. Handshake!

Then he began talking about what he was going to do to remove the extra tissue to smooth things out. I mentioned that the plastic surgeon was hoping that whatever he did would raise the tip of my brow a bit. Dr. Nixby said, "I think what I'm going to do will accomplish that." He proceeded to draw on me with dark blue ink.

He then told me that he would have to go into the eyebrow a little bit. This made no sense because he told me at the November appointment that the whole reason he wouldn't do any work on my <u>eyelid</u> was because he didn't want to go into the eyebrow area "because eyebrows won't grow back if you remove them." It didn't make sense when he said it in November because the eyelid is not the part that grows hair. And it made no sense at my February appointment because he had told me in November he wasn't going to do anything to my eyebrow. I foolishly hoped for the best.

Well, at least he was honest this time...so now it is <u>my</u> fault my eyebrow is too short afterward. Yah, it looks shorter now. I guess I should have RUN!

I told Dr. Nixby that I had begun getting consultations with plastic surgeons because I remembered him saying in November that he would fix the part <u>above my brow</u> but he told me I had to go to someone else for the rest. **I mentioned that my eyelid still looks puffy, has too much skin in the middle and doubles over since the procedure from last year.**

I was just stating a fact. I did not expect an explanation or admission or apology. But what the doctor said next floored me!

Dr. Nixby:	**"That's all you. You had that before. It's due to the aging process."**
Michele:	**"But this one's not that way."**
	(Pointing to my good eye.)
Dr. Nixby:	**"Yah I know."** (Said with recognition in his voice.)

He bolted out of the room and then came back 10 minutes later.

My doctor obviously wants to blame anything but his own judgment for how he messed up my eye. It's insulting when he tries to convince me that I was that way before. And that fictitious comment about "the aging process"...really? **Does he think I forgot what I used to look like? This all makes me wonder how he treats his even older patients!?!**

I will admit to having a lot of little glitches in my skin from five different bouts of really bad poison ivy on my face, but one thing I know for certain is that my eyes were looking good... not puffy, droopy, twisted. All of those things were things he snuck in on me! My cancer wasn't even on my eye!

Dr. Nixby's nurse injected me with numbing shots and prepped me to be cut.

She also covered a lot of my face, possibly because the doctor didn't want me to see him cutting close to my eye, I guessed. Thankfully I'm not claustrophobic despite how Marilyn died. (Talked about in another chapter.)

Mid-operation, the doctor and nurse were chatting. He also asked me about my weekend plans. I said that I was in a skin cancer support group on facebook and I mentioned the name of a doctor with the same credentials who sometimes gives advice. I think it made Dr. Nixby nervous. He said, "That can be dangerous."

I responded, "Well, you just have to take into account that most of the people there don't have medical expertise and they may not have had the same procedure. But doctors sometimes comment." I told him that I made a friend on the support group site and she went to a different local doctor. It's comforting to know you are not alone. (**I have never mentioned the doctor's name or his company while discussing anything online in an open format. But I do tell the truth about my trauma.**)

As he finished sewing me up, Dr. Nixby said he was going to send my medical information to the plastic surgeon I had mentioned earlier. He said it three times in fact. Maybe he wanted to impress the other doctor...I don't know. I was still unhappy about his earlier untrue comment about my eye.

What truly baffles me is that between my November appointment and my February appointment, I don't recall the doctor or nurse taking any pictures. It seems to me there was one point in November when I had my eye closed while they were looking at something, so for all I know may have taken a photo of my well healed scar. But it is odd to me that I don't think they really are interested in documenting how bad my eye looks as a result of the initial surgery. You would think that would matter!

After the revision surgery, the nurse began talking at a rapid pace, saying I was left with dissolvable outer stitches and some internal stitches. She rattled off care instructions...saying I could start massaging my scar in 4 weeks. I asked about an antibiotic and she said I probably wouldn't need one. She said if I got an infection it would be in 3-5 days and I should call. The nurse briskly shuttled me down the hallway and pointed towards the door. I never saw the doctor again... and didn't want to!

Gwen said, "Hi Michele"...as I almost passed by without noticing. She was at the front desk and looking pretty as ever and sweet. I couldn't help but wonder why she wasn't my nurse for that last visit, and two things came to mind. Either Dr. Nixby was training the other girl and wanted her to assist, or he didn't want me talking to Gwen about my Marilyn beliefs like I did in November before he came into the room.

I figured she might have told him what I said, and he possibly thought I was crazy. –I don't know.

My feelings toward Gwen are very muddled to this day. I wish I had met her in some other way. She seems like a very lovely person, but she is still the one who essentially lied to me the day of my operation. Her eyes are fine, one of mine is messed up. I know she was just doing what her boss wanted her to. Let's just say that her boss is not one of my favorite people!

Thankfully, I did not get an infection from my revision surgery. But again, the hell of healing started all over... and then a twinge of depression...although nothing as bad as before. I will never go back to Dr. Nixby's office ever again. I wish I never had.

The wait...again...

Waiting 4 weeks to massage my scar felt like a long time. The stitched up area faded extremely quickly but the big bulge coming out of my forehead right above my eyebrow looked like I was popping a vein or something. My bangs were getting pretty long and I walked around looking like a sheep dog because I didn't want anyone to wonder what the protrusion was.

Over time things did smooth out, although I clearly will need to hire a plastic surgeon because Dr. Nixby's tweaking procedure did NOT lift my brow up as he told me he thought it would. The corner of my eye still droops a lot. And the initial surgery left me with a messed up eyelid which hopefully the plastic surgeon can improve. Fingers crossed!

And why, you may wonder, did I go through with the revision on the lumpy scar tissue above my eyebrow if my doctor ticked me off and seemed illogical? I can only say this...if I had more money I would have gone straight to the plastic surgeon I had a consultation with and liked. I feel very sorry for people who don't have insurance and need a doctor.

I would say that during the first year after surgery, one of the hardest things to deal with was the <u>well-meaning people</u> who said things that just seemed patronizing. And sometimes they just came up to me and said them...even when I wasn't engaging them in conversation.

-I don't want to be told my scars don't matter or give me character.

-I don't want to be told my deformities are barely noticeable.

-I don't want to be told the doctor probably didn't realize how things would heal, because that is no excuse to not inform your patient of potential side-effects before the surgery occurs.

-And I definitely don't want to be told that basal cell skin cancer isn't like "real cancer" because I'm not going to die from it.

One co-worker told me that it wasn't like I had "real cancer" because she knew someone else who was having a treatment to save her life. This piece of wisdom came out of the mouth of someone who takes up-close selfies and posts them online on a regular basis...obviously showing off her big green eyes. So, don't try to make me seem like a crazy vain person because I don't want my eye messed up and I'm upset my doctor didn't properly inform me of the procedure he was about to do ON MY FACE!

If you are even thinking for a second, "I'm glad that didn't happen to me"....then don't act like it is nothing because it is on MY face and not yours. I just want to feel understood... not minimized. Don't tell me sugar-coated lies <u>even in the name of being nice</u>, please. Skin cancer is traumatic. Just tell me you are sorry I'm going through this, and you can see why I would be concerned. Or say nothing...shhh.

Bad past experience...

<u>Doctor visits during my 20's:</u>

I will say this. I feel very foolish for not going to the dermatologist years sooner about my curling iron burn. I probably could have prevented the degree of seriousness of the whole cancer situation. It was always a presence on my face and I just covered it up over and over again. I failed myself.

But here is the thing. When I was in my mid 20's I had a job with good insurance. I went to a dermatologist about my face because it was constantly becoming red. He prescribed some ointment that never really made a difference on me. But at least I had a dermatologist, I thought.

At the time, I had heard a lot about skin cancer in relation to moles and tanning. I had given up sunbathing years earlier because I knew my skin was light and prone to burning, and also I find sunbathing incredibly boring. But I did have a few moles I thought perhaps I should get checked out. They were small and didn't bother me, but were in places where undergarments rub. I decided to be cautious. So I made an appointment.

The dermatologist chuckled at me and acted like I asked him to do something silly. But despite the fact he didn't think my moles were of concern, he did remove one or two and had them tested. Not cancerous.

I then went back to him, maybe a year later, because I had two warts on my legs. The one on the front of my right leg was bigger. Both were pink, hard, looked like large bug bites, and had been a part of me for well over a year. **The doctor acted as if I was nuts.**

I told him I was only in my 20's, wore dresses often and wanted to be in show biz, so I needed to look my best. **He said to me, "Just because you have good insurance, doesn't mean you have to come in here for every little thing."**

I had him remove the warts and I never went back. His attitude was belittling. I feel that that doctor acted as if my concerns were trivial. I had good insurance and a decent job. Either way he was going to get paid. And I didn't go into his office very often. I have no idea why he was so dismissive when I was trying to be responsible about my skin conditions. That was his supposed expertise, right?!

In retrospect I realize I should have just switched doctors, pronto. I should have found someone who cares about people. And I cannot help but feel that that situation many years earlier, was part of the reason I was not quicker to take my curling iron burn more seriously after it began to look different during my 40's.

It really is up to patients to take themselves seriously, because some doctors will and some doctors won't. Thank God for the good doctors.

I am Michele...a real person...not just a patient number.

It was in the midst of my deepest depression that I began reconnecting with the Marilyn part of myself. I realized that in some ways the whole skin cancer surgery horror story was similar to the night of Marilyn's death. It was like an ambush.

Let me make this clear, it was <u>the reconstruction</u> portion of treatment that was extensive and unexpected and upsetting. I know I had no choice but to get rid of the cancer itself before it got worse, but I expected more explanation and choice afterwards and prior to "being stitched up".

On both August 4-5, 1962... and... January 23, 2018, I had a false sense of security and then BAM! Others took over and I experienced total loss of control of the situation. Nothing was ever the same and I felt surprised and disrespected. Other people had their own agenda for me. I was treated like a "thing". Maybe the medical staff hurried me through because their waiting room was crowded that day...? Maybe I misunderstood something.

Marilyn was killed as Bobby was nearby. Handsome Dr. Nixby rearranged my face without prior explanation. Even with Dr. Nixby, it is hard to stay 100% mad at him, like the way I don't want to be mad at Bobby for his part in Marilyn's death. I try to stay mad, but it is very hard to do.

I wonder if I knew Dr. Nixby during another life. Was he perhaps my brother during Cleopatra's lifetime or was he the hitman during Marilyn's lifetime? Those would be my guesses. **Isn't it interesting that he told me that he would have given his sister the same operation he gave me?** And Cleopatra had a bad relationship with her brother. (I don't know who anyone else was...I just guess for fun. I could be completely wrong.)

My surgery was in January. In May 2018, I made the decision to search for a <u>female hypnotist</u> and hire her to dive deeper into my past life memories. I found a wonderful lady named Toni who works not far from my job. I saw her three times in June and once in November 2018...and then again once in April 2019. I don't tend to go under easily, but sometimes during the weeks after a session more memories begin to come.

I had never hired a hypnotist before so I wasn't sure what to expect. My friend Tom believes it takes about 6 sessions for a person to reach the full-depth they are likely to go in the hypnosis process. Apparently sometimes it takes time to "go under". I also found out through reading that "going under" may not be the correct term. You never really lose control during hypnosis. It isn't like falling asleep or being unconscious.

Anyway, I do think being hypnotized helps me to remember things <u>after</u> the session. Maybe I'm less self-conscious exploring my memories when I'm by myself. It's been quite wonderful having someone I like and trust to hypnotize me here in Indiana...while also having a friend who is a hypnotist in North Carolina. I feel like I have two people to consult.

As I began to really focus on meditation I ordered some lovely healing stones...amethyst, red jasper, smoky quartz. I read that quartz is good for your lymph system. I found meditation tapes online, as well as sounds of waterfalls and thunderstorms, which actually speak to me on some level, if they are just the natural sounds without musical accompaniment.

Crossing the line...during Marilyn's time.

The reason I wanted a *female* hypnotist during my Michele-life was because I have <u>a vivd memory of being Marilyn</u> and seeing a doctor...psychologist. I think this was sometime mid-career, not towards the end. I remember having sex with the guy on a couch during a session and afterwards I walked down a long hallway to the ladies room. I was sobbing. In my mind I had such conflict.

I felt like I had put myself in the position I did because I hadn't actually said "No." But I also didn't know why someone who was "helping me" took advantage of me. I couldn't even figure out if he actually had taken advantage of me. **Where is my responsibility? Where is his?**

But sometimes you just want to know that someone won't even ask. Don't request or expect me to do something if you know I am vulnerable. Just because I am there doesn't mean I should be available.

I, as Marilyn, really deeply wished that someone had my best interest at heart. I wished that helping me had trumped going for an encounter with me. I knew my image in Hollywood set me up for this sort of thing. But I just wanted to "be a person". I remember that walk down the hall felt like forever, and I felt so incredibly stupid and alone. This is the extent of the memory, so I have no idea if I ever went back for "therapy". I hope not.

Despite Marilyn's negative experiences with therapy, she obviously believed it was still a good thing. I don't recall her other therapists but I continually hear that she had a counselor up until the very end of her life. I also believe that some therapists are good people and help clients. As with anything, you have to choose the right person for YOU.

In connection with August 4-5, 1962, I have read that apparently Marilyn's last doctor was dragged into the mix and some people even have tried to blame him for her death. I see this as a great big excuse. I see this as the real killers trying to deflect blame. They may have summoned him to the scene so he would take the fall for Marilyn's fatality. But make no mistake, he was not at fault for her death. If anything, he tried to help. But even if he was unable to do so, he did not kill her...he did not kill me that night!

Therapy during college...in my Michele-life...1982-83...

I am electing to give my doctor the code name "Dr. Painter", because he was an artist at heart.

Because I struggled with eating disorders, my first college roommate suggested I get help. Her sister had gotten treatment for the same thing a few years earlier. I began attending weekly one-on-one counseling sessions with a nice man named Dr. Painter. It was at the University's health center just a couple blocks from my dorm. (Later that same year, I also went to group therapy for eating disorders. Those sessions were run by two women.)

Finally after a good 6-months, Dr. Painter had me take some tests, such as an extremely long questionnaire, drawing pictures of a man and a woman, and reading ink blots. I assumed he wanted to see if I made the woman look thin, because I had issues with food. I remember being frustrated because my picture of a man looked girly, and I gave up saying, "I guess he is turning out to look like Jesus." The doctor assured me it was not a drawing contest and I should just do what came to mind and I was able. Maybe he was gauging my temperament and my tendency to expect perfection...? I don't know. But I'm no artist, despite drawing often as a younger child.

When the doctor seemed slow at getting me my results, I pushed for them. He told me he didn't find anything alarming and wasn't sure how he could help me, so I had to decide if I wanted to continue sessions or not. I figured I probably wouldn't go back because my parents were paying the bill. But in some ways he <u>did</u> help me, even if he didn't realize it. He pointed out things that no one had ever mentioned before, and I remember.

During one counseling session when I was being very chatty and coy, he told me I was a "brat". When I asked him what he meant, he said I used cuteness to manipulate conversations. I never thought of myself as "cute" or "manipulative" and it made me think about how I acted. But yes...he was right. I knew I certainly did try to be charming, especially when I didn't feel "pretty enough". I knew my personality changed a lot that year.

He also told me I gesticulate with my hands a lot. One time I did notice him staring at them as I spoke.—I thought I was just imagining it. It's true, my hands are always up in the air ...despite the fact they are big and ugly. I figured it might be a good quality to be demonstrative since I was studying acting. But it is natural. I do use my hands a lot to communicate.

Dr. Painter pointed out that it was odd to him that I never cried during a session, despite telling him how unhappy and broken-hearted I often was over boys or whatever else. He said most people cry at some point during counseling. He said in fact some patients cry a lot. I guess I was too shy to cry and it never occurred to me that I could or should. I would have died of embarrassment...especially in front of a man. But it made me realize that maybe I was short-circuiting my therapy because I was perhaps holding in my emotions. I guess I didn't want to bore him. I wanted to entertain.

Maybe I was tired of crying because Marilyn cried so much despite a number of therapists during her lifetime...? And I cried a lot as a teen.

Dr. Painter also told me this. He said he didn't know what he could do for me but that he thought I was very interesting. There was a moment where we connected eyes and it was strange. I made the decision never to go back. But the thing is, he was always very professional. There I sat across from him in a mini-skirt every single session. I was talking like a brat blabbing on-and-on about all of my stories...never crying. I could tell him things I couldn't tell college boys...and he listened...and I felt safe.

I asked him what made him become a counselor, because I think psychology is interesting. He said that he was the counselor and not there to talk about himself because he had to focus on his patients. So I asked him again. He said that he was an artist who went into psychology so he would have the money to buy paint supplies, because they are expensive. He said initially he figured he could make a lot of money but the profession didn't pay as well as he had hoped.

I asked him if he was still painting and he said he hadn't for quite a while. I thought that was an amazing story...but also sad. I realized then that sometimes people do what they have to do in life to make a living.

He was always so respectful of me, unlike some of Marilyn's professional support people. About 10 years down the line I was working at The University and saw Dr. Painter now and then, as he was on committees and projects and seemed well-respected. I hope he still gets to paint.

Have you ever found that sometimes you don't know what you want or need until you find it...or....it finds you?
Like a cat...me?

Once when I was in my 20's, I went to a new age place with a friend. A lady tried to do a past life regression on me but it didn't work. However, what I recall her telling me is that she felt my energy was like a CAT's. I told her that couldn't be because I love dogs. She kept saying over and over that she felt my energy was cat-like. At the time I thought of cats as cute but mean...always hunting. I didn't want one at all.

However, I have since come to see that cats can also be quite funny natured and cuddly. When I was in my mid-40's, a neighbor's old cat began hanging around our house in the fall time. Then a terrible winter came along. The cat was constantly on our doorstep. Turns out the neighbor's boyfriend moved into her home with several dogs and the cat was very frightened of one of them. I kept the cat for about a month until I found out who he belonged to, and by then I was already smitten. The neighbor said I could keep him. Alexander Whiskers was my new baby! He made me love cats. After he was with us, I went on to adopt more meowy children.

Spirits around us...

Because I know from my own past life experiences that your personal energy exists beyond the body, I believe some people have the gift to sense spirits around them. I do think some people who do this sort of thing are legit. I have never had someone give me that type of reading before but I would be open to it.

I have gone to different types of "psychic readers" before. Some seemed like nice people who had no special insight. <u>One seemed like he could read my mind! Another predicted a few things that really happened.</u>

There was one "psychic" woman, however, who I totally wasted my money on because she was making stuff up from one minute to the next and contradicting herself! I haven't been to a psychic in 16 years...just living life as it comes.

The Scammer...

One time while I was in my early 30's, my friend Tanya and I decided to go to a "psychic" who was advertising readings for $20. (Tanya believes she had been Vivian Leigh during one of her past lives.)

The psychic had just opened a new business in our area, and she was running "a deal". The woman had a sign hanging up on her house and that was where she was doing her sessions.

My friend and I went individually to this place after work...so by then it was dark out. Tanya went first and then I followed. Tanya said the woman kept telling her her husband was cheating on her and if she got Tanya's credit card she could tell her more. My friend was very upset.

Then I was told a whole slew of falsities. I called the psyshic on what she was saying and she was still very insistent. On top of that I kept hearing banging noises in the background and I asked what was going on and she said it was her brother. By the end of the session, I supposedly had a curse on me which was ruining my love life and she wanted me to come back with $250 for "a curse removal ceremony" in which she said I would lie down and she would burn candles and say some magic words. There was no way I was going to lie down in front of this woman while her brother was hanging out in the wings. I didn't trust either of them.

Well, needless to say my friend and I wanted to report the psycho-psychic to the Police. I talked to my boss and my boss' boss and they agreed we should. I was afraid for all the college girls in the town who might get trapped by the psychic and her brother. The lady was too intense and a liar. I just had a weird feeling about both of them. Better safe than sorry.

My friend and I went to the police station the next day during lunch hour, but after waiting around in a little room for an hour, my friend left to go back to work. I was working for someone who had been a sexual harassment help contact at The University, and she gave me permission to stay at the station as long as it took.

When the officer finally showed up to talk to me he basically was convinced I was trying to be like the woman on "The X-Files" TV show.—*That* is what he said. He even mentioned my red hair. He further said, "Anyone who goes to a psychic is a bit nuts." Some people automatically assume that.

I said to the policeman, "Maybe you should send in an undercover female officer." I handed him the newspaper ad for the psychic. He finally seemed convinced to check things out. All I know is the psychic's sign was down two weeks later. I don't know what really happened, but something.

This is really a problem I believe...there are people in the world who really do have "the psychic gift" but the cons of the world give a lot of people the impression that they all are scammers. Be open-minded... **be very careful.**

Mutually bored...agreed!

Typically I do not discuss reincarnation with my boyfriend Jay. I know he simply doesn't believe in it. But since writing the book, of course I have brought it up more often...just like he wants to go on-and-on about the stock market on a daily basis. One day I was in the middle of a story and Jay said, "Be normal." Well, this is my normal, dear.

Jay has said to me, "You know, reincarnation to me is what the stock market is to you...not interesting and I barely listen." This is fine with me! I'm glad he knows all that bull and bear stuff goes in one ear and out the other and sounds like "blah, blah, blah"!

June 1, 2019:

My boyfriend Jay and his singer gals were doing a band gig at some dinner party an hour from our house. This "disbeliever boyfriend" of mine IM's me and says, **"It's Marilyn's birthday and my gig is in Monrovia...put that in your book."** (Monrovia, Indiana)

Chapter Eleven:

MARILYN: UNDER THE PILLOW: THE CORONER GOT IT WRONG!

"Jack , do you know what your brothers did?"

 he story I am about to tell you is **NOT fiction. Yet I have no way of proving it to anyone.** I have no DNA evidence, I have no documents, I have no photos or surveillance video, I have no crime scene articles, I have no witnesses to corroborate what I say. **I have nothing that will hold up in a court of law.**

Truth...
Psssst...it wasn't "probable suicide"!

 You can believe me or disbelieve me. But I know that what I am saying is true. If people don't believe me, that is fine. At the end of the day, I can look in the mirror and say, "Norma Jeane, you did it.

You told the world." **I apologize to anyone who is hurt by the truth I am about to tell.**

AUGUST 4-5, 1962:

I/Marilyn had intense insecurities. I could go from full confidence bordering arrogance to completely being a crumbling tearful mess who had no control over my fears and emotions. My life was often extremely exhausting. **I decided to kill myself that night…August 4, 1962.** I was frightened that my career would not be stable in a few years…afterall, I was already 36.

I had a lot of pills and downed a handful, knowing that dose would not kill me. **But I told myself I was going to take control of my life, by taking control of my departure.** I told myself that I would just lay there and THINK for a while….and then I would take another round of pills….a bigger more powerful one…..later…..to end it all. I thought I had time to wait.

Apparently I became too groggy because the next thing I recall is waking up to someone coming in the bedroom door. I was bleary-eyed but tried to focus and got up a bit, just leaning forward. There was Bobby, Edward, and some stranger….a serious looking man in a suit and holding a briefcase. He looked like a hitman out of a movie.

I didn't panic because Bobby was there. (I hated Edward and he hated me….but that is a whole other story. He had raped me after a party a while back. He hated me because I wouldn't take on another brother.) I guess I had a false sense of security because Bobby was there. But then things got weird. Bobby began telling me that I need to get out of something. I don't recall what. I kept saying, "You can't tell me what to do." I was loopy.

Then I said I had to go to the bathroom. I got up and sort of walk/wobbled over to the bathroom and stood behind the inside of the bathroom door. I stared bleary-eyed at a shelf/cabinet across the room and wondered what I was supposed to do and why they were out there. I didn't actually use the bathroom….I just stood on the inside of the door. **I remember feeling hyper-aware and time seemed to stand still…until I decided I had to go back out. It was almost like I could sense**

something was about to happen, but what? I didn't know. Why didn't Bobby come alone?

Then I walk/wobbled back out and plopped down on the bed....but not in the position with my head at the top of the bed...more in the middle of the bed. Edward told Bobby I had had sex with him too.... and Bobby believed him! Bobby began slapping me and he called me a slut. **I kept saying "No Bobby I didn't do it...No Bobby."** Then suddenly it was like a switch flipped in my head and I suddenly realized Bobby would never believe me over his brother. I began laughing hysterically......I couldn't stop.

That is when I remember Edward reaching past me and Bobby and grabbing the bedroom pillow and saying, "There is only one way to shut up a slut.".....and he put the pillow over my face. I began grabbing at the pillow to try to pull it off but I couldn't. I couldn't breathe and I was panicking...... THAT was when my consciousness left my head. It was the strangest release. To be trapped inside of a head/ body for a lifetime and then to be out...on the other side... was very disorienting. I remember I saw myself and it was so perplexing.

My consciousness then moved around the room like a frantic ball of energy. **At one point it smashed up against a mirror and I was startled but I don't know why.** I didn't go into the mirror but something scared me at the mirror.

I then noticed Bobby pacing around the room...moping...looking so sad......just gloomy. **My consciousness went up to his eyes as if to appeal to him and say, "Here I am...here I am!!!"....but then I realized he couldn't see me. I was out of body.**

Then Edward said, **"You'll get over her Bobby, she's just another girl."** This was very strange. I don't think there is ever such a thing as "Just another girl"...because every girl is important!

My consciousness then went up behind Edward and I wondered what he was doing. My white negligee was hiked up to my armpits, and I realized he was jerking-off on me. Afterwards, Edward struggled to remove the right side of my gown (on his left), so the hitman bruskly tugged at my left, pulling it up over my head. That was a moment of true despair. I was outside of myself and watching these men treat me like a mere object. I couldn't say anything ...I couldn't do anything...I

261

couldn't stop anything. It was all happening to ME, and I wasn't even "there" anymore.

The serious man then began taking stuff out of his briefcase. I think there was a metal box with gauges and knobs.....and some tubes....and some little containers with different colored things in it....something pink...something green... I didn't know what that was for. But when he took out the green one he said, "This one will really make her pop." Edward chuckled and flushed some of my pills in the toilet.

I remember trying to get back into my body again, and thinking I looked older than I used to think I did....and also sweaty. I needed a manicure. I hovered near my body and also went back into my body a while longer.

I know I saw someone find my diary but I'm not sure where it was, or if it was a red one. I believe it was in some lower level cabinet drawer. I know it was hidden low...not high. **I remember thinking, "No, no... that is mine, you can't have it."** But I couldn't stop anything that was going on. I also believe I witnessed someone burning my diary...but I'm not sure where that was.

I remember seeing a needle on the floor and thinking maybe someone would find it after the men left and know that something bad had happened to me. I don't know if they found it themselves or not. I was in and out of clear conscious thought.

At the very end, as I left my body for the last time, a dark liquid squirted out of me suddenly...onto a white sheet hanging in a clump at the foot of the bed. It was disgusting and I remember being fearful that that would kill my image. —How strange that I had just been murdered and I gave a damn about my image...my IMAGE.... Who cares about my image! I am sure Mrs. Murray had to clean up the mess.

Over the years, Mrs. Murray has not given a consistent account of what really happened that fateful night at Marilyn's house. However, I empathize because poor Mrs. Murray was probably scared out of her mind. Afterall, I ended up dead. Would she have survived if she had told the truth?

I thought I was taking control of the last night of my life...but alas all control was taken from me and I felt traumatized, frantic, disgusting, ashamed ....and the deepest feeling of being discon- nected and alone.....and betrayed.

For some odd reason, I think I remember actually following the stranger with the briefcase into a completely other building quite a distance away.....I saw him get into an elevator and I kept wondering who he was and what he did to me and WHY. He had no expression on his face. It was like he was barely alive himself. He looked like he was devoid of feelings of any kind.

Sometimes I also believe I returned to this plane...and was there in the autopsy room, but then my consciousness left because I couldn't handle it. I think my energy was especially attached to my body/face during this lifetime...because I was known for my body. As my consciousness was processing the shock of all that had happened so quickly, I do remember feeling very sorry for myself.

In my mind I want to believe that Bobby was there that night to reason with me and keep Edward and the hitman from killing me. He did, afterall, start out talking to me but I wouldn't listen...I was already doped up. I have a very hard time disliking Bobby even though he was there and looked the other way. I saw his sad eyes and it's very hard to forget that up until that night I thought that he was special. Bobby was personable.

I am sure I am being delusional though...he knew why he was there. He knew what the plan was. He got others to pull it off. My feelings are still all jumbled up about that man. I don't actually remember a whole lot...other than he used to sit on the side of the bed and talk to me and that made me feel important. And he was very give-and-take. Not self-centered.

One of the other "Marilyn Claimers" has said that Bobby was more fun than Jack, and on that point I do agree. Jack was somewhat handsome and had "the big title" but overall Bobby was a lot more fun.

I am sure Edward wanted to kill me no matter what. He probably came to my house pretending to be supportive of Bobby, but meanwhile he had his own axe to grind. Because I never confided in Bobby about that, he didn't know. Edward gave me a strange vibe from the beginning. Bobby and Jack were attractive. People have the right to choose who they spend time with. But maybe within the same family it is hard not to compare what you get (or don't) to what your siblings do.

I also remember that when I was Marilyn, I was not particularly nice to Bobby towards the end. I was flippant. How exactly did I expect to threaten him and think that things could turn out well? Doesn't a bunny know not to take on a tiger? I might as well have worn my diary around my neck...perhaps with that sequin happy birthday dress. I was being so blatantly foolish. I should have walked away.

I/Marilyn honestly think that I was under the impression that I got to choose between Bobby and Jack because I had dalliances with both of them...eenie-meenie-miney-moe! But what I didn't see was, because they both played the game of sexopoly with me, neither one of them wanted to claim the prize. Even now when I think about all of this situation from a life-time away, I have great inner conflict about everything and every one of the players...the men, and myself. Utter nonsense. All of us completely foolish.

By the current year, (2019) we all know Bobby and his brothers are gone. I wonder if the stranger with the briefcase is still walking around? I'm guessing he was in his early 40's back in 1962. I'm guessing he is gone.

I remember the odd piece of equipment the hitman used was confusing at the time. But it perhaps explains why I/Michele used to feel "off" when I would visit my Father at his various work places during this lifetime. As an engineer he had machines all around and I used to feel strange but couldn't figure out why. I just reasoned it was because I'm not very scientific.

After my/Marilyn's consciousness first left my body, I was never connected to it the same way again, and things were more and more confusing. I feel that my consciousness was hyper aware the first minutes after leaving my body, but then actual clarity came and went.

I vividly remember the color of Bobby's eyes. That is something above all else that really stands out to me. My desperate attempt to get his attention. My consciousness going up to his eyes. Very blue with a fleck of something else. Very, very blue.

At the risk of sounding disrespectful: I wonder if Bobby thought about Marilyn during his final moments of life. It's not that I think he loved me, but did he realize the position he had left me in while his brother and the hitman killed me? I'd like to think it dawned on him.

I also have this other nagging thought: If Bobby's wife never remarried does immunity still apply as far as testifying against her spouse? I mean, if by any chance Bobby did confide in her what happened to Marilyn on August 4-5, 1962? I would never want her in that position of testifying against people in her family. But still... I can't help but wonder. Selfish perhaps.

As for Edward:

Although I do not like Edward Kennedy in the least... **I am sorry if my telling the truth about what happened back in 1962 hurts anyone in his family today.** It is beyond me that so many "witnesses" claim to have seen Bobby near Marilyn's house on the evening that she died, but no one seems to remember seeing Edward.

My friend Tina said that Bobby was more well known and maybe people didn't even know who Edward was if they did see him. That seems like a stretch, because I am sure Edward was seen in many photos with his brothers. However, somehow he has seemed to escape being linked to Marilyn's murder. Nothing could be further from the truth... he was there!

The letter...

I will tell you this...when I was 20 or so, I did write Edward an anonymous letter. No threats, just informing him that I was back and mentioning a couple things...being smothered by him and that he and I both knew who I really made love to (not him!) It was handwritten and just one page....it might have been front and back...it's so long ago and hard to remember now. I didn't have much to say to him, and **I knew**

he would kill me again if he believed I was her and he could find me.
I didn't keep a copy of the letter...kind of wish I had. I have no idea if
he ever received it or if it was disposed of by some clerical worker who
opens mail and thought it was junk. I don't recall what address I used
either. An older friend suggested he would be at some certain place and
I looked the address up and used it. If he had seen it, I am sure he would
have known......and been a little scared. But then perhaps towards the
end of his life, he might have been relieved, knowing he could possibly
come back. It's hard to say. I don't know how his mind worked...only
that he was scary.

"The pen is mightier than the sword"..... Edward Bulwer-
Lytton in 1839

Rape is a 4-letter word... (I cannot prove this, I just remember it.)

**So, why would Edward want to kill Marilyn and be happy to
participate in her murder you might wonder?** I don't think he was
there just to support Bobby.

One time during a party, Edward cornered Marilyn in the middle
of a large staircase. I was halfway down and he ran halfway up and prop-
ositioned me. **I told him I wasn't interested in getting together. And
he said, "Come on, what's one more brother?"** That really unnerved
me. I managed to push past him and went downstairs and had another
drink and talked with a small group of people for another 20 minutes
or so...but I felt self-conscious. I then decided to leave.

As I was leaving I had to walk past a string of cars which were on
my left. Edward must have noticed me exiting and followed me out on
purpose. The next thing I knew, he tackled me and pushed me into the
backseat of someone else's car and raped me.

So, I think it was pure jealousy and envy that motivated him. I
think he was anxious to get rid of me, although I never told either of
his brothers what he had done because I was so humiliated. **But I also
don't know what the hell I was thinking, wanting to stay involved
with Bobby or Jack after that occurred because clearly "the bad guy"
was always going to be around.**

So let me say this blatantly, the person known as "The Lion" was really "The Liar". Yes...that's right. I am saying it clearly. This isn't just an opinion, this is an experience. I was under the pillow. I was pushed into the back of a car. **I cannot prove anything but know it. Marilyn knows!**

All the theories...

I have read that some people think Marilyn was killed because she had information about aliens in Roswell that were studied. I have read that she supposedly had inside information on attempting to kill Castro. Who knows what the Kennedy's may have confided in her, or what she may have kept note of, or what she may have lorded over Bobby's head and threatened to tell. Whatever it was, Marilyn <u>never should have been told,</u> and she never should have used that information as a weapon. And...she/I paid for it.

Let me make this clear. I have absolutely no recollection of WHAT could have been in Marilyn's little red book that supposedly had big secrets written in it. I'm completely clueless and have furthermore never attempted to remember any of that ...not in waking life, not in meditation, not through hypnosis. I don't want to know, I don't care. It has never just come to me like other memories have. The information is old now. Moot!

It doesn't last forever....

Even though we get many lifetimes, we only live our current lifetime once. Life is short. It may not seem that way while we are going through it, but when time runs out, we suddenly feel the coulda'/shoulda'/woulda's.

When I/Marilyn died, I remember thinking, "There are <u>no more tomorrows</u> to finally take charge of my life and straighten things out." I always thought that I had "tomorrow" to take the steps to be taken more seriously. But it was easiest to go down the most obvious path. Be pretty. Be sexy. I remember wishing I had the courage to reinvent myself...but I didn't. No courage. I was afraid to take really big risks.

And then two months after turning 36, it was all over...in a way I never expected. It was like I fell through a trap door...down down down...the end. No more time. Gone. Over! And then, on top of it all, my murder has been a cold case for decades. But many thanks to those who tried to uncover the truth. Thank you.

Some may wonder WHY I would even be upset about dying that night...the very night that I myself had chosen to depart. Afterall, I did take a round of pills with the intent to take more. So why? Why?

I'll never know if I may have changed my mind. Or perhaps I might have just not awakened until morning if those men hadn't startled me awake as they walked through my bedroom door uninvited.— So I may not have had the opportunity to take more pills that night. Maybe I would have attempted to kill myself at a later date anyway. Marilyn will never know. I can only speculate. My fear of aging would have still existed on August 6 and 7 and 8 and 9 and 10........ 1962. ...1963...1964...

But even if I had killed myself that night, at least it would have been my choice, by my method, and without being bullied or shamed and called names, and stripped naked. Perhaps I'm only kidding myself. Perhaps things were going to end messy regardless. I just imagined going out with more dignity. I wonder how Bobby managed to pretend he wasn't there.

If DNA evidence had existed back in 1962, I wonder if this case would have been solved? Or was "that family" just so powerful, that the evidence would have been lost before it ever made it to a lab for testing?

I bet those three boys really enjoyed the headlines the very next day. But, now you know...it was a set-up. Marilyn found in the nude...wasn't Marilyn's choice. I can't relate to the posed crime scene photos of my former self... I refuse to.

Somebody found me alive and made sure I was dead, before they left my bedroom. Somebody got away with it.—All three somebodies got away. And my soul moved on. **And now writing this book is the only way I know how to explain it.**

So the question is…. "Do people care more about writing more stories about how I *might* have died? Or do people want to know and accept what really happened?"

I won't get my hopes up. I expect to be called a variety of things… crazy…ugly…a wannabe actress…looking for 15 minutes of fame…a hack writer…slut. I've seen what people have said about another Claimer and Marilyn herself.—Oh well!

When I was in my early 20's…

I was grocery shopping with my Mom and I noticed a book about Marilyn on a shelf. I picked it up in anticipation of reading an interesting blurb or seeing some glamour shot I might or might not remember. But…I was horrified! There in front of me was the most personal and disgusting photo. It was an autopsy picture that I can never get out of my mind. WHY do people want to see that? Are they jealous because Marilyn was pretty? Do they figure someone out there in the medical profession will be able to read purple blotches and determine the cause of death? Why are photos like that not protected and confidential like medical records of living people? Why?

PLEASE STOP!   PLEASE STOP!   PLEASE…

When I/Michele was 19, I saw a photo of myself sleeping. Someone had taken it in the back of a car when I was coming home from spring vacation. **It scared the heck out of me…I looked dead.** I was seriously stunned and felt a shock go through me. Now my boyfriend takes them to be funny. But at least my cat is in them too.

Chapter Twelve:

MARILYN: INFATUATION WITH THOSE TWO BROTHERS: BOBBY AND JACK.

*I*often recall **Marilyn's thoughts.** I saw a video where another "Marilyn Claimer" was asked if she thought Marilyn really expected to be First Lady someday. She seemed unsure but hopeful Marilyn was smarter than that. I'm sorry to say, Marilyn was not! I was not!

I, as Marilyn, remember thinking that maybe it was a long shot... but still, I was not smart enough to just dismiss the idea. I really thought a chance existed. I remember thinking, **"Wouldn't the kids back in high school be amazed if that happened?! Blond movie-star becomes First Lady! Just little 'ol Norma Jeane moving into the White House."**

Perhaps because I had made it out of a childhood filled with so much chaos, and had become a movie star at some popular level, I actually thought I could pull this off too...becoming First Lady. It seems so insane now.

I also recall that Marilyn used to compare the two brothers. "I like Jack's body ....I like Bobby's eyes.....Bobby talks to me more..... Jack is President." As superficial as this is, the title trumped every-thing...and I knew that made no sense because I actually felt closer to Bobby. A lot of people say they remember where they were when they heard the President was shot.—I think that whole situation is very sad. But, in reality I feel 10-times sadder about what happened to Bobby. I guess in the long run I felt more bonded to him than I was willing to admit, when I was trying to impress the kids back home and I was chasing a title.

When you love someone, you don't screw their brother. For Marilyn, this was all about going through a phase in life which was rather desperate...reaching for something big. What if she turned 40 in a few years and her career faded away? I remember thinking the worst and not having the guts to reinvent my image. I was afraid people would only accept me in one way...sexpot. I also liked immediate grat-ification and "working on things" takes time. (This is interesting to me now because during this Michele-lifetime, my ex-boyfriend Kyle was the same way. He wanted everything ultra fast without too much work....and it led to huge problems.)

I would say there was some kind of love in both of Marilyn's affairs with Bobby and Jack, but it was not mature. It was flighty. Intense infat-uation, perhaps. It was more than just a one-time fling with either/both of the men, but still it was all about "the lies we tell ourselves". Make-believe overall. Grasping....grasping... grasping ...for something that really belongs to someone else. **These men were married.**

When I think about all of the headlines for decades and decades, I sometimes feel badly for the Kennedy children and wives who have had to endure the continuing public interest about Marilyn and Bobby, and Marilyn and Jack. I am especially sorry to Bobby's wife who has had to deal with it all the longest.

Marilyn has been gone since 1962, but yet their families still have to hear about the Marilyn affairs. **I'm sorry that it is still a topic of conversation. It was selfish on my/Marilyn's part.** And the fact that Bobby and Jack were messing around with a bunch of other girls anyway, doesn't change that. Marilyn played a part…it was wrong. In the end I really felt like a fool.

I feel badly because Marilyn's name has so much staying power, so she is perhaps the ONE GIRL who people won't drop from the headlines. **But really, why are we still talking about "Marilyn with Bobby and Marilyn with Jack" anymore? They aren't good role models in terms of relationships.** The media loves pretty looking people and status and drama. But all three adults were behaving badly. **And I'm sorry.**

Seeing your past life self, doesn't mean always agreeing with your actions. Marilyn knew better too, she just wasn't mature enough to walk away. I know I knew better then. I remember knowing it, but I was full steam ahead in delusions.

I read an article once where someone was discussing past life experiences and they said that if you pursue your past, you better be prepared to discover that you were not always the hero in every life.

<u>**So here goes…My Confession:**</u>

I/Michele am not a saint. One hopes to improve from one lifetime to the next but we all start over when we come back, and therefore make our own errors in judgment.

A foreshadowing of events….

I remember when I was 16 and working evening shows at the community theatre. A beloved older actress was taking a break on the deck right off of the crew's quarters. As she was smoking she was looking me very seriously in the eyes. **She said, "You know Missy… there's more to you than people think. You know…they say you always have to watch out for the quiet ones. Wait 'til you mature.**

You'll see. You always have to watch out for the quiet ones." I timidly said, "Oh not me." I've often wondered what she thought I was going to do someday.

Then when I was 21, I went to the country club close to home to fill out an application. I was wearing a dress and standing around waiting for someone to fetch me paperwork. An attractive man about mid-30's came up to me and looked me up-and-down. He beamed and inquired about what I was doing. I explained I was hoping to get a job. **Then his smile turned to a smirk and he shook his head and said, "The wives around here better beware."** I asked him what he meant. He just repeated himself and walked away. I didn't get hired. At the time, in my young foolish mind, I thought that what he said was flattering...I guess he thought I was pretty. I also thought he was way-off-base and read me completely wrong!

As I've indicated before, my 30's was a real time of experimentation. This period was partly driven by depression and partly driven by hormones and desire. I was basically floundering around in the wake of what seemed like a shortage of available appealing men close to my age... and then, a couple married men entered stage right....(wrong!)

I am using code names for these men for very obvious reasons.

PART 1:

In my 30's, I was divorced and depressed...and watching way too many movies about illicit love affairs. At age 29, I went into my relationship with Demetri thinking things were going to be great, but a couple years in, I felt like his cynical nature was constantly trying to suck the joy out of my hopes for a happy bond between us. I guess I should have just broken up then. I was beginning to feel a deep, deep sense of despair.

I admit I had hopes that my relationship "with a mature man" would "fix" everything for me. But he had his own issues. I know that cheating fixes nothing. I know that communication is the only way to get back on track. But getting side-tracked seemed easier and more fun than talking to someone who was often grumpy. I made up excuses when someone began to show interest. This was not the first time someone did, but it was the time I permitted myself to step-out. I allowed myself to believe that it would be ok.

This situation actually overlapped with part of my relationship with Demetri. I hate to say it, but it is true...and I know that wasn't fair to him. I'm guessing it was about 3 years in. In the midst of dealing with grave disappointment, temptation came along...in a power suit.

Walden and I worked in the same town and we crossed paths several times a week. He definitely stuck out in the crowd. He wore spiffy suits, and had a unique and commanding voice. He was a gentleman ... always very polite. Also in his thirties. Typically our conversations were cordial...just cordial. At the time, he was married and I was struggling with my own lifestyle issues.

After a year, something changed. Walden seemed to take a sudden peculiar interest in talking to me about personal matters. He would phrase things he said as if fishing for explanations without really directly asking. He seemed to want to know who I was with and how things were going, and I thought it rather odd. During one veiled interrogation he made the statement that whoever I was with was lucky and he complimented my skirt. I knew I was no longer imagining this extra attention. At this point, I pondered..."Am I really actually attracted to this man? Or am I just flattered to be noticed? I knew he was attractive but I had never given him a real thought before. Afterall, he was married. Off limits, right?

One day Walden approached me and mumbled, "I can rent a room at the hotel across from your apartment." I responded somehow, but I really don't recall what I said. I simply remember several days of speaking in choppy sentences and nervous looks and acting as if we were "doing something top secret and clandestine". He could have dropped the issue and I would have been fine. He could have pushed the issue and I would have gladly gone along. He was taking the lead. It was a bit tantalizing.

Bored in my life. Still feeling the emotional fall-out from my failed marriage. Disappointed in my relationship status. Completely stressed at my job. **How do I recount the many excuses I could make for doing what I did?** Just being a follower, just following the perceived excitement that had presented itself in my path, I was essentially allowing another to make my decisions for me. I am responsible for my own actions, but …I let him decide if we would actually follow through. He decided. We did.

We got together on a chilly rainy night and I was freezing just crossing the street. I wore a lace negligee under a raincoat and was attempting to conceal how surprisingly nervous I was. When I got to the room, he said he had just gotten off the phone with his wife. Walden had a pizza waiting on the bed and he asked me if I wanted a beer. He then proceeded to look beyond the lace and offer me what I had come there for. Our encounter was brief, and a couple positions later, I practically bolted out the door. I remember the perplexed look on his face, as I was quickly making my exit.

Walden :	**"Why are you leaving so soon?"**
Michele:	**"I don't want you to get sick of me. As the saying goes …'Always leave them wanting more.' Besides your wife might call again. Bye."** (Something lame like that.)

The books I read…

For many years I had read self-help books and articles about why men are often more emotionally detached then women. A common theme seemed to be about how most men are afraid of being smothered. I think this is why several men have told me, "You kind of really think like a man." These manuals taught me to be both genuinely and calculatingly aloof.

I once read a most intriguing article which claimed to be a real life story. A man who lived in a lighthouse said that his most memorable encounter was when he made love on a cold stormy night to a woman he had just met, and she touched him all over, whereas most of his lovers had been very timid. It was just a one night affair, but it made an impression he never forgot.

The point is, all of this reading material formed a large part of the personality I brought into relationships by the time I was in my 30's.

Ask for little. Expect little. Bend over backwards. Forgive repeatedly. And for God's sake, most of all never be boring in bed. It's all just a theory, easier to play-out with some partners than others. And I am not a robot...I'm a GIRL! Ideally, with the right person, all this bookish advice comes naturally.

After the tryst at the hotel, I ran across the street to my apartment and spent the night watching TV. I wondered why I hadn't stayed longer. Let the inner conflicts begin! And the unrealistic fantasies flourish!

I remember a time a friend and I were discussing men, and I asked her if she thought that Walden was handsome. She immediately snapped, "Yuk, I'd never *do* him." I thought she was crazy and never said a word. I admit I gave him sort of a "Kennedy-esque status," and I had him on a pedestal for a while. At first I thought he was suave and powerful... an authority figure in his job and definitely appealing. Absolutely no one knew about us.

Walden and I continued to interact as we still crossed paths. At first our little "inside secret" seemed rather sexy, as we perpetuated the ruse that we were non-sexual casual acquaintances. However, sometimes I wasn't quite sure how I really felt. I thought he was attractive, but was I blowing things out of proportion just to justify breaking the rules? One moment I felt like I had to continue because I told myself he was amazing. The next moment I thought I was simply concocting a semblance of passion because my everyday life was so boring and frustrating and nobody datable seemed to be on the horizon. Just because someone is attractive or <u>you</u> want to be attractive, doesn't mean you have to "prove it" by getting involved.

One day I saw Walden's wife from a distance...she was wearing bright red lipstick and a frightening scowl. Her sour look confirmed it all. In my mind I thought, **"Walden deserves to have a good time ...he needs it. She has driven him to do whatever he has done! How on earth did he ever end up with *her*?"**

I reasoned that we were doing nothing wrong...and continued. As a matter of fact, her bitchy look made me feel as if I owed it to Walden as if I was somehow offering aid to the suffering. (Things we tell ourselves!) The things he said also supported this notion as well. I excused all the inappropriateness of my actions by mental gymnastics that tallied up all the bad things in my life, therefore making Fate and The Universe owe me some kind of leniency. I thought Walden and I each deserved some kind of break. I tried to imagine myself as a woman from a Lifetime movie.

As time went on, Walden and I got together during evenings after work hours. It was always him calling me when I least expected...and all to *his* convenience. I could never call him, of course. I knew "all the rules" from things I had seen on TV. As a matter of fact, there were times I thought Walden was a bit giddy and haphazard out in public, and I would rein him in and say, "People are going to catch on if you do this or that." As miserable as I was with the restrictions I was also playing that part of the "smarter one," constantly safeguarding our secret and enforcing the limitations. It was kind of like shooting myself in my own foot really.

Walden would call, I'd take a shower, greet him at my door, and foreplay consisted of him smoking a cigarette and griping about his wife. (Cigarettes and kissing don't mix.) He claimed he was living nearly celibate and his wife "rarely gave him confirmation as a man". –He liked to use that phrase. From the time he showed up at my door until the time he left, each encounter was maybe 90 minutes. We were never together more than that.

Despite being at odds with his wife, Walden said his family really adored her. It was becoming clear I didn't belong. His wife was loved... they had a history together. Furthermore he said his wife's temper was horrible, and she really would kill us if she ever suspected anything. He assured me he wasn't kidding. I began to picture myself on the news ...the camera panning towards my car lying in a ditch. Nevertheless, we got together here and there for a little over a year ...but less than once a month.

One night Walden came over and we got a bit careless... I ended up with a couple big hickies on my neck and one near my chest. I panicked because I was used to getting together with Demetri on the weekends and that was only a day or two away. **I called my friend Meredith and she seemed full of advice, but none of it seemed like it could get me out of the jam.**

"**Wear a turtle neck**"   —**I hate them and don't own them!**
"**Just have sex in the dark**" —**Uh, semi-dark maybe but can't guarantee it won't be the middle of day.**
"**Put cold water on it and hope that the marks shrink.**"

We did get a few chuckles out of it all. I ended up telling Demetri I was sick and couldn't see him on the coming weekend. I didn't know what else to do. I figured he might end up competing with Walden's wife to see who could kill me first.

But back to reality. The terrible truth is, no matter how sexy Walden was, several encounters in, I realized we just didn't quite sync physically. I clung to the idea that his attractiveness still made it all worthwhile. Kind of like when actors have terrible chemistry, but the movie viewers don't feel the negative tension,...all they see is the lovely images. Things <u>seemed</u> like they <u>should have been</u> perfect. Two dynamic people, close in age, excited to get together, sneaking around, last-minute encounters....never having to deal with daily real life together.

But, over time, I had to concede...none of this was working for me on any level. I considered throwing in the towel, but it took me over a year to do. Because Walden was charming I kept hoping for the best in the sheets. But I don't know what I thought would change...we never talked about anything sexual...positions...preferences...nothing. We just "did-it".

So...exactly what was the problem? "**His thrust killed my lust.**" (Yep, I made that up and it really describes what happened.) Walden and I were not compatible. I have no idea if he even noticed. Maybe bad sex was ok with him....better than nothing? Maybe if I had been taller or he had been shorter...maybe it would have been better. Maybe he was just nervous because we were sneaking around. I really don't quite know how to describe it..."battering ram?"

I'll never know if he was only that way with me, but at that point, I realized perhaps I owed his wife a little empathy. Maybe that was just his style and her experience too. **BATTERING RAM! Need I say more?—Well I will. It was very hard...it was fast ...and a rhythm that never felt sexy. Sexual but not sexy. Hard but not deep.** I really don't know if it was better during our first couple of encounters or if I was just so mesmerized by his presence that it didn't yet matter. That is all a blur.

One night I remember standing on my apartment back deck and looking over the parking lot. My assigned spot was "lucky 13". I remember thinking, **"So this is the way it is...being the 'other woman.' Aren't I supposed to feel like I won a prize?** Why do I feel like a big dummy waiting around for someone I rarely see? And why am I waiting for someone I'm not compatible with?"

Sex with Walden wasn't the thrill I hoped for, but despite trying to be emotionally detached, I had developed somewhat of a crush on him ...or "the him" I imagined when he wasn't around. **So there was the big irony: I wanted more time with someone who screwed me funny. I wanted ....more time........with someone........who screwed me... like a <u>maniac</u>. WHAT was wrong with me?!**

In the end, I was watching TV and my answering machine picked up a call. ...four times. I was tired and not in the mood to make any last minute plans. Walden had called me over and over and told some corny joke. The desperation hit me like a ton of bricks. He wanted to get together with me way too badly and he had a wife. I emailed him the next day with my regrets. I told him it was over. He seemed to take it in stride. I'd like to say that I had a moral epiphany, but that was only partially true. I simply couldn't continue to see someone I didn't have the guts to talk to for real. I simply couldn't continue the way things were on any level. And I had no right to ask for more time...and <u>if sex had gotten better</u> I would have probably ended up attached to him and heartbroken. Time to say good-bye.

As time went on, crossing paths was rare, although it did happen occasionally. Several times we said hello and made small talk. He looked uneasy and sad, I felt guilty. But at least we got out alive. I never wanted to hurt his wife. I don't want to die fighting over a man. But if I die for a man... he would have to be MY man...not someone else's.

Despite all the awkwardness, I still think of Walden as sexy and cool, all these years after our encounters. I really can't imagine it was all that good for him either. I just think he wanted to know someone found him attractive. I have no idea how he remembers it all. He talked about his wife, not about us. I think he griped so much about her, because he really loved her.

What stands out in my mind is that I felt a certain torment during this period because I knew my behavior was not just. When I would leave my boyfriend's house, it seemed that "Don't Go Chasing Waterfalls" by TLC was constantly on the car radio. And I felt like I could relate.

Part 2:

I had enjoyed ...or survived...my previous encounters with a man who I knew up front was married. I had absolutely no intention of getting involved with another married man. However, here is the thing: I don't chase the "bad boys"... the "bad boys" pretend to be "good guys" and then they drop the act when I'm intrigued and hooked. So...here goes...another sordid tale...this happened a couple years later. Enter the guy in the blue plaid flannel shirt who lived in another town.

At one point I met this guy online through the local personals ads. Sheldon was near my age, he emailed me often and had a good sense of humor. He sent me a photo of himself and I thought he was dressed like a lumberjack. The picture was awkward, yet somewhat cute. I told myself he would look better in person...and he did...a little.

Sheldon told me he fantasized about having sex in a public place. We talked about many things, but as time went on it was obvious it was leading toward making that reality. We made plans to get together the

next time he was in town on business. Finally our plans were in place....
and then...he confessed.....he was married. He told me <u>the night before</u>.

I was surprised, disappointed, irritated, and confused about what
to do. Yes, confused. **There should have been no confusion! I should
have said, "Morally this is wrong, good-bye."** But I didn't. For weeks
I had believed he was single. I wanted to unhear what I had heard. I
liked being uninformed. I felt all the anticipation of our tryst sliding
down the drain.

Sheldon told me he loved his wife but was bored with their "predictable sex life". He said he had already had one affair and his wife
found out. He commented that he seemed to have a pattern of falling
for girls with the same name, so he wasn't worried about slipping-up
talking in the middle of sex. The big question was....did I want to join
"Sheldon's Michele Club."

Sheldon continued to bemoan his situation and I mulled things
over. I, of course, felt sorry for him. Sheldon was going to be in town
the next evening whether we executed our plans or not. I figured he
might have confessed because maybe he wanted a way out. I told him
that would be fine, we could call things off. But he assured me he still
wanted to make things happen.—We did.

**Sheldon came to pick me up at my apartment. I was wearing
something short and ready to hike up to my hips.** We went a couple
blocks away and drove to the top of a parking garage. We did **whatever** relatively fast, but mission accomplished. As we pulled out of the
parking spot, someone else was coming up to that floor. We exited
the garage.

**Then we went back to my place where we proceeded to break my
bed!** Yes, broken. Sheldon was not small in stature and somehow the
double bed I grew up sleeping in had buckled...and crashed. At some
point in time during the weeks following, my Dad offered to repair it,
and I sheepishly stood by as he reinforced the slats under the mattress
while he had no idea why it gave way in the first place. At least I don't
think he did....?

For about a year, Sheldon and I continued to get together. It was
not often, and probably less than ten times. At one point I recall he said
he was trying to meet a tall Asian woman online because that was one
of his other fantasies and rare. I remember feeling jealous and calmly

telling him that. But the truth is I had no hold on him. We weren't boyfriend and girlfriend.

At one point, Sheldon said he was coming to town for a meeting. He picked me up around 6:00AM. It was barely light out and a bit chilly. I was wearing my flimsy, little burgundy colored sundress. He took me to a park a few miles away, and we found a spot to mingle barely off a beaten path. We had no sooner gotten done, when we discovered the park was more popular than we suspected. A couple joggers just missed the show! We were quite surprised and laughed our way back to my place where I was let off. I then got ready for work that started at 8:00AM. Yes, I was in the middle of a mid-life crisis!

There was also the time we had chocolate syrup and whipped cream. I remember we spread out a big beach towel, and used it on the floor just inside my apartment door. It sounds better than it is. It's really just a mess.

On a different occasion Sheldon told me he would bring some pot. I told him I had never had it before and didn't think I should ever try it. (I had that engrained in my head as a teen.) He insisted...he told me it would "make me feel really relaxed and it would <u>enhance everything</u>". I contemplated how forbidden it always seemed to me, although I know for a lot of people it is no big deal to smoke a joint. The idea seemed as monumental as losing my virginity at that point...I was 35. But it never happened. Sheldon was going to stop by my place after work and bring it with him. However, he had to leave town earlier than expected.

I never asked for a rain check. It was really a relief not to ever cross that line. I guess it was some part of me pretending I was really "still a good girl". I don't think that smoking pot for medical reasons is wrong... let me make that clear. But I don't really want to live in a world where people who are stoned are getting behind the wheel of a car. I'm glad I have never tried it. It's just not necessary for me.

One of our craziest ideas was the time we decided to "stage a fight" and we emailed each other ground rules for about a week. No gouging eyes, no punching, no kicking in the balls, no biting...etc. He was supposed to walk through the door and "attack me". When we finally got together we wrestled on the floor and he *came* just before he could stick himself inside me. I could tell he was embarrassed. But Sheldon was over 6' tall and far from wimpy...obviously he could have done whatever he wanted to to me if it were not just a fantasy. We managed to squeeze in a quicky about 15 minutes later. Sheldon recovered quite well from Round 1. He was fun.

I remember I barely had time to wash up between the time he left my apartment and the time I went to work. I went to the office in my little flowered sundress and feeling flushed and clammy the rest of the day. I told my co-worker what we had done. She told me a year or so later she was very jealous of my sex life. She had been trapped in a turbulent marriage she eventually got out of. She met the man of her dreams then.

But seriously....

The whole idea of being attacked is simply not funny or cute or even sexy. I have no idea how we even came up with that idea in the first place...I'm sure it must have been his. (It was not at all a nod to violent behavior...especially since in the midst of writing this book I began to remember a past life during the 1880's in which I was beaten to death in a brothel by my client/lover.) I have never tried any S&M stuff...never will.

I suppose to some people my acquaintance with Sheldon sounds like a fun little romp...something maybe from a TV movie. It was fun...now and then. But I really wanted a RELATIONSHIP. **I wanted someone I could be seen out in public with and see at least once a week.**

The big revelation for me came through a couple different circumstances. After seeing him sporadically a bunch of months, I suddenly had not heard from Sheldon for two weeks. This was very odd, because he had emailed me five days a week, multiple times a day up until that point. Finally Sheldon sent me an apology and said that for several years he had been having some reoccurring health issues and a flair-up kept him at home. He told me his wife was really great at keeping things around the house going while he was in bed due to pain. And he said that he could be quite frightening at times because suffering made him cranky. **I started to think of his wife as a person who was a saint…we weren't in a movie, but real life.**

Then a month or so later, Sheldon told me he had gotten a great job offer and was for sure going to take it. This meant moving further away. He said his wife was amazing and generously offered to leave the neighborhood and job she loved to allow him to pursue his opportunity and he had not expected her support. She was making it easy for him.

I pointed out these positive qualities his wife had, and Sheldon agreed she was great. I began to wonder, "How much does someone have to do to keep their mate at home? Is nothing enough?"

Despite this fact, he still seemed to think we could/should continue to get together.— *That was it!* **I really didn't get it. HOW could he risk hurting her by seeing other people?** How could he risk losing her? His wife sounded like a wonderful lady. I told Sheldon that I had fun seeing him but it was over. He said he understood, but then he called me again when he was in town. I just didn't answer the phone. I couldn't.

When it's over….it is OVER!

Thus concluded my intimate associations with men who belonged to someone else. It's shameful even to put into writing, and certainly not something I'm proud of. I hope both men worked things out in their relationships. I hope they learned something from our encounters that made them try harder to make things work at home.

Emulating Marilyn's worst behaviors is NOT progress! There is nothing "cute" about threatening someone else's world.

I'm sorry if either of the wives of these two men ever found out. And God knows, I had a screwed up marriage, so why would I want to tamper in any way with someone else's? Marriage is supposed to be between two people. <u>And if multiple people are involved it should be by complete upfront agreement</u>. I can't even begin to pretend that getting involved with either of these two men was "right".

I love the TV show "Sister Wives":

The Brown Family is beautiful and entered into their marriages while everyone was completely upfront. I've watched them for years. I wish Kody, Meri, Janelle, Christine, Robyn and all their kids could live free of judgment and persecution. They deserve the very best!

Interestingly enough, I have seen online where people claim Marilyn has Irish roots. On the "Sister Wives" program, each wife receives a claddagh ring when she gets married. I think that is charming.

Go figure!

Sometimes when something seems like a good idea...it isn't! When I was in my early 30's I bought two life-size cardboard figures of Marilyn. On one she was wearing the red dress from the opening act of "Gentlemen Prefer Blonds" and the other was her in a white one-piece bathing suit. They stood in my bedroom and livingroom. On a regular basis I would forget that they were there and I would darn near have a heart attack as I entered the rooms. My brain would register "big object...intruder" and send fear down my spine. Then I would laugh it off and vow to be prepared the next time....I usually wasn't. After several years of jumping out of my skin, I gave them to Goodwill before I moved to California. If those cardboard Marilyns could talk...oh what stories they could tell!

Chapter Thirteen:

HALLUCINATIONS: SEEING WHAT OTHERS DON'T.

Oh Mother....why?

<u>Genetics to begin with</u>.

When I was Marilyn/Norma Jeane, I was very conscious even as a small child. I recall waiting in a long line with my Mom and she had me in a basket, as she was sitting down while waiting. I was practically smothering from the blanket she had on me. But people would stop and ask to see "the baby" and say how pretty I was. I was just tiny but I knew it was a good thing.

I also remember that even as a baby, I hallucinated...I saw things that weren't really there. Not sure how I knew since I was little. Maybe I had some special sense because I have lived so many other lifetimes before Norma Jeane/Marilyn's? But at that point, the extra things I saw seemed amusing and not harmful. Of course, as a baby I had no responsibility so I didn't have to function at a high level.

The incidents made things worse.

The tirade:

When I was about 1 1/2 years old, my Mom was very happy and giddy because some doctor boyfriend was coming to stay the weekend. He took us out. **But he also took me alone into a room with a clock on the wall and put me up on something and molested me with his finger.** I remember I peed my pants. I am not sure my Mom knew he did that to me.....but when the doctor left, she turned from very happy to very dismal in a matter of moments.

My Mother suddenly turned to me and looked at me with mean-ness and began calling me "a bad woman". I think she was jealous of any time he spent with me, because she wanted him all to herself and she wanted him to come back and he left in a hurry to go off to work despite her pleading with him to stay. I think she was jealous when people said I was cute...proud, but jealous.

My Mom began to rave at me and repeatedly told me I was bad and a "bad woman". I knew I was just a child. I could walk and run but hadn't been doing it that long...I was small. I ran past my Mom to get away from her and she grabbed my arm and picked me up and she threw me on the bed and was saying something about <u>something in my head</u>. I didn't know what she meant. <u>She said I needed an operation on my head</u>. She hit me and tried to smother me but stopped....then she turned to the dresser where there were scissors and she picked them up. I must have passed out.

When I woke up I had something tied around my head and a mark on my face and a chunk of hair missing. I remember trying to focus on a wallpaper pattern on the wall but it was blurry and then I had dou-ble-vision. And after that day I remember I had daily hallucinations ...both visual and also audio. Random things would appear and I knew no one else could see them. They were 10 times what they used to be. And I remember imagining that I had a twin, who looked different than me but was still my twin.

It was especially hard when I was a teen because I also felt energy swirling around as if something was touching my hair and playing with it...yet I would look in the mirror and none of my hair would be moving or out of place. **Whenever I read people describe Marilyn as possessing a "luminous quality" I can't help but feel that what they are really seeing is the result of energies that actually were attached to her/my being.**

This made life constantly a challenge to focus. And I always felt as if my mind was going to collapse in on itself...into the void of utter nothingness....and I would cease to exist anymore.

And as a child, I often was OCD about blinking my eyes or having a sniffle. –I hid it as best I could. I guess they were ticks.

Hot towels:

I remember when I was Norma Jeane, my Mother would take me to some religious ceremonies. Afterwards, other ladies would make plans to meet at a restaurant for a mid day lunch and my Mom would always tell them that we would join them too but we had some things to do first. We would go home and she would heat up the towels. I was starving and just wanted food. I had to wait. I hated it. It wasn't a one-time thing.

My Mother would take little towels and they would be damp and hot. We would sit on the floor in the bedroom and I always sat with my back up against the wall. She would sit across from me. She would put the towels on me and on herself and it was sweltering and hard to breath. She would hum some low type chant...almost moaning. She would talk about how we had to purge the evil in us so we weren't "bad women". I could never understand this because I knew I was just a kid, so how could I be bad...bad for what...what made me bad? I/ Michele have only ever been in a sauna one time and absolutely hated it. Maybe this is why.

Did my Mom convince me at a young age that I was unpure? Did my Mom feel guilty for her own urges and drag me into her self-purifying ceremonies because she was afraid I would turn out just like her? I am sure my Mother wanted love and to be desired, but then again, here she was with me. She was stuck taking care of a small child which made it harder to meet new men. Most men probably thought I was "a responsibility". I suppose she even thought sometimes that I was her competition...and I was just a child! I am sure to her I was both a blessing and a curse.

I loved my Mother and felt very bonded to her the first couple years, but I didn't understand her, and I was aware that things were very strange, even though I wasn't far into that lifetime yet. During later childhood I felt abandoned but it was probably for the best because God knows what she might have done to me next. I always felt as if an ominous cloud was following me around...hovering. I was always waiting to get caught in a downpour. Overly sensitive, overly fearful, overly emotional...that was me.

I remember being little Norma Jeane and having these two experiences...1) The Tirade...and...2) The Towels. But during Norma Jeane/Marilyn's lifetime I didn't recall these things with the clarity I do now. I honestly think I forgot about them because they were so disturbing. And that is part of what made my inner conflicts and mental state so much harder to figure out when I was her. I wasn't quite sure when my inner turmoil really began. What was the origin?

I/Norma Jeane figured genetically I was doomed. I didn't quite remember there were these interactions with my Mother. I would sometimes be on the verge of "remembering something" but it would hurt so much deep inside my being that I would push the memories back to the black hole of forgotten things. I possibly would have benefitted quite a bit if I could have just realized the things that had happened to me. But facing painful things is difficult. I believe these incidents were some of the nasty things that sent me into tears as a young adult. I always knew my problems were deeper than whatever I said they were. I always knew I wasn't facing something. It was like trying to see through a thick fog.

I know that even I/Michele can't remember all the past life things I want to know. Sometimes a past life person's face will begin to come into my mind's view and it will scare me so much or I will feel such overwhelming love and sorrow that it is too strong to process. — Consequently, what was about to materialize evaporates. Fear drives it away. I have yet to figure out how to over-ride that reaction, so that I am able to see more of the people in my past clearly.

The late 1970's:

I remember during my 7th grade I saw a three-part mini series on TV. It is called "Sybil" with Sally Field and Joanne Woodward. I loved it and oddly felt I could relate to it although I wasn't sure why. It was completely different than my current lifetime, yet I had no idea it was dangerously similar to my previous lifetime. The main character had multiple personalities after severe abuse by her Mother. A doctor helped her remember what had happened to her. Very good movie.

So I can understand why, during my other lifetime, I couldn't quite ever allow my mind to go back to those terrible, emotional incidents enough to deal with them. I, as Marilyn/Norma Jeane, suffered for not knowing.

During adult years...

When I/Marilyn would go to photo shoots....even then, doing something that came naturally to me was so hard. I always wondered if people could tell I was on the verge of insanity. I was always relieved that my craziness didn't show in the pictures of me. And at night I was terrified to be alone...needing someone to be present so I could talk, or be held, or just feel like another living someone was there to pull me back to reality. The nights I spent by myself were excrutiating. The dread was unbearable until I'd fall asleep. I would replay the day in my head and wonder how long it would be until someone would figure out my secret...I was losing my mind!

This need for company is part of what accounted for my countless indiscretions with men. I didn't want to be left alone to deal with the inner-workings of my own mind all by myself. I wanted someone to play off of. It wasn't just an emotional issue due to the lack of a father-figure. **During that lifetime men were both perpetrators and security blankets.** I was always trying to lasso someone to spend the night with, while also trying to break free and be independent. I was a mess! I didn't want men to define me and yet I begged for them to use me, so I didn't have to be alone.

When I was Marilyn, my ongoing mental illness was stressful daily. It is very, very degrading when you feel you are going to lose your mind and totally disappear. People knew <u>something</u> was wrong, they just didn't know how much.

When I said I saw and heard things other people didn't, this is an example of what I mean:

- If I were indoors, I might suddenly hear a train whistle and know there is not a station nearby.
- If I were talking to someone, I might suddenly see polka-dots or flowers behind their head but know they just appeared and aren't really there.
- I might see a bird land and then imagine it was speaking directly to me in a chirping only I can understand...or even a human voice.
- I remember when I was under a stressful situation, sometimes I saw a bee in my right eye...but knew it wasn't real. This first occurred when a man attempted to rape me in his tool shed. I was quite startled and kind of in shock and thought I saw a bee in my line of vision in my right eye. It happened on some other occasions also. Maybe it represented fear, but it looked like a solid visual thing, and it was very annoying. I would blink my eyes a lot when I had this vision. I'm just grateful that at least I knew the hallucinations were just that, but I lived in fear of the day I slipped deep into another reality and wouldn't be able to distinguish. Ignoring the visions was exhausting.

It sounds crazy but it is the way it was for me when I was Marilyn.
I appreciate that after my death, many people really tried to understand
me. I read that some people think I might have been undiagnosed
Bipolar or had Schizophrenia.

So... as I said earlier, I know that I/Marilyn used to see things other
people didn't, <u>even prior</u> to the incidents with her Mother. I would say
that I must have inherited at least some helping of mental complica-
tions. However, maybe it would have been managed better if not esca-
lated by my Mother's violent tirade or my Mother planting ideas in my
head about "being bad". It seems that "Nature versus nurture collided".
The trauma lingered.

**When I was living Marilyn's lifetime, I remember thinking I
had everything, but could barely enjoy it.** And although "being an
orphan" didn't help, and was painful in other ways, it was the hallucinations that were the real thieves, which robbed me of normal deci-
sion-making and enjoyment. I looked great on the outside but I was
devastated daily on the inside. I made up excuses for things too easily.
Even special events were made harder and it is so surprising when I see
the array of photos where I had a smile on my face, because I know the
anxiety I was concealing.

**If you want help, you have to actually <u>tell people</u> what is wrong
with you, and you need to be an active part of your own treatment
and not live in denial.** If the Dr. Phil show had existed in the 1940's
or 50's, Marilyn would have probably felt far less disconnected with her
mental issues, and I/she could have admitted them out loud, sought
help, and been a much more confident and focused person who made
different choices. Now people discuss things that were taboo half a
century ago.

Marilyn felt frightened at least some part of every single day. Her
pills were part of her coping habit, but in the long run they hurt as
much as they helped her. **Today there are many more medicines for
very specific needs.** This is important. People need specific treatment,
not a blanket "knock yourself out" or "make yourself high" approach.

**I have seen people improve their lives with the right medica-
tions.** And I have seen people mess up their lives because they went

off their medications. Some people don't need medication. Every circumstance is different. People who need help require understanding and compassion ...they are worth it.

I am sure I was a completely exasperating creature. But I never felt like I could truly help it. Between emotional issues about relationship abandonment and sexual violation... coupled with hallucinations...I couldn't be the person I wanted to be. It was easier to fall into usual behaviors. And it was easier that everyone think my problems were all because of my lack of a father-figure. **Blame him...not my "crazy mind" ...because if they blamed MY MIND, I felt it was like saying I was worthless.** I felt defective....flawed. I felt alone.

I didn't want to be "just a body" and yet I wouldn't hesitate to pose nude again and again if that got me attention, a paycheck, a headline ...and possibly another lover to take on my issues when my loves were exhausted and heading towards the door.

It was like I was slamming the door on someone's face, but then opening the window and waving at them. I often felt like a big fat liar because I knew I contradicted myself. And I would say things to the press but often I would ask myself what I was really doing to support the statements I made. I acted like I wanted equality but I would beg for approval.

Really, this reminds me of my own life as Michele where my ex-husband would tell me to dress up and be sexy but then he would be angry if other men noticed me. Do this but don't. Contradictions. Makes no sense. Maybe I went through this during my current life so I could truly experience how frustrating it is when someone at my side is pulling this kind of nonsensical, illogical, infuriating, maddening crap!

They paid for loving me...Marilyn...

I remember one time Joe was banging and banging on the bathroom door, which I had locked. I was sobbing about some sorrowful childhood feelings that were bubbling up to the surface again. He just wanted me to come out and was begging me to talk to him. But I just couldn't. And I felt so low because I knew he deserved better. I was a girl-woman...a child in a woman's body, expected to behave and even perform like a WOMAN. But I was unable to live up to even reasonable expectations much of the time.

I knew that anyone who was with me was probably considered one of the luckiest men on earth while I was at the height of my career. However, I knew that that was just the public perception. Lucky... was probably not the experience of any of my husbands. And for that I am truly sorry. They have gone on to say quite nice things about me after the night I died. I don't know if it made them feel less guilty, or if they figured it made them seem more popular, or if they truly loved me. I believe my first husband James really did love and respect me. And I believe Joe did in the end. I might have stayed with James had I been more "normal".

I am not sure about Arthur, but since I know I was far from perfect, I will read only the best intentions into whatever he has said about me since my death on August 5, 1962. I read that he didn't attend my funeral. I think if Joe was big enough to invite him, he could have been big enough to attend. But what difference does it make. Maybe Arthur just didn't want to be around Joe...who knows! And I am pretty sure James didn't attend because he was so soft hearted my death possibly broke a piece of his heart. And also he had another wife who probably didn't want him anywhere near my body, even if I was stone cold. Not everyone loved/loves Marilyn Monroe!

Imagine if the story had been completely different and articles had claimed that Marilyn and Clark Gable had a great working relationship. That would be a wonderful story, instead of always hearing that my behavior on-set stressed him out, helped lead to his demise and he died before his baby boy was born. I remember being Marilyn and sobbing over the loss of Mr. Gable. That was a deeply heartbreaking tragedy...for everyone.

Yes, Marilyn had mental health issues, yes! I don't take clarity for granted during this lifetime. I remember my many other past lives and during them I never experienced what I experienced throughout

Marilyn's life. Unfortunately I had things unusually rough during that lifetime.

I very clearly recall being Marilyn and the kindness that was extended to me by some of the professionals who I worked with. I remember a situation where I was expected to go in front of the camera. I don't recall what movie I was making but what I cannot forget is that I was emotionally paralyzed. I sat in full make-up and gown in a room with a mirrored wall, such as you find in a dance class studio. I felt powerless to pull myself out of my chair, as I couldn't stop sobbing. And the mystery of it all was I had no idea what I was crying about. I simply had no strength, no confidence, no ability to get a logical grip on things and to fulfill my obligations of the moment. I knew others were waiting and I was letting them down. I had to walk down a long hallway...and hit my mark. I felt complete inability to function. And others waited for me... for that I am truly grateful.

Perhaps people believe they already know all about me/Marilyn... but I can tell you this, the lows in my life were worse than all the stories. And now in the Year 2019, I want to say "good-bye" to that pain. I only borrowed it...I do NOT want to keep it any longer. Even just remembering it for a few moments feels too diminishing.

I have often wondered how I will feel once the world knows all of this about my former me. I have often pondered how Marilyn would feel knowing I am spilling her secrets. I am sure the 1962 her/ me would be mortified. But my soul is in this Michele-life now....and I am in charge. If I can use Marilyn's name to help someone than that is the least she/I can do. Afterall, by the time this book goes to print, the world will have kept Marilyn a relevant figure in the media for 57 years beyond her 1962 death. Marilyn owes the world something...about kindness and understanding. EMPATHY is a beautiful gift.

Chapter Fourteen:

MARILYN: MY BABY BOY...VANISHED.

I have read a few articles that claim Marilyn told many people she had a baby girl when she was a teenager. I read an article that said she told a housekeeper she had a baby boy. Some people believe this was all a fiction and Marilyn merely told this story for attention. I am here to tell you the truth. Yes, I had a son when I was still Norma Jeane. Here is what happened.

Marilyn's baby boy:

*I*t was October and warm. I/Norma Jeane was wearing shorts. I was 14. I/Michele do not know who I/Norma Jeane was living with at the time. But the lady at the house told me to go out and tell the man that we were eating dinner soon and he should come in and wash up. I went out to a tool shed and knocked on the door. He opened it up and I said what I was supposed to. He grabbed my arm and pulled me inside the shed and slammed me up against the wall. I was in shock. He undid his pants and tried to rape me but instead he just made a mess on my stomach and ran out the door.

I went into the house all bewildered and confused and went to the bathroom to wash up. I saw the cum on my stomach and was curious....I knew nothing about how life really worked. I touched it. (I don't know why I did this.....it was stupid. I suppose it could have been because I had been molested by my Mother's doctor boyfriend years earlier.) I touched the stuff.....and then stuck my finger up inside me. I ended up pregnant! Can you believe that!?

I had the baby....I believe it was during the first week of July when I was 15. I think I had him on the livingroom couch and several women helped me give birth. It was painful. A few days later, they sent me to the store or up the road to a neighbor's house to get something....when I came back, I went to check on my baby in the crib and he was gone.

I ran downstairs and asked where he was and was told he was taken away and gone for good and I couldn't get him back. I cried, and screamed and pleaded...... he was gone. I don't know what I named him.....I keep thinking Charles Edward, or Brandon, or Clark. I don't recall. I know I was trying to pick out a good name....I remember thinking about names.

Years later, when I was famous, I thought about finding him..... maybe I could have hired a detective. But since being a sex symbol is both prestigious and also condemned, I figured he was better off not knowing who I was....maybe he would have been embarrassed....? I didn't know. I have to hope that my son did not inherit mental health problems and he had a good life. I had to hope he had a real family.... and didn't hate me. I would never know.

Today DNA testing can be done. With more resources offered to trace your family tree, more people are interested in their own DNA analysis. People want to know their own ethnic backgrounds and who their relatives are. I wonder if anyone has ever gotten Marilyn's analyzed. I wonder if her living relatives have ever had their own put in an ancestry database. I wonder if Marilyn's son is still living, or if he had any children. I wonder if they would be glad to know they are related to Marilyn...or not. Questions......

Where does this come from…? Who believes it?

I know there are all kinds of other speculations written about Marilyn. How many abortions, what about a love child with this person or that. I have no recollection of any of such situations…none. During this Michele-lifetime I made a decision not to have children and got my tubes tied six months into my marriage when I was 26. I think it is funny when people claim they are the children of high profile people like Marilyn and The President. Marilyn tended to wear pretty tight clothing. And I really don't think it would be possible to sneak their love-child around for decades. People really come up with crazy stories! I have absolutely no recollection of a love child.

Adoption…..rescue…love…..

I saw an interview on youtube where a bunch of celebrities were discussing Marilyn. And Jane Russell was advocating for adoption because all children deserve a loving home. She wasn't just saying it, but she was also working with an organization to help find children homes. Jane was such a special lady. Jane was a real classy STAR.

I also very much admire Julie Andrews. She is extremely talented and you never hear her name connected to a scandal. She is attractive, sophisticated, and a treasure to the movies she has been in. When I was a kid, I loved "The Sound of Music" and my friend Mrs. White and I eagerly read a magazine article on Ms. Andrews and her husband adopting baby girls. We both thought Julie Andrews was one of the greatest entertainers. But clearly she is so much more than that. She is a really good person. She is the kind of person you would want to adopt you, or adopt your child if you can't keep them.

As a shy teen, I also loved singing to the stage version of "Camelot" on record…and Ms. Andrews made that musical amazing! She was in the successful play…she should have also been cast in the movie. Someone in Hollywood really screwed up there. Then again, Hollywood screwed up before as well.…Julie Andrews should have been in "My Fair Lady" too!

Chapter Fifteen:

MICHELE: WHAT DO I MAKE OF THE OTHER "MARILYN CLAIMERS"?

A while back…

I can't recall the exact year, but about 17 years or so ago I first heard that someone else was claiming that they had been Marilyn Monroe during their last past life. At the time it was just a blurb on my TV set…a story to come, like a teaser to keep you on that station. I didn't even watch the actual segment about it because I knew my soul had been Marilyn's. What could somebody else possibly have to say? I chuckled to myself and I dismissed the idea and didn't give it another thought. What was the point?

Just last year...2018...

Then over a decade later I had my skin cancer surgery and I thought a lot about killing myself, but I didn't want to leave people behind all hurting and mad...including my cat. I also found some support groups online and conversing with other skin cancer patients was helpful.

Anyway, contemplating death lead me back to Marilyn. I began to meditate on Marilyn's life and hired a hypnotist in an attempt to shake-up more blocked information from the past. **"Did I need to do anything during this lifetime to fulfill my karma carried over from Marilyn's?"**...that was the big question. It is also one that really saved me, because it gave me an adventure and also a purpose other than staring in the mirror at my scars all the time. And also, I really knew the answer all along. I had had the nagging feeling for the last three decades.—Do something! I knew Marilyn had expectations when she sent her soul into this Michele-life.

I googled **"woman who believes she was Marilyn Monroe during her last past life"**. When I found a handful of people who claimed they had been Marilyn, I was alarmed! Most were women, one a man. I ordered books about three of them, although I have read very few pages on any of them...it's just hard. But here are my thoughts about some Claimers.

1) **Why did the information about the one most publicized Claimer make such a big deal trying to draw comparisons to the way the Claimer and Marilyn looked?** I remember multiple past lives myself and have looked a variety of ways throughout the centuries. And although this claimer is attractive, she doesn't really "look like Marilyn" anyway. I guess you have to start somewhere, when attempting to prove something that is un-provable. Unfortunately it's un-provable for us all... none of us can outright prove our past lives.

I also saw this Claimer on quite a few interview videos and I don't understand why this claimer has used the word "haunted" when explaining her past life memories of her supposed self. This Claimer also seems to be under the impression that Marilyn merely killed herself...that's it. So even if she is tapping into some "Marilyn energy" somehow, she must only be remembering the first half of the night I/Marilyn died. It is true I started out taking pills on my own.

I heard that this Claimer made the statement "Marilyn didn't reincarnate because she was famous, she did because she was human." And that I do whole-heartedly agree with. It's a "soul-thing" not a "fame-thing". This Claimer also loves animals, as do I...good for her.

2) **And why did another Claimer actually write in her book essentially about how she was hoping the first Claimer would prove to have been Marilyn so she could exit herself? Huh?—I read these pages over and over in disbelief.** I also disagree with the idea expressed that Marilyn was murdered to "send a message" to the Kennedy brothers. Two of the brothers were present at the murder, that I am sure of. And who knows... maybe the third was aware of what was going to occur...seems most likely.

However, the same lady does state that despite the fact she wasn't completely interested in going public and writing her book, she did it because she wants people to know Marilyn didn't just kill herself. And *that* is true! And *that* matters. And *that* I appreciate! And for that I like her a whole, whole lot. That point in-and-of-itself is very powerful. Because to me it is proof that somehow this Claimer does have some connection to Marilyn...I'm just not sure what it is. Maybe she is just kind-hearted. But to put yourself out in the public eye for scrutiny to stand-up for someone else is really brave.

3) **And then there is the third Claimer. She appears to have self-published her book.** The book has a cute cover. The text was more like an outline of ideas, and I was baffled because

I wanted to know her own personal current thoughts about things. I wasn't sure if that lady really believes her soul was Marilyn's or not. But...and this is a big but......she gave me the idea to self-publish, so I appreciate her inspiration. She is also in show biz, as are the first two Claimers mentioned...and unlike I am. She seems to be talented with make-up.

Here's the thing:

"Either your soul was Marilyn's or it wasn't."

It isn't a choice and it isn't dependent upon whether or not someone else tells a better story. You can't wish it away. It is the most deep inner connection. For better or for worse my soul was Marilyn's. And I have great empathy for my former self. My past lives are sacred to me. I was those people, I lived their lives, I lived their deaths, and I have never for a moment wished I could detach from them. I wished their lives were easier sometimes, or that I had more discipline, but never have I for a single moment wanted to wish them away. To me that would be like cutting off my own arm. I strive to understand them and to help those other parts of me come to peace regarding situations where maybe they felt they lacked the ability to reach peace on their own. I can no longer imagine not remembering them now.

Even when I have a difficult time remembering my blustery life as Bach, I know that I will deal more head-on with his issues during a future lifetime...probably when I am male again. But he is a piece of my soul's history too. He is a part of my "historical family of selves". And I am very sure some things I have gone through during my Michele-life are directly related to him. But I don't want to discuss that...it's private. Some things have to be!

Who will believe me now...?

I will admit, I feel somewhat as if the array of other "Marilyn Claimers" convolutes any chance people will listen to me...and the truth. I am afraid we all look like fools now. **But I am hopeful truth will out.**

I have heard that actually many, many young actresses are under the impression that they were Marilyn previously...it's just that most might seek a counselor, but not necessarily write a book or give an interview. I believe that we all...*especially aspiring actresses...* know what it is like to feel... often vulnerable... lost in a big system... dependent on the judgment of others higher up the ladder... treated like "a thing"... abandoned by someone whose love or approval we crave...dependant on the kindness of strangers... and occasionally heartbroken for reasons that are strangely illogical and hard to explain. In that way we all know what it is like "to be Marilyn". Marilyn felt these things often, perhaps extra-intensely and more regularly than most. But I think this is why so many actresses can relate to her...and feel a connection. And it is sadly sweet. People like to say "misery likes company", but Marilyn would not want others to feel the pain she did...not even a fraction.

In the final analysis, I would like to THANK all the "Marilyn Claimers" who put themselves out there. You gave me the idea to come forward with the truth. Otherwise I might have continued to be my reserved philosophical self and found a million different reasons to avoid the karma I was born to fulfill. **And that would be truly sad.**

An unsolved murder is always sad. And make no mistake, Marilyn was murdered. I was murdered. I, as Marilyn, lived a very interesting life, which came to a dismal end. The final act in my life was one in which I had lines no one listened to, I was stripped of my costume, and my co-stars stole the show. I was just a prop. Somebody rewrote the script on me. I was waiting for the director to yell "cut!"... but that didn't happen. (No one saved me.) And then publicity....ah, publicity.....all it cared about was my costume....again. Cause afterall, that is more important than the plot.

<u>I wonder how the lives of the other Marilyn Claimers have pro-
gressed: Questions come to mind. This is what I would ask the
group of them if I could.</u>

-Did you ever regret going public? If so:
>   —why, was it just because you are a private person afterall?
>   —why, did something negative happen as a result?

-Did you find that a large number of people who read your book
seemed to believe you? If so:
>   —do you think it was just initially after reading/hearing
>   about your story?
>   —do you think people continued to believe as time went by?

-Did you since realize that your soul had not actually lived as
Marilyn? If so:
>   — why did you imagine a connection in the first place?
>   — would you go public and admit your change of mind?

-Did you find people wanted to hire you or date you based on the
premise that you had been Marilyn? If so:
>   — do you feel appreciated as "your current self" then?
>   — do you think those people had expectations you
>   couldn't meet?

I often wonder what the true impact of "coming out as Marilyn"
has been for those who have dared to come forward. I hope someday
I understand if we all are actually connected through Marilyn's lifetime. If I found out today, I have the feeling the explanation would
be fascinating. Because I know my soul lived her life, I am baffled
by it all.

Chapter Sixteen:

MICHELE: ANOTHER LIFETIME REVEALED: LOST, BUT FORGOTTEN NOT.

Remembering Lizette:

T he strangest thing has occurred. As I was writing <u>this part of the book about my forbidden dalliances during my 30's,</u> I began to remember another past life. This has caught me totally off guard! I never would have imagined another one would appear...because all the other past lives I've remembered came to me about 30+ years ago. At first it was really hard for me to believe I had not remembered this lifetime sooner, as it occurred within the last 150 years. (I think my death during this lifetime radically affected my current lifetime for many years.)

The memory of this lifetime came to me in an interesting way. I kept feeling as though there was a man in a blue soldier's jacket standing diagonally across from me, facing me. His presence was strong and I felt as though he was with me for several days. I did not actually see him with my eyes but in my mind's eye...and he was very, very solid. I didn't know what to make of him and surely wasn't thinking it could be past life related. He was not scary, just *there*. But then I began to see objects as well...a blue glass bottle and a gray handled broom. I also began to remember feelings of great grief, shock and pain. Then he stopped "being there".

I know some people do a thing called "automatic writing" to try to free-flow think and put things on the page and then allow whatever information comes into your mind just happen...maybe from the spirit world even. Well I have a hard time purposely doing that. I don't stick with it. **However, it seems that writing this book has had the same affect somehow. Especially as I analyzed my sexual encounters, I think a "memory portal" has opened up. Perhaps there were a couple other contributing factors as well.**

1) About a week prior to my beginning to recall this other lifetime, my ex-boyfriend Demetri contacted me out of the blue. I had not heard from him for several years. As we traded a few emails, I told him I was writing a book. Being his usual cynical self, he proceeded to heavily imply skeptical and negative implications towards the idea of reincarnation. Now, I get it that not everyone believes in it, but I have no mind to keep corresponding with someone who repeatedly expresses doubt about it. Friends don't have to agree, but they can show interest in finding out why something is important to me... or bring up a new topic to discuss. I feel kind of bad, but I dropped contact with Demetri.—Bye. I believe the strife I felt with my ex fed into the return of my latest memories coming alive. Conflict with a man I both care about but who also makes me feel as though I'm walking on gravel in my bare feet...seems somewhat familiar to my past life.

2) And then there are the shoes. I am definitely not a "shoe horse" as people say. I actually think shoes can be very pretty but I almost always spend my money on something else. I have very few pair compared to most women. I love basic stage actress shoes that have a 2" heal and strap. They are the kind you can put taps on for dancing. Anyway, I have many in black and several in different colors. And I finally bought a tan pair. When I recently began wearing these tan shoes they made me feel "different". I believe I was wearing light colored heels in the past life when I was killed during the late 1800's.

Mary Virginia Wade's lifetime ended in 1863. So in this other lifetime I am now recalling, I had to have been born after that. I believe that during this newly discovered past existence that I died during the mid to late 1880's. I was 16-18 years old. But I think I was 18 when I died.

My friend Tina has some psychic ability. Between things I remember and her input, we feel pretty sure we know the full names of the people I remember from my past life. We have been able to find some material on the man, but then came to a mysterious dead-end and drop-off in information regarding the later part of his life. We only found one photo of him...wearing a Civil War Union Soldier uniform. But I will just use first names. I don't want any great living relatives of the man in this story to be upset. And I also can't prove anything. I have found nothing on the person who I believe I once was. But I know I was real.

This is the story I remember... I was Lizette. This story ends in violence and I do not condone violence. I only am writing about this because I completely believe it is a past life memory and I feel

that my past life selves deserve to be heard if they attempt to resurface. I am pretty sure this can be considered another unpunished/unsolved murder case. But this girl who I was had a life...way before she had her death.

I am not sure what town I was in but I feel certain I was in the United States...most probably Kansas. My name was Lizette.

My Mother and younger sister had red hair. My little brother's was kind of sandy brown/red. My Dad's hair was dark brown or black.

Both of my siblings died of some illness but not at the same time. I think my sister died a year or two after my brother did. I believe my Mother died partially of heartbreak over the loss of two of her children, and also because as a result of that she stopped taking medicine for some condition she had...maybe a blood disorder ...and she fell.

I feel there might have been some question as to whether the man I knew as "Dad" really was my father. I looked different than my siblings. I feel that my Dad and I had a very close relationship. The kind where he would stroke my hair and tell me I was pretty long after it is "cute" to do so. However, I have no real memories as to the extent of whether or not things became highly inappropriate.

I came from a show biz family and I even placed second in some big singing competition at a fair. I had aspirations to go to a big city and become a stage performer and star. My Dad was a real charmer and entertainer on stage, maybe even a magician. But he made some bad business deals and was somewhat of a con artist and he was put in jail.

And so it began...I somehow ended up in a "house of ill repute" at about age 16...during the mid 1880's. I always believed I would get out of that house. Why no relatives to take me in? Maybe my relatives were ashamed of my Dad and therefore didn't want ME to ruin their reputation by association. Maybe the family name had a stigma. This is uncertain. But I feel that this was probably the situation.

I had very pale skin, light green eyes, and blond curly hair that I had to brush often. I had high cheekbones and a slight build. I remember I had a box and in it I kept a very special hand mirror and brush set. It was a connection to my mother and my most prized possession. I took it to "the house".

I believe I was in the house for two years. It was more like a big redbrick 4-story business building than an actual home. It had long hallways, several community areas, and every girl had her own room which doubled as living quarters and "place of transactions".

I had a room assigned to me on a higher-up floor and it was a little claustrophobic but beautiful sunlight streamed through the window and I loved it. The room was not overly small, but imagine if you had only one room to call your own and had to share it with clients every day. I believed this accommodation was temporary and I had high hopes that my Father would soon be released from jail and I would no longer be on my own.

When I entered, I was one of the younger girls and not yet brazen and sassy and loud. I was still more "girly" and not quite "the woman". I was eager to learn what the other girls knew...tricks of the trade...the inside scoop on the clientele. There was a sisterhood among us. We owned little and had no place else to go. Fake happiness. Curves of the flesh. Men. Money. Every day pretty much the same...accept on days I still took singing lessons.

I learned quickly to set aside my emotions and feelings towards adult activities in order to keep up with all of my transactions. Quite frankly a few of the regulars were good 'ol boys who were a whole lot of fun. But then there was the one dark-haired man who paid me a visit with two of his friends. He was a little bit kinky and he also beat me up. I wondered who would slap me next. More than ever, I was determined not to stay forever.

Among them all there was one man who really stood out... "the bearded man who wore the blue coat". He had very blue eyes and blondish hair. He was probably mid 40's. He had broad shoulders and was very strong. Not fat, but a bit stocky. I think he had some skin condition at times. He was average height but taller than I was. I will call him "William". The truth is, he was my first lover. I gave him my virginity...he gave me money. He had all the control to come and go as he pleased, as I was in my room...always waiting for the next guy.

Once I entered the house William forwent visiting the other gals and I became his sole entertainment. His fixation made me somewhat uneasy, although flattering. Sometimes his intensity scared me but he was a client so I complied to keep a roof over my head. He was quiet and seemed to have a deep internal struggle. As time went on I had conflicting feelings about him. I still felt somewhat uncomfortable in his presence and yet part of me grew rather fond of him as he began to confide in me and become more a "person" than a "mystery".

Perhaps while seeing William on a regular basis, some part of me even unexpectedly fell in love with him. But my profession made such an idea awkward. I would never admit any real feelings for him to myself. Besides I was a teenager and William was much older.

At some point a cute, well-mannered and well-off, brown-eyed, brown-haired boy about 24 came into the picture. He wanted to take me away from the house and I was very fond of him and grateful. I thought he was my salvation. We made plans. I was to meet him at a specific time on a specific day at the railroad platform. We were going to leave town and start our lives over somewhere else. I had so much to look forward to...love... a new profession...the world. I hoped his family wouldn't disown him for affiliating with me...should they find out where we met or that my father was in jail. But he didn't seem worried one bit.

He gave me two flowers and I put them in an empty blue glass soda bottle and placed it on the bureau in my room. I packed my bags, and could barely sleep the night before we were leaving town. When morning arrived, I tidied up and swept the floor. I placed the gray handled broom in the corner of my room.

I was walking down the hallway with my suitcase in hand. Ready to start over. I was on a deadline...on a mission. I had to get to the train on time and meet my brown-eyed guy. But then I saw William coming towards me. I nervously turned around and went back to my room and closed the door, but then I had to open it because I had to get past him and make it to the railroad on time.

William was in the doorway and I couldn't get past him. His broad physique blocked my exit. We were at an impasse. He wanted to talk, I needed to go. I had to explain that I was meeting someone and couldn't stay. He seemed baffled. I admit I had not told him of my departure, but had no real sense that I needed to because, afterall, he could buy another girl. He was "just a client". Maybe I was devaluing the role I played in his life...and his feelings. I was young. (Besides, it was not an era where I could have called him up on the phone and told him I was leaving town. There was no hi-tech way to give him prior notice.)

William refused to budge. I remember being extremely frustrated and panicked that I wouldn't make it to the train on time. I also recall looking at him and thinking he looked "older" and also knowing he was a "real person" in that moment. (These moments at the door remind me of the night Marilyn died and I was standing inside my bathroom door...in heightened awareness and a feeling of suspended time.)

Finally, I pushed William a bit to get him out of my way. I gave just a little push on his upper chest because he wouldn't allow me out. My hand was on his blue jacket. He did not like that. William punched me in the stomach, slapped my face...and as I attempted to straighten up he pushed me forward towards the bed. Completely flustered and trying to grasp what was happening, I struggled to straighten up...and then I shrieked, "What are you doing?! Are you crazy? Get out of my way... I have to leave!"

William then grabbed my arm and threw me on the bed and began raping me. It was the oddest thing...this man who I had done *everything* with for nearly two years looked so completely different to me all of a sudden. I stared at his face and tried to reconcile the mild-mannered guy I had come to know with the person who was on top of me against my will.

At first I was pushing on his chest and trying to get him off of me, but he slapped me a couple times in the face and it was no use. He was hurting me more than I was moving him. I managed to slap him on the side of the face near his ear and that is when he began choking me. This was suddenly extremely frightening. William was not only willing to hurt me, but obviously willing to kill me. I gasped for air and could feel his hand pinching in on the sides of my throat. But he stopped short of strangling the life out of me. William got up.

I turned away and laid on my right side half curled up, tears dripping down my cheeks, looking away from him. I was ashamed I had been over-powered and I refused to even look in his direction. I didn't want to see him. I told myself that if he left now I could still possibly make it to the train on time. I just wanted him to get the hell out!

But then as he was adjusting his pants, William noticed the flowers in the soda bottle. He asked if they were from my new lover and I told him I was getting married. William did not like that, and dumped the flowers and water on the floor and came toward me. I tried to roll off the side of the bed to my right but he was very quick and so much stronger. **William grabbed my left arm, pushed me flat on my back, and assaulted me with the bottle.**

It was a most painful and <u>incomprehensible</u> thing. I closed my eyes and thought I was going to pass out and wished that I would. I hoped that when I opened my eyes it would all be gone and not real... however he persisted...in and out. I looked downward on the bed and I could see him manipulating the blue glass object in his hand. The very rigid top of it kept disappearing inside of me. The shame itself nearly killed me. I closed my eyes again. Thoughts of my siblings' and Mother's deaths drifted through my mind...all painful losses. And my own pain was unbearable. Only minutes earlier life seemed very normal...didn't it?

When William was finally done with that, he got off the bed again. I felt very cold and couldn't actually move any part of my being at will... only shaking with chills, as I tried to speak and could barely form words. I stuttered ..."You'll pay for this. They'll lock you up in jail for what you did to me." (I should have kept my mouth shut.)

William noticed the gray handled broom in the corner of the room, and he picked it up...came over to the bed, and with a very strange smile he called me a "whore". <u>I knew at that moment I was going to die</u>. As I was still lying there weak from his bottle torture, I kept saying, "No...no."

Pleading did no good ...he had the upper-hand. I expected him to beat me with the broom, but instead he pushed the tip of the handle into that space between my legs where his cock had been. Every breath I took was possessed with sheer primal fear and getting heavier and heavier.

William hesitated and I looked at him and thought for a moment about saying that I loved him, maybe to change his mind. Maybe he was even *expecting* me to give him a reason to stop. But I just couldn't say the words, I simply couldn't.

This seems somehow reminiscent to my life as Charlotte, where I was about to be burned at the stake. I was asked if I had anything to say and I could have possibly pled for mercy or feigned love towards my husband who instigated the whole scene. But even then, I said nothing. (Am I stubborn or just honest?)

William defiantly rammed the handle so far up me that I could feel everything rupture deep within. It was too late to lie...too late to beg...too late...no escape. Showing no mercy, he persisted with several more unrelenting thrusts as if to drive home the message that *he* was in control.

I was released from my body and my consciousness went frantically spinning around the room... freed but confused ... ungrounded... in anguish... towards the light at the window.—Stop! I didn't even notice when William left the room.

Out of body, my consciousness had to make sense of the departure and come to the true realization that my body was no longer life sustaining and there was nothing to belong to. I was afraid to look but did...I did. I had to say good-bye. Good-bye to a life that seemed like it was just beginning. I returned to see the wreckage...my body lying on the bed.

My eyes were closed and I looked peaceful as if I was merely sleeping. And I thought, "How can that be, after all I just went through...how can that be?" I was sorry I couldn't see my light green eyes for the very last time. My golden hair was tousled but seemed so lovely and normal, until my consciousness noticed a little drop of blood. A drop of blood...just there...up in my hair?

I then looked down to see the rest of me. Beneath my chest there was so much blood...so much blood. And around my thighs there was a pool of it...blood, blood, and pieces...pieces of ... And the broom was still on the bed and red...blood red. **And I thought, "How ironic...I'm wearing my favorite spring dress with gold and orange flowers. I felt so pretty in before...but now everything seems so *ugly*."**

I noticed the blue glass bottle on the floor...the one William *fucked* me with. And the flowers not far away. And then my consciousness spun around the room and fixated on my suitcase...packed for no destination. Blunt as it was, I had to come to grips with "never" and "forever". **"I'll never get out of the house...I almost got out of the house. I'll never meet my guy at the train. I'll never sing again. I'll never see my Father again. I'll be here forever...................."**

And then as those frenzied thoughts calmed, my consciousness was overtaken with an overwhelming deep despair. "HOW could that man do this to me? I gave him *everything* I could...I did everything he asked of me...whether I wanted to or not. HOW?" I suppose the one thing I never gave him was my heart. Was I supposed to?

My consciousness was stuck in a loop, "If only I hadn't pushed him. If only I hadn't pushed him. What if I hadn't pushed him? Would things be different if I had just stayed? Why can't I start over? I wouldn't push him! I wouldn't push ...him." **HOW did this happen on the very day I was supposed to get out....HOW?**

I would never know:

-I wonder if William ever had to account for what he had done?

-I wonder how my brown-eyed guy heard the news about what happened.?

-When and how did my Father hear?

-And most of all, I wonder who inherited my brush and mirror set, sitting in that special box, all packed up in my suitcase. I never took it to the city.

I have a dim recollection of coming back to the earth plane at night and knowing my body was in a box or bag outside of a stone building ... seemingly abandoned in the dark. It was very, very dark. I don't know if someone was digging me a poor-man's grave? Who would really claim me?

Back to my Michele-life...dealing with the story.

I didn't want to believe the nasty death I envisioned for Lizette. The memories came to me over about 5-7 days and when all the disgusting pieces fit together, I emailed Toni, my hypnotist. I just couldn't ignore what I felt were true memories, although I tried to live in denial and tell myself I might be going bonkers a bit. I didn't really think I was though, because I manage each day to work a very detail oriented, demanding job.

I confided in a friend that I thought I was remembering another past life. But I also said, "If I'm losing my mind, I must be a high functioning nut." **I tried to laugh off all the signs pointing towards another past life where I had been murdered.** I mused about which would be worse...."having died in such a terrible way during the 1880's".... or..."having these strange thoughts for no substantial reason and possibly losing touch with reality during this current lifetime".

Thankfully Toni responded to my email for help. She was willing to see me again. "Hypnosis will clarify everything," I hoped. I had not seen Toni for several months and when I went in April 2019, it was only my 5th session.

I want to make this perfectly clear, hypnosis is not the cause of my memories. I have gone to hypnosis to talk to someone else who really believes reincarnation is possible, since so few people I know in-person do. And also I have a wish to uncover more information and clarify what has come to me on my own. But hypnosis has not fed me these memories nor fabricated the storylines.

As my appointment approached I felt more and more uncomfortable with the thought of explaining outloud the rape, bottle torture, and grotesque demise of my former self.

I kept thinking, "Tell Toni everything and don't forget and leave anything out." I wanted to tell her, but truly wasn't sure I could even manage an explanation while she was sitting across from me. I warned her a couple times that I would be talking about something perverted, embarrassing, and seemingly far-fetched. But I also figured she had already listened to my "I was Marilyn and this is how I was murdered," story...so she is open-minded.

I told her that I had "pain memory" too. That is when you don't feel the actual real pain of the experience but yet you have an odd sensation and you *know* there was pain. Kind of like when I had my skin cancer operation and the doctor pulled my skin up my cheek and to my forehead. It didn't hurt at all and yet I felt something really odd was happening on that part of myself.

Toni was kind enough to see me after work hours. Again I kept prefacing what I was about to tell her with, "This is going to sound crazy." I even told her that I was afraid she might not want to talk to me anymore after she heard the story I was about to tell.

Toni said, "Usually when people tell me that I won't believe what they are about to say, it is because they know I really will." I told her right-off that I never took drugs and hadn't had alcohol for over a year. I felt I had to make that declaration in case she thought what I was about to say sounded insane.

Then... I told her everything. **She said she could hear the emotion in my voice.** I kept looking to the side as I spoke ...mortified that I was even verbalizing the brutality...let alone claiming it happened to former me. I used the "f-word" a couple times instead of the "r-word" because "fuck" is easier to say than "rape". It was my desperate attempt to control the conversation and not melt under the degrading pressure of it.

I told her that it was hard to talk about Lizette, and sometimes my "big Michele voice" comes to the forefront to be tough and cut embarrassment off at the pass. But I really didn't do that this particular time, like I had when I told her last year about how Marilyn had died.

After this part of my session, I went to the restroom and my face and neck were broken out in huge crimson-red blotches. I told Toni that I figure this happens to me because I burned at the stake during Charlotte's lifetime. But honestly, I was just so incredibly embarrassed to speak of Lizette's experience. I felt her humiliation all over again.

Toni even brought up the idea that maybe my bladder issues are connected to this specific past lifetime. **She said, "You know, if that man really did what you say he did...your bladder is up there...and maybe that affects this lifetime."** So we have speculated that maybe Marilyn's lifetime or Lizette's could have influenced my current physical conditions.

After Toni's acceptance and also being put under hypnosis, I felt more at peace, despite the unsettling nature of it all. I now continue to pursue the details of Lizette's lifetime, although I know the truths won't come out until they are ready to be revealed. It's really give and take. Lizette has to trust me to know her story. And I have to understand her with empathy. She was a real person...just like we all are. Just like *every single one* of us is. I want to know more about her life before she entered the house.

Marilyn and Lizette:

Was Marilyn's ambition driven by a subconscious dream... Lizette's unfulfilled aspirations...the wish to "be somebody" and perform for a big audience? Well, Marilyn scored there! People still associate her with singing "Happy Birthday" to the President of The United States.

And did Marilyn stutter because she remembered what happened to Lizette...her former self? It's hard to say, but I think perhaps.

I DO believe that during her teenage years Marilyn awoke from an early morning dream...a nightmare... about a brightly lit room and blood. I dimly remember waking (as Norma Jeane) and knowing something bad happened but not knowing what exactly that was. I can't help but wonder if Marilyn's own insecurities and energy imbalances stemmed from Lizette's lifetime.

This could mean Marilyn's own childhood traumas were compounded by her soul's past traumas. All of which are also somewhere in me...waiting to be dealt with now...or to pass forward into the next incarnation.

Back to the Barn Hook Incident...early 1930's.

Two things come to mind when I ponder this tragic incident:

1) I wonder about that little boy who fell on the barn hook during Marilyn/Norma Jeane's childhood. Had HE been William during Lizette's lifetime? Some people believe a soul can enter into "learning contracts" during future lifetimes. But alas, all of this is something I can never know for certain...I just question.

2) One of the Claimers has said that she recalls experiencing a crushing feeling in her chest ...and she seems to equate it with dying as Marilyn. But I have even wondered if she could have possibly been the little boy in Marilyn/Norma Jeane's childhood. Afterall, he fell face down and the hook was somewhere in his chest/stomach region.

WHY... WHY... WHY... WHY... WHY?

Why meditate or go under hypnosis to get a clearer view?

One might wonder. WHY on earth would someone want to "walk through the pain" and relive a traumatic past life event in any way shape or form ...especially something that was simply disgusting.

Well, I think it has something to do with "inner self-preservation". Remember we are talking about THE SOUL and its life existed prior to and extends beyond each individual lifetime.

When you are at your most vulnerable and in the most pain (emotional and/or physical) your inner dialogue and energy muster to keep you "the most you" and able to get through the event. Although on the outside it may not really seem that way, because a person's body can be hurt or die, the essence of the person's energy will go on.

Also, even if your final moments are horrific, they are "your last moments"...they belong to YOU...and they are the last time your consciousness remembers living that particular lifetime. I think people love themselves or find reasons to love themselves during those moments. It comes down to self preservation...on a deeper level than ever before.

So for me at least there is a very strong wish to *go there* again and know what I knew before...my past me...during traumatic events.

Maybe in doing that, I not only understand my core self more but also desensitize myself to being overly influenced by that past event any more. I suppose it is about "facing the pain". I've heard people talk about snake venom injections to build immunity to snake bites. Maybe it is the same premise.

During one past life I was a Siamese twin girl, my sister was on my left. We each had dark curly hair and blue eyes. This was during the Renaissance period and we were the children of very important people. When we were small our parents loved us, but as we got older they seemed embarrassed by the gawkers. They removed us from the main part of the home and we were only allowed outside under certain circumstances. An older gentleman supervised our outings and we wore a long dark cloak and were instructed to be quiet. Now and then we were taken to a fair or the market place. However, my sister almost always threw a tantrum, which resulted in severe scoldings and being locked up alone for longer and longer periods of time. Our existence grew increasingly dismal. Finally, when we were 11 years old, three men with an axe came to the dungeon where we were hidden away. They were quite rough. They grabbed us...tore our clothes...and bluntly separated us! The blood splattered against the wall...as my sister screamed. I passed out for a time. When I awoke, I was alone accept for a spider on the wall. I was completely traumatized...half naked and shivering...cloth wrapped around my chest...tied to a chair...and left in the dark. The next morning they took me to a nicer part of the castle and attempted to converse with me....but for many days, I remained silent. I saw their disappointment, but I didn't care. I was returned to the room of damp stone and solitude. Every day someone came to feed me....but I refused to eat or speak, to protest my sister's death. I died of starvation. I never understood why my sister had such outbursts and I didn't really miss her because I was always punished for her behavior. However, I hated what they did to her. Stubborn!

Chapter Seventeen:

MICHELE: WHAT ABOUT NUDITY, WEIGHT, AGING AND IMAGE?

Nudity:

*O*bviously I don't think nudity is a bad thing…as long as it is in the right context. As I have said earlier in the book, I have posed nude before, when I was younger. I simply don't have any of the photos to prove it.

The thing is, any time you take a nude of yourself, you must ask yourself:

1) What if someone I don't want to see it sees it?
2) Could there be any repercussions?
3) Can I live with either of the above happening?

320

When Marilyn died, apparently people knew that she was found in the nude. That really isn't so bad...I mean, that was one of my better looking lifetimes for sure. **But the thing is, I wasn't sleeping in the nude.** I was wearing a small white night gown and if I had been the cause of my own death, well I certainly wouldn't have taken it off before taking more pills that evening. **But here is the thing...there is not a damn thing I can do about how those men left me.**

So...instead of getting mad about that aspect of things, I will just do this. I'll imagine hearing the "Candle In The Wind" song, if you replace the "Marilyn found in the nude" to "Marilyn found in a gown... or teddy...or nighty...." Yah, get the point? It doesn't flow. I guess if nothing else, those men who murdered me helped make a better song. On the other hand, Elton John is such a genius, I am sure he could have made it work beautifully no matter what. He would find a way. He is The Master of Music.

I have never been a real model, but one of the most flattering things a guy has ever said to me was, "My friend and I call you 'Miss Face' because I like your face." Funny....see, no nudity necessary. "It" is in the face.

Was Marilyn's lifetime under the influence...?

Since starting this book and remembering the lifetime of Lizette, I have come to a very strange feeling. Is there a relationship between Lizette never making it out of the house of ill repute where she died so young and Marilyn never escaping her sexpot image either?

Marilyn never aged in front of the camera and she never took the steps to cultivate a different image. She attempted to take her own life before she aged-out. I wonder if subconsciously Marilyn felt she was "not allowed" to move on. Was it sheer laziness that prevented her from seeking a new image....or....maybe Marilyn felt the consequences of Lizette trying to make it out of "the lifestyle"...?

I do think Marilyn remembered being Lizette. Her own Mother did a number on her also at an impressionable age. But I don't like the "perpetual victim role". People sometimes have the right to say they are a victim, but who wants to live there forever...? Enough about that.

During that final year of life as Marilyn...I told myself I should take the steps to change my image:

1) Stay away from cameras for 2 years (which scared the hell out of me)
2) Go to some small town with great community theatre and just act
3) Darken my hair to medium brown
4) Wear more sophisticated clothes, not so revealing
5) And most importantly, get a vocal coach to help change the cadence of my voice, because I knew in my heart that my speaking voice was keeping me from becoming a serious dramatic actress most of all.

Personally, I do NOT sleep in the nude. I have a hang-up about it. Maybe it is leftover from 1962? I like nighties that are like short small v-necked mini-dresses. Soft material...not always lace, but could be.

Weight:

I have heard people mention Marilyn's fluctuating weight. Even one of the "Marilyn Claimers" mentioned it. Well it is better to be heavy than to kill yourself losing a few pounds. In college I went from skinny-skinny to pudgy-pudgy. I fluctuated throughout those years.

It was mostly an emotional thing and I used food and exercise to deal with intense feelings.

While in college ...

For a while, I kept wearing my smaller-sized jeans even as my weight went up. I began to realize that this was an issue and I started carrying safety pins and an extra pair of pants in my backpack. One time I was in Michael C's acting class, with just him and a girl named Sherry. We were doing Shakespeare, which Sherry and I were both quite bad at. Then as I was spouting "thous" and "shalts" ... I felt the button on my jeans snap off...and "ping" on the floor. I hoped I was the only one who noticed. Then, I could tell the zipper was zip-zip-zipping downward. Thankfully my winter sweater was long enough to cover my crotch**! But as soon as the Shakespeare fiasco was over I blurted out, "Michael, I'm going into the next room to change my pants."** He gave me the weirdest look. I grabbed my backpack and scrammed. I can only imagine what he and Sherry thought!

The point is, don't live in denial. Embrace yourself as you are and swap out the skinny jeans if you have to for a while....or forever. A person is about more than their weight! The only time to really focus so much on weight is if it is causing you health problems and you will lose a limb or die because of it! And if your job is dependent on it, do it safely...and even slowly if that is the only way to stay healthy. Or... look for another job.

I am not going to say that weight doesn't matter. I'm just going to say that it is ONE part of life...it is not the meaning of life ...it is not the thing that determines whether a person deserves love...and it is not the thing that your loved ones will miss about you on the day you die, even if you are the "perfect weight" according to elite standards. ONE part.

Thoughts about aging:

Well, I don't like the idea in general...I'd rather continue to look 36 forever. But, this is what I tell myself. "My beloved Nunny was

47 when I was born. I never knew her at a younger age and I thought she was amazing and beautiful." She was wonderful at 87 too. We all get older and we all wish we would look young forever. It isn't happening.

So...stop looking into the mirror and start looking outward. Adopt a pet and take good care of them, and you will have someone in your life who never notices, minds, or leaves you because of your wrinkles, gray hair or extra pounds. Unconditional love. (But don't adopt a pet unless you really want to take good care of them...they are living beings who do require daily care. Relationships require nurturing.)

Image: My June Allyson Moment.....

I remember many years ago reading an article that talked about the cute blond actress June Allyson. She was born the same year my Nunny and President Kennedy were...1917. She became a popular movie star with an attractive clean-cut image.

In the article it talked about how Miss Allyson was up for a movie and assumed she would play "the flashier sister" role. But that went to Kathryn Grayson. (Oddly enough Peter Lawford was their love interest.) The movie was "Two Sisters From Boston". In the end things worked out well cast the way they were. But at first it was a bit of a jolt because Miss Allyson was very pretty herself and anticipated getting the opposite part.

Early 1980's:

I remember one time in college I was in a theatre class for scene directing...which required acting. I had to rehearse a scene with a girl named Cory. I don't recall what play it was from, and we were only doing one scene. The teacher assigned the parts. I was supposed to be the "built girl" and she was the more "intellectual and plain" one.

We were running through a rehearsal and I had some short, tight little light green outfit on. Cory only had sweats on. But all of a sudden it was quite obvious, she was hiding a knock-out figure much more curvaceous than mine. She just wasn't dressing that way so I guess it took longer for people to notice. But they noticed! She also had longer hair and green eyes but wasn't all into make-up like I was.

I remember hearing the teacher **Wayne** say, "Things should be the other way around, it looks like we got things reversed."

I couldn't deny it. Yes, it hurt my feelings even though I pretended that it didn't. But at some point I found the article about June Allyson and it was kind of like a band-aid. It was like, "OK, so some major star experienced the same thing, what are you going to do? Get over it."

Cory and I didn't exchange parts cause it wasn't for a real performance and it was just some scene in the class that we didn't spend too much time on. **But I guess God and The Universe were telling me something that day... "You may have *been* Marilyn Monroe...but darlin', you are NOT Marilyn Monroe!"** —Got it! Loud and clear!

*** Oh...let me amend what I said above. Every performance is a "real performance".....you have to commit to your role!

Get over yourself!

It was probably two years later in my college career that my favorite acting teacher Michael C. told the class to listen up. I remember him stopping us in our tracks and he gave us a lecture on "type". **He said, "I know you all don't want to hear this, but 90% of the time, directors cast parts according to type."**

I knew I was sitting in a class of students, some of which were desperately trying to break out of "their type" and wouldn't want to hear that. As for me, I had no clue what my type was anymore.

Michael continued, "Take a good look in the mirror and be realistic. What do you see? What kind of parts are you made to play? Most of the time you will be cast according to the way you look. I hate to say it, but that's the truth. And it's also better not to be gaining weight."

I felt like he was saying that last part for my benefit because I had gotten a bit chunky. But see, he was nice, he didn't say it right to me. He just gave advice to us all...and I knew what he said was true.

Acting is different than a lot of other jobs in that "your body is your instrument". That is what people see…they see YOU. It isn't like typing a letter or making a piece of furniture or painting a house, where people see a product. Actors are seen … looked at …. viewed… photographed… filmed… judged… criticized…hired and fired…and weight could matter.

I remember two fellow actresses telling me their stories:

1) The one refused to take that dreaded look in the mirror and come to grips with her "type-cast type". She would wiggle her butt when she walked and had a lot of confidence…yet refused to take that realistic look. She asked me one time what I thought she could do to help her get cast. I told her maybe get braces. She flat-out said she didn't need them. I liked her but she was struggling and I didn't know what else to say. She was nice and a fairly decent actress too. Her butt was definitely cuter than mine… I guess she had that.

She continued to get her hopes up, but not to get the parts she wanted. One time she was particularly unhappy and in tears. **I just thought, "Uck…that can't be me. I don't want to cry over not getting parts. I don't ever want to take all this so seriously that I'm that upset."**

2) My other friend was someone I palled around with a lot and really admire. Her name is Sue. She said she was liberated once she took that realistic look.—Smart! We are still friends several decades later. She is pretty and kind and a damn good actress too!

Chapter Eighteen:

MICHELE: WHAT DOES IT MEAN WHEN I SAY, "MY SOUL WAS MARILYN MONROE'S"?

Michele was born July 10, 1964.
Marilyn's lifetime: June 1, 1926 to August 5, 1962.
I've lived...I've died. My soul has been here many times before.

I think all of these memories from the past are a combination of things. They are the chance to be entertained by stories long forgotten. They are opportunities to review past struggles and triumphs. In some cases they may provide a release from pain and fears held onto. It is as if your former self is confiding in your newer self. I think a person's former self sometimes wants to explain the reasons for their mistakes. The former self wants to know they still matter....especially if that person died an unjust death or had some other unusually painful experience. The former self is a piece of who the current self is. The former self may still wish to live out an unfulfilled dream...now.

The current self may be called upon to befriend the former self (or selves) by empathy and to deal with them. Sometimes the memories are a real mixture of pain and pride. For instance, two lifetimes ago I had a naturally powerful opera singing voice, however I had so many family and health problems that I stabbed myself and died at about age 20.—This is the lifetime right before Marilyn's. Maybe Marilyn's lifetime was such a struggle, because in the previous lifetime I had simply thrown everything away...?

During one lifetime I had red hair and I was an actress who practically lived in the theatre because I was used to getting lead roles. During that lifetime, I died on stage because of a freak accident when something fell from the rafters. It's amazing to reconnect with experiences beyond your current lifetime. Pride and humility. Joy and despair. It's all a part of every life.

When I went to my hypnotist, I initially had the intention of going deeper and retrieving more details of Marilyn's life. Then I got sidetracked with Charlotte's. I think Toni could sense the obsession for the past growing...it was in my eyes.

Toni said to me several times, "This lifetime as Michele is the only one that matters now...it is the most important. This is where you are living now, and this is the only lifetime you can still affect anything."

I resisted that. I felt like my other lifetimes needed me. I also concluded that my other selves were so much more interesting than I am. But, I know she is right. Live in "the now". Grieve some for the past if you must. But...only current lifetime has control.

In writing this book, I am fulfilling Charlotte's dream to be an author. I will do my best to appreciate the resources I have as a person alive in the 21st Century. But also...this experience isn't a one-way street. In-turn I am finding the process of writing fascinating although somewhat tedious at times. (The technical aspect is irritating!) **This is an example of the circle of healing between the lifetimes. Helping myself, may help her...and she is still a part of me.** If my past self is more at peace, this is good all-around. I never wanted to write a book before...ever. **Maybe Charlotte's energy has unblocked my Michele-hang-ups. But then again, in doing that, Charlotte is also helping Marilyn to tell her own story.** We are all one. This is a soul thing. This is a continual traveling life energy experience. The soul lives in the body, but it also lives beyond the individual lifetime.

Despite my belief in multiple lifetimes through reincarnation...and despite my lack of discussion about heaven and hell...I do believe in God.

What Karma Matters matter?

So...getting back to Marilyn...maybe she did have plans for me to follow-through on in my Michele-life. But maybe it is alright if I improvise now that I am here. Maybe I don't need to win an Academy Award this time around. Maybe I can be forgiven for not putting Edward in jail. Maybe it's good enough that, through me, her consciousness got to visit planet Earth and see what impact she left behind.

Speaking of impact: My apologies...

I saw an interview where actress Hope Lange said that Marilyn had tried to get her fired from the "Bus Stop" movie. I feel very badly about that. I am sure Marilyn was probably jealous of the younger star's cuteness and afraid she might steal the show. Miss Lange seemed quite understanding in the interview...but I'm sure back in the 50's it wasn't so nice. I personally have no recollection of this incident, but yet I don't doubt it either. I could see it happening...especially if I was on a lot of pills that day...or something tripped me off and I was in a petty-petty mindset!

I also feel very badly that Marilyn left so little money behind and her sister Berniece and niece Mona Rae had to help pick-up the pieces of Marilyn's Mother's care. I am sure that was a constant struggle. I feel completely horrible about it. I do not remember a lot, but I do remember the things my Mother did to me during that lifetime, and I can only imagine things got worse with her as time went on, even though she might have been more frail with age. **I'm very sorry that those two women had that hardship. Very.**

And I am also extremely sorry to Ethel Kennedy. I am sorry I was an intruder and a major pain-in-the-ass...especially since she had so many beautiful children. There is really no other way to put it. **I would want to say to her. "YOU are the one Bobby loved....period. I'm sorry."**

I would say the same to Jackie Kennedy also if she were here. I have only a dim recollection of making a phone call and being extremely nervous. I have read that Marilyn called Mrs. Kennedy and Mrs. Kennedy had a very clever quip in return....basically telling Marilyn to go ahead and take over the President and the White House, <u>and all the problems that go with it</u>. She sounds pretty smart and quick witted! **Marilyn *should have* felt dumb.**

I want to also say that I am sorry to anyone in Edward's family, because you probably think I'm making things up, although I'm not. I'm sorry. I can't pretend the past didn't happen. Only the individual is responsible.

The upside of Marilyn...

Marilyn would be thrilled people still find her so pretty and more fascinating than ever. I am happy for her. Part of me is also very happy for me too. I'm proud of some of the things my past self accomplished! Maybe it takes the edge off of being a BIZ-drop-out in this lifetime. It's truly a strange thing.

Part of me is occasionally even jealous of my former self. Then again, I know how difficult that lifetime was and I take it all back! How can I possibly be jealous of someone who was tortured by her own mind, didn't know her father, and was methodically murdered as one of her lovers knowingly stood by! Forget I ever had that thought... banish the thought...banish it! Nope, no need to be jealous.

But getting back to the upside, Marilyn has the best fans ever! Fans from before...and new fans who were born long after 1962.

If there's one thing I am sure of, it's Marilyn's determination to set the record straight about how she died. And, who knows, maybe a future self will be an amazing serious dramatic actress. Maybe they will remember Marilyn and Michele, and maybe they won't.

Maybe today... in this Michele-life... it is just my job to live.... be alive ....do ....thrive.. celebrate ... enjoy ...and hope. And to remember Marilyn the person, who started out as Norma Jeane ...and not worry about following in her footsteps in any way shape or form.

Afterall, I have much to be thankful for. Both of my parents are still together and alive... my sister and I were raised together and get-along well... I have been with the same clever, handsome man 16 years... my "step-daughter" is beautiful and talented and sweet ...our pets are cute and funny ...and my Nunny in heaven said she wants to meet me in another lifetime. **It doesn't get much better than that!**

Author Jacqueline Susann wrote best-selling novel, "Valley of the Dolls"...it's about starlets and their relationships with pills. Marilyn was familiar with that concept. When you are forever-36, people can project all kinds of magical scenarios onto you...and they will never be proven true or not. Here is the truth. **If you like Marilyn and want to honor her...be sober. All the friends in the world can cocoon you with acceptance and advice and assistance, but if you aren't sober, it will probably never be enough!** And love affairs...are not the same as love. And if you suspect you are sleeping with someone you shouldn't be with....say "good-bye". If Marilyn were still alive, by now she would have more than a few wrinkles, and it would be her turn to allow someone else to shine in the spotlight...and she would be one of the elders to give advice. **Be sober! You cannot become your best you, if you are constantly avoiding yourself.**

Chapter Nineteen:

MICHELE: FINAL THOUGHTS...CUT, AND THAT'S A WRAP.

This is why...
I called the book "Marilyn: Not Just Another Girl"

*T*he reason I only put my former first name in the book title...
and not the last... was because <u>this book is personal to me</u>.
"Marilyn Monroe" feels like the title that belongs to a supposed "legend" and "icon". Marilyn was "a person". That's what I remember.

The reason I used "Marilyn" and not "Norma Jeane" in the title... well, it's because this far into my Michele-life, I'm kinda partial to "M-names". They feel like "me".

I knew immediately that I wanted to put the "Not Just Another Girl" in the title because those words of Edward's pierced my soul when I heard him say, "You'll get over her Bobby, she's just another girl."

However, I then considered that perhaps I ought not give Edward's words that much attention. I thought about changing the title and played around with a few options for a couple days. But then I returned. I returned to that place in my mind when I knew that my Marilyn-life was slipping away ...and I was startled and sad. I felt I just had to use the title I originally wanted. It felt so profound to me. **Those words... *those words.......*are so "of that night".**

Yes, while I/Marilyn was one of many pretty actresses....and one of many flings, I was not "just another" anything. And neither were any of the other girls who the brothers came in contact with. None of the women were less important than those famous brothers. And let's face it, their wives were saints for being so devoted to them. Very strong.

Each woman deserved to be treated with respect....each one deserved TO LIVE ...and there is no such thing as "just another girl". Just like there is also no such thing as "just another boy". Each person is important. Each person has a mind, feelings, energy and a soul.... and deserves to be treated with RESPECT.

In the immortal words of the magnificent Julius Caesar, I do make this proclamation now. Much to her own surprise, "Marilyn came, she saw, she conquered." But I know, nobody does so much all alone. Many writers, make-up artists, wardrobe crews, lighting designers, fellow actors etc. work together to create a star. Marilyn's photos weren't selfies...talented photographers took them. Among her good friends were celebrity photographer Milton Greene and his wife Amy. **And the most obvious statement...Marilyn's career was nothing without her FANS.**

I remember during the early 80's, I saw a profound TV movie called "Miss All-American Beauty" with Diane Lane and Cloris Leachman. Diane's character wins the crown and in the end she puts it on the woman who has been truly beautiful and supportive and hard-working on her behalf.

When I/Michele was 16, I decided to be an apprentice at the community theatre a few miles from home. During the day I helped paint and assemble the backdrops and props. During the evenings I helped change sets, run sound effects, or assist with quick costume changes executed in the wings. This was all volunteer work for the love of art and experience. There was also a lot of joyful comradery among the group who volunteered as well.

It was an extremely sweltering hot summer and I was assigned the task of ironing the clothing for the lead in "The Prime of Miss Jean Brodie". There was barely any air flowing through the theatre. As it was, the theatre was converted from an old barn and it had been very minimally upgraded. My forehead dripping with sweat, I toiled and toiled to get things ready every night. I went through a couple weeks of rehearsals...ironing in the heat and in awe of the three teenage girls who were co-starring in the show. They were about my age, and very talented.

Then, on the eve of opening night, the actress I was preparing the costumes for gave me a lovely delicate vase of flowers and thanked me in a very heart-felt manner. I had admired her before that night, but then I really did. She completely touched my heart when I realized that I wasn't invisible.

I think that that is one thing that reincarnation does...it teaches your soul how to be on both sides of the fence. In one lifetime you may be the star and in the next you may toil the in the support crew. Some people might be tempted to live their life thoughtlessly and recklessly because they think this one life is "it". However, because you don't know what form or position you will come back in, it is still best to strive towards kindness during every single lifetime...and hope others do the same. We all are in this world together.

Two good friends I made since starting this book:

My Friend Tina:

A few months ago I posed a question on a Marilyn Monroe facebook site. I was attempting to be as neutral as possible and simply ask what all the Marilyn fans think of so many people claiming they had been her. With thousands of people on that site, I was hopeful to get a discussion going. However, I wasn't getting any responses, so I forgot all about it. I figured I had just asked diehard fans something they might find in violation of their late icon's honor.

Then finally someone replied. I wasn't sure if I would get a positive comment or a snippy one, quite frankly. Thankfully, positive. Tina is 5 years younger than I am, very pretty, says she has some unexplored spiritual gifts ...<u>and she has felt connected to Marilyn since she was a child.</u>

Tina said she always felt she could relate to Marilyn and she has been including Marilyn in her prayers since childhood. I asked Tina if she prayed for her because she suspected Marilyn had been murdered. She said she did believe Marilyn was murdered, however she prayed for her because Marilyn seemed very nice... particularly so in photos with animals.

Tina and I are having ongoing conversations, as we both feel that God and The Universe wanted us to meet. Another friend is always a very good thing. And I am also very humbled and honored on Marilyn's behalf, to have had someone praying all these years for my former self. It actually boggles my mind...and I thank her for it.

Tina and her spirit guides have helped me as I recently remembered my past life as Lizette. (I talked about this earlier in the book.)

My Friend Tom:

I also have another new friend named Tom. I met Tom through a reincarnation website because one day I decided to google "Does anyone believe they were Sharon Tate during their last past life?" Sharon is in one of my favorite movies, "Valley of the Dolls" written by Jacqueline Susann and also starring Patty Duke, Barbara Parkins, Lee Grant and Susan Hayward.

I emailed Tom one day and he and I have been having interesting online conversations ever since. So nice to chat with people who know reincarnation isn't just a goofy thing people make up. As of today, Tom has no definite past life memories of his own but still believes and also conducts hypnosis. Tom is like my hypnotist in Indiana...he points out that "this lifetime" is the one to focus on most and live.

Tom often will talk about how he believes he might have been a number of well known people in his past lives...specifically men who were in the military. He often will talk about "being nobody now". We have had discussions about how "being famous" doesn't make you more a "somebody" than someone else. We are all somebody...especially to our families. Tom is intelligent and intriguing...a very wise soul.

As far as this goes...

I heard that Hugh Hefner is buried next to Marilyn now. I read some blogs where people with rather definite opinions on the matter were expressing themselves. I have an opinion too, but I'd rather talk about what I wish was, instead of what I wish wasn't. I was a Doris Day fan, and wish that that beautiful lady was Marilyn's new neighbor. Miss Day was so talented and she really loved animals. I watched some of her movies at my Nunny's house when I was a teen. Oh well...whatever will be, will be.

Mr. Hefner has a family and families are important so we should all just be happy that Mr. Hefner got to choose where he ended up. I am sorry for his family's loss. Can you really blame him for wanting to be next to Marilyn?

Suicide: I read that following right after Marilyn's death, the suicide rate went up drastically. This is NOT a good thing. This is not dramatic and cool, this is traumatic and sad. Personally I am not completely against people having some choice in the matter as to live or not. I understand feeling heartbroken, betrayed, "less than empty". But I do think one has to consider that there may be people affected—people who love you deeply, <u>or are dependent on you</u>, or who will help you. What will happen to people dependent on you?

When people say they love you, choose to believe it. If people offer help, choose to take it. Imagine what your life could be like if you got the right help. **Ask for help. Marilyn would NOT be happy to know** people died because they thought she was a role model. Suicide is not fashionable.

Marilyn would not wish to be responsible for influencing other people's decisions on this particular matter.

No OUT about it!

As far as past lives go...I think they are a new opportunity for THE SOUL to live again and to experience the joys, sorrows and accomplishments of being human. But a new lifetime is NOT an "out".

It doesn't mean that if you are unhappy in this lifetime you should just go on to the next. That is kind of like when people use abortion as a means of birth control, instead of actually taking responsibility for fertilization potential before they have sex. You don't just casually kill a living being....

When you do come back, you start over. You may be motivated by your past self but that past self is in the past. No one is going to make me a model just because my soul used to be Marilyn's...see what I mean?

You have no guarantee that the life you will come back to will be better. You may come back richer but in poorer health. You may come back with a special talent but a family that is in chaos. You may come back as the opposite gender...which isn't a bad thing, but I'm just saying you may not come back similar to your current self. You may be luckier or terribly unlucky in the next lifetime. Does someone really want to gamble? Be who you are NOW.

I tell myself all the time, "current lifetime has control." That is what my hypnotist said to me and so did my friend Tom. So...I don't want anyone to take reincarnation as an excuse to end their current lifetime. Just wait until things happen naturally. Work on this life now. Sometimes life is work! But, there is a future. Reincarnation IS real. I can't prove it, but I promise I know.

Remembering a Star...

There was a pretty lady named Peg Entwistle who was a talented woman best known for jumping to her death from the Hollywood sign in 1932. She was upset because her luck in show biz wasn't going the way she hoped.

Ironically, the day after she died she got a letter in the mail which offered her a starring role in a play. Just imagine if Peg had just held on... simply imagine. I think about her often. God Bless Peg.

May 2019:

I went back to Pennsylvania to visit my parents. I told them I was writing this book. I reminded my Dad of his reaction a couple decades ago, when I told my parents I had been Marilyn and he said he preferred another blond starlet. **He instantly said, "It's my prerogative to change my mind...and I do."**

I'm not sure I believe him...but that's my Dad.—Supportive. He did mention that one of the things he preferred about Marilyn was that she seemed more down-to-earth. He is very pleased I am working on a project even if he doesn't believe in reincarnation himself. **I am sure it is a challenge for him and my Mother to see me as anyone else but their daughter...Michele Marie.**

So, here is the deal:

I, Michele, am as vain and insecure as ever....but despite that, I have chosen to self-publish this book <u>before</u> I hire a plastic surgeon to fix my eye. Why? Well...it's a hard call...but then again, it really isn't. **Life is about choices ...and I owe Marilyn this much. Lest I perish anytime soon, I want to know that Marilyn had her say....it's a "soul thing." I don't want to disappoint her...because I still remember what it felt like to *be her*.**

Epilogue:

THINGS I DON'T KNOW.

Back in 1962:

As my soul belonged to a weakened and dying Marilyn, my consciousness was in and out of body. As you can imagine, it is hard to see all detail and understand everything when you are drifting off to another part of The Universe. I was used to men doing many, many things to me...but this I was completely unprepared for. It's called MURDER.

With so many people speculating about how I/Marilyn died, I feel almost a need to attempt to explain every little thing about that night...yet I cannot. And I feel I owe many people an apology because I have held the answer to this mystery all along. Truthfully, I was pretty oblivious to how many people were still investigating for an answer, until I woke up to the headlines during this last decade.

1) I know some people believe that Marilyn had no pills in her system. To that I can only say that I know I had taken probably about 5 pills earlier in the evening. I remember spreading a bunch of pills out before me and knowing I had "enough".

But then I only took a small handful and put the rest back in their bottles with the intent to take more after several hours. Unfortunately, I fell asleep....and I lost control of my own destiny. I know I took them with water. Did Mrs. Murray pick up after me one last time, and walk my drinking glass to the kitchen, as she stripped the bed to wash the sheets before the onlookers descended on my home? I believe the glass of water was on the floor. I believe I drank nearly two glasses.

2) So, I/Marilyn was found in the nude. Where did my nighty go? I have no idea. The last I saw it, it was tossed aside in my bedroom. Did the Police ever find it? Maybe it was stashed some place in my house, or maybe taken as a souvenir by one of the men who took my life...or even investigated. I was dressed when Bobby, Edward and the third man arrived. No panties, but definitely a white nighty.

3) And why did Edward do what he did on me, right after he smothered me? Had DNA technology existed at the time, it is highly unlikely he would have, but perhaps he hoped to make it appear that I was distraught after being dumped by a lover...I don't know. Was that move a planned thing? Did he walk into my room knowing he would do that to me? And that Bobby let him baffles me to no end!

4) Why do some people blame Dr. Greenson for killing me? The way I look at it, by the time he arrived on the scene (so I've heard), I was already given God-knows-what and poisoned with the intent to kill. If Dr. Greenson arrived with the intent to help, but neither Bobby, Edward, nor the hitman with the briefcase informed the doctor I had ingested much more than my usual prescribed medications, then those three men, Bobby, Edward and the hitman, are the ones who are responsible for my death. They were purposefully negligent. They administered something toxic without my consent and against my will. And they withheld information with the specific intent to point their fingers at the man who merely walked into the scene with the best of intentions to rescue me. Most likely, Dr. Greenson was encouraged to take action. And there is also the distinct possibility he was afraid for his well-being if he didn't.

Present time:

I have recently begun looking at a number of online Marilyn Monroe fan sites. So many people on them are WONDERFUL, but why are some of them bullies to the others? I have no idea. Not impressive, not at all. There are tactful ways to share information or discuss differences of opinion. Kindness trumps all. Marilyn would wish for kindness while discussing her. Kindness is the truest beauty.

And lastly...a new online friend has very strongly argued that he does not think I know how Marilyn really died. I have tried to assure him that I DO know what happened to me...ME...MARILYN...MY SOUL...I WAS THERE.

I must say this...no matter what sharks may have circled around Marilyn and taken advantage of her, or maybe even wanted her gone, I know what happened that night in August 1962. And that is what I am talking about in my book. That night.

I am talking about WHO showed up...who slapped me, who smothered me and who administered toxic substances into my body. All the various conspiracies, I knew nothing about at the time...or give credence to now, because my soul was there, in that bedroom, with those men. And I will never forget WHO showed up.

Furthermore, my friend does not believe I/Marilyn even associated with any of the Kennedys. I did, I paid for it. But I want to make this point very clear: What certain members of a family do is not to be blamed on the family as a whole. We are each responsible for our own actions as an individual. I blame no Kennedy family member alive during this present day. I believe they are good people.

I hope that moving forward, people will write only about Marilyn's career. But I don't know if anything I say means anything to anyone else but me. Does it?

Thanks a Million!

To all of the Fans who see Marilyn as a real person who was smarter than the parts she played...and who also watch her movies. You have breathed life into Marilyn's career long after she was gone...and really, because of YOU, she has never really been gone.

<u>You are dream-makers.</u>

To my Parents who told me I was intelligent and that I should write a book someday...and send me care-packages...and let me study theatre in college!

To my sister Chris who took me on Spring Break to Florida with her... and let me wear the red dress in her wedding.

To my sista' Mere who offered to drive to Indy and take care of me when she heard I needed an operation...(but I'm glad you were with Miles.)

To my orangy-porangy Catsby who crawled on top of my laptop many times but never was mean and erased Mommy's book.

To my boyfriend Jay who helped me every time I had computer issues while I was typing this book...and always looks cute.

Your support is priceless.

And to my beloved Nunny...who I will definitely see in another lifetime.
I can't wait!

Special thanks to the Lee Strasberg Theatre Institute for honoring Marilyn with a theatre named after her. The photos of Marilyn walking up to the Actors Studio sign are the best in my opinion, because they represent her dreams. They represent that period in time when Marilyn demonstrated her sincerity toward her craft. They represent the beginning of new friendships with others who understood "there's no business like show business" and lived it. Marilyn wasn't just a model. She wasn't merely hopeful...she was motivated. Marilyn was an ACTRESS... and she was proud of it!

I also appreciate Mr. Strasberg's moving eulogy. He knew the person as well as the performer. Clearly to him Marilyn was not just another girl.

My first baby picture. Did I know what happened to me in 1962?

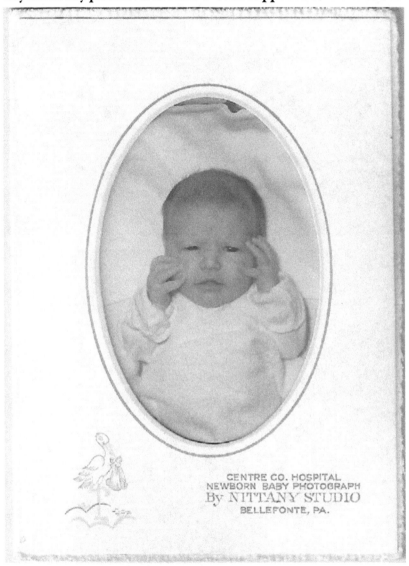

CENTRE CO. HOSPITAL
NEWBORN BABY PHOTOGRAPH
By NITTANY STUDIO
BELLEFONTE, PA.

**My favorite childhood doll-children. Mary and Emily.
Subconsciously Marilyn and Me?**

Bunny Doll painting by Nunny.
Looks like she has radiating light like Jesus.

2nd grade picture. I had a crush on a boy with freckles.
I already had braces and got them again as a teen.

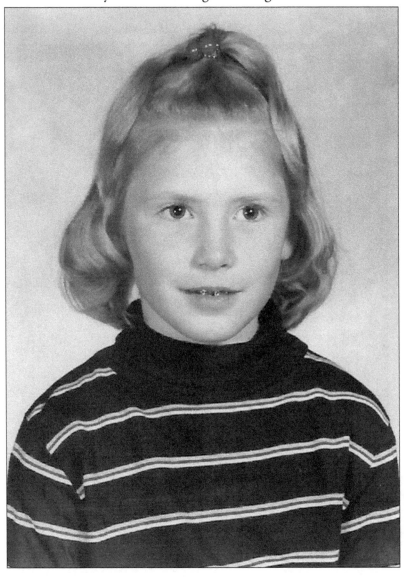

Senior portrait that was in the Newspaper.
Photo by Bill Coleman.
Class of 1982.

Photo by Bill Coleman.
Age 17.

The year I began to remember my past lives.
Photo by my Dad.
Age 19.

My last year in college.
Photo by my Dad.
Age 22.

Photo that won the Marilyn contest.
I look more like Jane Russell in the blond wig during the
Courtroom scene of "Gentlemen Prefer Blonds".

October 30, 1987 - The Daily Collegian.

Article by Ted M. Sickler

Photo by Susan Farr

Monroe look-alike chose

M IS a Boalsburg resident who graduated from the University with a bachelor of arts degree in theatre last spring and now works as a bookkeeper on campus.

Contest prizes included a dinner for two at the Nittany Lion Inn, a copy of Eve Arnold's *Marilyn Monroe: An Appreciation*, a Monroe coloring book and a Monroe calendar.

The look-alike contest was held to draw attention to a special display of Monroe memorabilia including calendars, posters and books that includes new information about Monroe's personality.

Wilson said the judges looked for an entry which portrayed the All-American girl closest, not necessarily the look. Wilson said the bookstore holds two or three promotional events a year.

Wilson said Monroe's

353

December 26, 1989
Las Vegas
Age 25.

Do I look a little like Joan Crawford here?
Some people think Marilyn had a fling with her.
I don't know, can't recall.
People think about the oddest things! Who cares?

I had a pencil with a troll on it.
You can see the troll and his shadow.

Visiting my boyfriend's family in Indiana our first year together.
I met the love-of-my-life at age 39!

Catsby and Timmy protecting me from my
photographer boyfriend.

Indianapolis Airport during November.
Flying to Pennsylvania to see my folks.
Age 50.

After basal cell skin cancer surgery on my temple.
January 23, 2018.

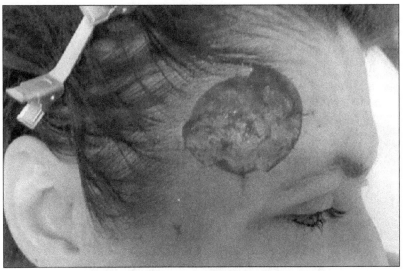

I named these two photos: Condemned and Survived.
Forward Advancement Flap reconstruction.
Skin pulled up from side of face to cover temple.

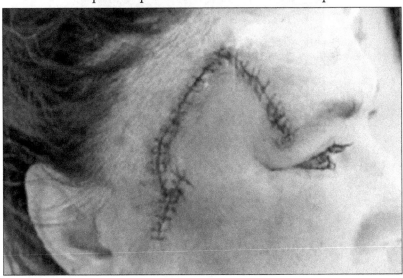

Scar healed amazingly well within a couple months.
Can barely see it if not looking upclose for it.
Right eye still looks strange well over a year later.
Plastic surgery needed to fix it. Right eye-lid droops.

Skin cancer IS "real cancer"!
Get suspicious marks checked out and ask lots of questions
throughout treatment if any kind of procedure is necessary.
Get a qualified doctor...but still ask questions.

October 2019

Catsby thinks he knows this lady.

Think long-term. Protect your skin!
Thankfully, I never was into sunbathing...cause it's BORING.
And I have never been to a tanning bed.
It's hard to tell what skin cancer I could have ended up with.
I've never smoked.

Lifetimes are like cats.
When you lose one it is sad. But then you go on...
and another one comes along and steals your heart.

Daisy (top), Alexander Whiskers (bottom)

CPSIA information can be obtained
at www.ICGtesting.com
Printed in the USA
LVHW010205280120
645026LV00001B/60